Women, Gender and Rural Development in China

Women, Gender and Rural Development in China

Edited by

Tamara Jacka

Sally Sargeson

Australian National University

Edward Elgar

Cheltenham, UK • Northampton, MA, USA

Published by
Edward Elgar Publishing Limited
The Lypiatts
15 Lansdown Road
Cheltenham
Glos GL50 2JA
UK

Edward Elgar Publishing, Inc.
William Pratt House
9 Dewey Court
Northampton
Massachusetts 01060
USA

A catalogue record for this book
is available from the British Library

Library of Congress Control Number: 2011924189

ISBN 978 1 84844 682 3 (cased)

Typeset by Servis Filmsetting Ltd, Stockport, Cheshire
Printed and bound by MPG Books Group, UK

Contents

PART III   THE GLOBAL, THE LOCAL AND THE PROJECT

Figures

Tables

Contributors

Laurel Bossen is Professor Emerita, Department of Anthropology, McGill University, Canada and 2011–12 Radcliff Institute Fellow at the Radcliff Institute for Advanced Study, Harvard University, USA.

Lisa Eklund is a PhD Candidate, Department of Sociology, Lund University, Sweden.

Yuqin Huang is Research Fellow, Max Planck Institute for the Study of Religious and Ethnic Diversity, Germany.

Catherine Ingram holds a PhD in Ethnomusicology and Chinese Studies from the University of Melbourne, Australia. She is currently an Endeavour Australia Cheung Kong Research Fellow, and a visiting scholar at the Shanghai Conservatory of Music.

Tamara Jacka is Senior Fellow in the Department of Political and Social Change, College of Asia and the Pacific, The Australian National University.

Heidi Ross is Professor, Educational Policy Studies; Director, East Asian Studies Center; and Co-Director, The Australian National University-Indiana University Pan Asia Institute, Indiana University, USA.

Sally Sargeson is a Fellow in the Department of Political and Social Change, College of Asia and the Pacific, The Australian National University.

Sharon R. Wesoky is Associate Professor of Political Science and Women's Studies at Allegheny College in Meadville, Pennsylvania, USA.

Song Yu is Lecturer in Management, Zhejiang Sci-Tech University, Hangzhou, China.

Yang Lichao is a PhD candidate in the Department of Political and Social Change, School of International, Political and Strategic Studies, College of Asia and the Pacific, The Australian National University. She holds the position of Assistant Professor in the School of Social Development and Public Policy at Beijing Normal University.

Zhao Jie is Professor and Director of the Gender and Participation Research Centre, Yunnan Academy of Social Sciences; Council Member of the Chinese Women's Studies Association; and Deputy Director of the Yunnan Women's Theory Studies Association, China.

Acknowledgements

This volume is the product of an international symposium titled 'China's Rural Development: Gender Politics, Social Equity and Citizenship', held at The Australian National University 14–15 August 2009. The symposium involved scholars working across a range of disciplines and we wish to thank all the participants in the symposium for sharing their research findings, knowledge and critical skills. That we were able to hold such a successful symposium was largely due to the generous financial sponsorship provided by the ANU China Institute, and Nathan Woolley's administrative assistance. Thanks also are due to the contributors to the volume for the care and patience with which they addressed our editorial suggestions. Finally, we are grateful to Allison Ley for her editorial assistance.

Tamara Jacka and Sally Sargeson

Introduction: conceptualizing women, gender and rural development in China

Tamara Jacka and Sally Sargeson

Between the 1980s and the first decade of the 21st century, China's rapid, sustained economic growth brought great benefits to rural citizens. According to the United Nations Development Programme (UNDP), for example, between 1978 and 2007 the real annual growth rate of rural per capita net income reached 7.1 per cent, and the number of rural people in absolute poverty declined from 250 million to 14.8 million (UNDP 2008: 10–11, 13). Rural life expectancy and literacy rates also improved dramatically. To many observers, these changes constituted nothing less than a 'developmental miracle' (So 2003). It was also noted, however, that China's rapid economic growth had coincided with an increase in the types of rural–urban, regional and social disparities, environmental degradation and unrest that characterized other developing countries. Of particular concern to women's advocates, some achievements that had been made in previous decades in reducing gender inequalities in rural political representation, income and education were being reversed (Tan Lin 2006; Tan Lin and Bohong Liu 2005).

Growing concern about the scale and severity of these issues prompted what has been represented widely as a major re-orientation of approaches to rural development by China's leadership. In 2003, the incoming Chinese Communist Party regime led by Hu Jintao and Wen Jiabao committed itself to shifting from a focus on promoting aggregate economic growth, to placing 'integrated urban–rural development' at the forefront of state efforts to create an harmonious, 'people-centred', 'well-off' society.

For development scholars and women's advocates alike, one of the key questions to emerge from this reorientation is whether or not we are witnessing a shift from a model in which gender equality in rural areas is viewed largely as a concomitant of economic growth, to an approach that enables rural women to pursue their own development goals. This is the overarching question that we seek to address in this book. More specifically, we ask, how are women and gender conceptualized in, and mobilized by the rural development policies and projects issuing from

1

the state and international and domestic organizations? In what ways is rural development reducing, transforming or reinforcing gender inequalities in power, resources and opportunity? To what extent, and with what consequences, are different women able to bring their own understandings of, and desires for development to bear in the momentous changes being wrought in China's countryside? To paraphrase Klenk (2004), who *is* the gendered subject, 'rural woman', that figures in contemporary approaches to rural development in China?

Despite differing in their focus on the actions of women from disparate areas of China and on a variety of policies, campaigns and projects engineered by different agencies, the contributors to this volume share the common view that in order to address these questions we must consider how gendered power relations interact with development discourses, institutions, policies and interventions, to influence the desires, agency and dispositions of different women in rural China today. It is from this perspective that we engage with arguments advanced in three influential fields of literature. In the first of those fields, theorists of development have articulated an incisive critique of development as a modernization telos that is instrumental in expanding the power of the state (Ferguson 1994) and reinforcing neo-colonial power relations between development agencies and subject-beneficiaries (Escobar 1995). The second body of scholarship deconstructs the Western, liberal masculinist models of individual agency and empowerment that underpin, and are deployed in, contemporary strategies of 'participatory' development, and illustrates how these simultaneously serve to represent women as vulnerable, passive victims of patriarchal traditions and instil in them aspirations for independence and power, whilst distracting attention from contemporary political, economic and institutional sources of gender inequality (Green 2000; Parpart 1993). Thirdly, China analysts have criticized the organizational and institutional frameworks created to serve the developmental goals of the Chinese Communist Party (hereafter, CCP) and government for failing to admit villagers' participation in 'problem identification', as well as the planning and implementation of rural development solutions (Chen, Lanyan 2008; Ho et al. 2004).

The contributors to this volume offer some qualified empirical support for each of these sets of arguments. Equally importantly, however, their analyses demonstrate that many women are making use of the material, discursive and organizational resources produced for and by rural development for their own purposes, in ways that shape different local processes and outcomes of development. Furthermore, development has facilitated the dissemination of gender equality as an ideal and institutional norm in the countryside, increased the channels through which women can advance claims for gender equal rights, resources and treatment, and expanded the agentic roles available to them.

What are we to make of this apparent contradiction? In keeping with other feminist analysts (Ortner 2006; Tinsman 2000), we argue that development involves projects that simultaneously might extend the power of the state, organizations and activists to discursively construct the subjectivity of development participant-beneficiaries, while also expanding the capacities of those participant-beneficiaries to conceive of, and pursue goals that are not mere reflections of, or reactions against, the ideologies, goals and methods of the powerful. This point is most clearly illustrated by the contributions of Sargeson and Song, Huang, Ingram, Ross and Wesoky, which detail how, in the course of dealing with the expropriation of their land, commodification and exploitation of their labour, and insertion into 'civilizing' educational and political programmes, women have claimed rights, resources and positions that have enhanced their ability to reflect on and pursue choices, and exercise greater influence in their households and communities.

The aim of this introduction is to outline how the contributions to this volume illuminate how women's agency is being scripted, resourced and reconfigured in the course of contemporary China's rural development. We begin by examining the role of key development actors – China's state, the All China Women's Federation (hereafter, Women's Federation),[1] the key authority representing women's interests, and non-governmental organizations (NGOs) and international donor agencies – in the making of a 'new' approach to rural development in China at the beginning of the 21st century. Much of the extant literature on this 'new' approach focuses on the extent to which it actually is 'new', and whether it is effective in achieving pre-determined development goals. From our vantage point, however, a critically important feature of this approach is that gender relations have largely been elided in the identification of rural development problems, and in the formulation and implementation of development solutions. In the guise of a backward, vulnerable and underutilized group, however, rural women are central to both. We interrogate how this representation of rural women informs development policy discourses, projects and practices, and what these mean for the ways in which rural women envisage and enact roles as development participant-beneficiaries. In the second section of the introduction, we explain how these themes are illustrated in the subsequent chapters of the book.

A 'NEW' APPROACH TO RURAL DEVELOPMENT IN CHINA?

Although the 'miracle' development of rural China became a staple of media and scholarly commentary in the 1980s and 1990s, it is worth recalling that for much of the 20th century, China's leaders viewed the countryside as a brake on the country's modernization (Wen, Tiejun 2001). The persistence of 'feudal' patriarchal relations in rural production, social reproduction, governance and citizenship was held up as emblematic of all that was pre-modern and antithetical to China's development as a strong nation (Edwards 2008). In the words of Qin Hui, Professor of History at Qinghua University, 'Before we had the saying "The Chinese question is essentially the problem of Chinese peasants." Now we should rather say "The peasant question is essentially the problem of China's modernization"' (2003: 139). The problematization of rurality in this teleological discourse was temporarily suspended in the 1980s, when the dismantling of communes, the liberalization of prices and the expansion of markets, along with the contracting of collectively-owned farmland to households, acted as a stimulus to agricultural productivity, rural industrialization and villagers' incomes. Indeed, in 1984 the State Council, the highest organ of executive government in China, announced that rural industry had become an important driving force of the national economy (Zhang, Zhihong 1999).

At the end of the 20th century, however, a series of reports and bestselling books in Chinese focused the attention of both policy makers and the public on three problems that were contributing to an unfolding 'rural crisis' (see, for example, Chen Guidi and Tao Chun 2004). Summed up in the pithy phrase penned by Li Changping, Party Secretary of a township in Hubei, in a letter directly addressed to Premier Zhu Rongji in March 2000, 'villagers are very poor, rural life is hard, and agriculture is in crisis' (Li Changping 2002: 20). Pointing to growing rural–urban inequalities in wealth, consumption and welfare, widespread protests against the arbitrary and excessive taxation of villagers and the emergence of a burgeoning village population deprived of their farmland by developers, some commentators went so far as to warn that a rural lumpen proletariat was threatening the nation's stability and security (Sargeson 2004: 648).

These exposés prompted China's leaders to concede that a new approach to rural development was needed, one which focused on creating a more harmonious, equitable society and employed 'a different kind of government intervention, from developmental and command-and-control to more targeted, decentralized and consensual approaches' (Ho et al. 2004: 7; Su, Minzi 2009; Ye, Xingqing 2009). To encourage farmers' investment in agriculture, the Rural Land Contract Law of 1998 lengthened the duration and strengthened the security of land contracts. Beginning with tax reforms in 2000, and proceeding through to the introduction of subsidies for agricultural production in 2004 and the nation-wide elimination of the agricultural tax in 2006, China's government sought to alleviate the costs of agricultural production. Township governments were directed to consult with villagers when transacting collective property, and new regulations required transparency in village elections, decision making, management and supervision. In 2002, the 16th National Congress of the CCP resolved that, henceforth, rural development would be central to China's efforts to create a 'well-off', harmonious society.

It was under the leadership of President Hu Jintao and Premier Wen Jiabao, however, that in 2003 a multiplicity of ad hoc initiatives were knitted together into what Christiansen and Zhang (2009: 7) describe as a 'strategically coherent, ideologically justified and practically coordinated approach' to rural development. Practical 'people-centred' (*yi ren wei ben*) strategies to promote rural development through the integration of urban and rural areas were set out in the six consecutive No. 1 Documents issued annually by the State Council, from 2004 to 2010. The comprehensive, far-reaching nature of what the leadership envisaged for rural China was first conveyed in October 2005, in the CCP Central Committee's announcement of its commitment to build a 'New Socialist Countryside' (Wen Jiabao 2006; Wu Yunhe 2008).

In the following State Council No. 1 Document of 2006 and 11th Five Year Plan covering the years 2006–2010, strategies were outlined and new funds allocated to: modernize agricultural production; raise rural incomes through increases in agricultural productivity and non-agricultural employment; reconstruct villages and provide physical and communications infrastructure; protect the environment; eliminate fees for compulsory schooling; create universal rural cooperative medical insurance and social welfare systems; and improve democratic grassroots governance.

In a second set of announcements in 2008, the CCP Central Committee proposed stepping up the reform of three institutions that had underpinned systemic structural bias in the economy and reproduced rural/urban inequalities since the 1950s: the systems of residential registration (*hukou*);[2] the rural collective land regime; and political representation (Ye, Xingqing 2009). A new set of reforms to the *hukou* system was intended to enable people registered as rural residents to enjoy equal labour rights and the same access to education, housing and social welfare, as urban residents. The relaxation of restrictions on rural collectives' transfer of rights to use and develop land were aimed at consolidating landholdings, facilitating agricultural mechanization, and enabling collectives to invest in rural infrastructure and social protections. Changes to the Electoral Law, to provide for equal proportionate representation of urban and rural delegates in China's legislature, the People's Congresses, would ensure that people from the countryside would enjoy commensurate input into key appointments, budgets, legislation and policy (Nilsson 2010).

This 'new' integrated approach to development through 'urban–rural integration' was justified ideologically by reference to the leadership's socialist 'scientific development outlook' on the country's historical progress. China, reasoned Hu Jintao, had reached a stage in its evolutionary modernization when industry must support agriculture, and urban areas support rural areas (Chen, Xiwen 2009). In domestic media, much was made of the extent to which the approach reflected the leadership's respect for Confucian '*minben*' (people as the foundation) principles, according to which the people constitute the foundation of the state and the primary responsibility of government is to ensure social harmony by meeting the people's basic needs (see, for example, Huang Hui 2006; Wen Jiabao 2004). For foreign audiences, emphasis was placed on the overlap between China's 'new' strategies to improve villagers' livelihoods and participation in decision making, and the humanist plans of global development agencies, manifest in the UN's Millennium Development Goals (UNDP 2009: vii). For example, measures aimed at improving villagers' participation in poverty alleviation, agricultural extension services and governance were incorporated into China's national development plans.

Few have questioned whether government investment in rural development increased under Hu and Wen's leadership. Rather, the scholarly debates sparked by their prioritization of rural development centred on whether or not their approach was, in any meaningful sense, novel, whether 'people-centred' rhetoric had translated into popular participation, and whether 'urban–rural integration' would effectively alleviate the problems of poor villagers, rural hardship and agricultural crisis (Ahlers and Schubert 2009). Su, Minzi (2009) and Smith (2009), for example, argued that despite the new stress on participation, interventions continued to be characterized by top-down paternalism, and the government's campaign-style approach to mobilization, obsession with quantifiable outputs, and investment in already well-endowed model villages. In contrast, a World Bank report attributed lack of participation not to the government's authoritarian methods but, rather, to 'a paucity of incentives for local people to organize' (World Bank 2007: 83). In assessing outcomes, Guo, Xiangyu et al. concluded that 'only the few relatively strong industrial provinces show significant development in their rural economies' (2009: 324), while Chen Xiwen accused local governments of using 'urban–rural integration' as an excuse for further land grabbing (Li,

Xing 2010). Conversely, Liu, Chengfang et al. (2009) argued that both infrastructure quality and villagers' level of satisfaction with development projects had improved.

What we find remarkable about this diagnosis of a 'rural crisis' and elaboration of a 'new' rural development approach, however, is, first, that the designation of development continued to reflect the valorization of a particular trajectory and form of modernity, by urban and predominantly male policy elites. State promotion of agri-business, industrialization and urbanization still comprised the main strategies of rural development, and the end remained the creation of a modern citizenry whose 'responsible' agency would be directed towards strengthening the nation (Lei 2010: 325). Second, and most importantly for the subject of our inquiry, gender has largely been overlooked. Nowhere, in either the leaders' major speeches identifying items of concern, or the No. 1 Documents setting out the framework for promoting rural development, was mention made of widening gender disparities as a serious development problem or a major focus for policy intervention. Indeed, as Ross points out in Chapter 6, even in the '2020 Blueprint' for educational reform which sets 'overcoming disparity' as a key goal, gender is ignored (China, Ministry of Education 2010). Nor, according to some of the leading Chinese development experts involved in an impact assessment for the UNDP, has gender routinely been incorporated into domestic policy analysis (UNDP 2010: vii; see also Song et al. 2006: 136).

On the other hand, although gender has been disregarded in the 'new' approach to rural development, rural women have been singled out for a great deal of attention. A growing body of literature has represented rural women as a burdensome, backward group impeding modernization of the countryside; a 'vulnerable group' (*ruoshi qunti*), characterized by lack, insecurity and helplessness; and an underutilized population whose labour should be deployed more effectively in the construction of the New Socialist Countryside and the nurturing of a 'modern' citizenry. In this multi-layered, gender-freighted narrative, lagging agricultural productivity has been explained as a consequence of the purported 'feminization' of farming following increased male out-migration from villages. *China Women's News* (2006) and Zhong and Di (2005), for example, reason that village women's internalization of 'traditional' gender norms, their limited education, 'low quality' (*suzhi di*) and inherently risk-averse character, slows the take-up of new technologies in agriculture, limiting productivity and profitability and so constraining families' investment in the education of children. Rural women thereby play a role in perpetuating the vicious cycle of rural underdevelopment. Meanwhile, women 'left behind' (*liushou*) by migrant husbands have been grouped together with 'left behind' children, the elderly and infirm, as a category of vulnerable dependents – akin to what Enloe (1990) refers to as the infantilized collective subject 'womenandchildren' – that is 'accustomed to being helped by society or men' (*China Women's News* 2006; see also, Xu Chuanxin 2009). To benefit from, and participate as agents in development, this group requires protection, instruction and 'empowerment' from a paternalistic state. In this regard, the masculinist state agencies involved in rural development are to rural women what urbanization is to the countryside: a means of modernization.

This discursive problematization of rural women as a backward, vulnerable, but also potentially instrumental group is consistent with the practical and theoretical positions historically taken by the state organizations involved in rural development in China, including the Women's Federation. Since the early 1990s, the centrepiece of the Women's Federation's work in rural China has been the 'two studies, two competitions' (*shuangxue shuangbi*) programme, which focuses on vocational training to raise women's 'quality' (Judd 2002). Through these activities, the Women's Federation has sought simultaneously to improve women's status by increasing the visibility and remuneration of their work in income-earning production, and mould them into rational, entrepreneurial citizens who possess the human capital necessary to compete in a market economy and participate in self- and community governance. These twin goals correspond with the key materialist propositions of both Marxist emancipatory theory and liberal feminist Women in Development (WID) discourse,[3] that women's economic participation is a precondition for equality, and women's equality is conducive to development. These instrumental links are made explicit in Section 2 of China's White Paper, *Gender Equality and Women's Development in China*:

> The state has made the guarantee of equal employment opportunities between women and men and the sharing of economic resources and results of social development the top priority for the advancement of gender equality and the development of women, and has worked out and adopted a series of policies and measures to ensure that women can equally participate in economic development, enjoy equal access to economic resources and effective services, enhance their self-development ability and improve their social and economic status . . .
>   Government departments and Women's Federations at all levels have jointly organized activities to encourage rural women to acquire knowledge and learn science and technology, and compete in their development and contributions, so as to bring their role in invigorating and developing the rural economy into full play. (People's Republic of China, 2005).[/quotation]

The above quotation, however, also is suggestive of a subtle but profoundly important shift in the Chinese state's representation of gender inequality in economic participation, and how it relates to rural development. It was a common refrain of the state led by Mao Zedong, that 'what men can do, women can do too'. In post-Mao era slogans, in contrast, 'women and men are different'. Hence, although laws consistently affirm gender equality, the role women are encouraged to play in 'invigorating and developing the rural economy' also, 'naturally', differs from that of men's. The focus of Women's Federation work consequently has moved away from remaking the structures, institutions and norms that produce gender inequalities in rural economic participation, towards remaking rural women. Ergo, women are being trained to develop themselves, their households and communities, by cultivating a new, open, 'mind-set', acquiring the technical skills suited to commercial agriculture and in demand from employers, and parenting more highly educated, civilized children.

This emphasis on the need for rural women to develop themselves reproduces three key elements of the powerful neo-liberal ethos that swept the world in the late 20th century. As in neo-liberalizing polities more generally, the Chinese state's role in development has increasingly centred, first of all, on 'freeing up' and providing infrastructure to support market forces. Second, it vests responsibility in individuals and encourages them to exercise a narrowly defined form of economic and civic agency, to participate in markets and self- and community governance. Third, some individuals are viewed as more capable of competition, self-development and self-government than others (Hindess 2001; Ong 2006). In particular, as Tomba (2009) has written, the urban middle class is being groomed by the state as the model of self-government, market rationality and national modernization. In contrast, in both official and popular discourse, the rural population, especially rural ethnic minority groups and women, are regarded as lacking the 'quality' necessary for self-development. Consequently, they are to be subjected to more direct forms of state regulation, paternalistic discourses of 'protection', 'assistance', 'education' and 'empowerment', and, of course, the salutary influences exerted by processes of urbanization.

The Women's Federation has responded to this developmental discourse by attempting to get a 'bigger piece of the pie' for rural women, in part by emphasizing where women are excluded or lacking, and their vulnerability. Parpart (1995) has noted that use of the term 'vulnerable groups' was first promoted in the 1980s by the Commonwealth Expert Group on Women and Structural Adjustment as a strategic way of drawing attention to the adverse effects of the World Bank's structural adjustment policies for women and other disadvantaged groups. There was a similar rationale for the term's take-up by women's representatives in China, and it has had similar effects: strategically, it served as a cover under which the Women's Federation bids for additional funding from the state, to direct much-needed resources into programmes for poor, rural women and 'gender-mainstreaming'. Simultaneously, however, it has 'further entrenched the image of the helpless premodern, vulnerable Third World woman' (Parpart 1995: 229; see also, Jacka 2006b: 74).

The Fourth World Women's Conference on Women, held in Beijing in 1995, heralded two important shifts in the approach to gender issues taken by the Chinese state and Women's Federation. The first was a tolerance of growing numbers of NGOs and foreign donor-funded projects working to overcome gender inequalities in rural China. The second was a commitment to 'gender mainstreaming'. At first, these two new initiatives seemed to promise more effective approaches to overcoming gender inequalities than those previously pursued. As we discuss in the following paragraphs, however, their recent progress and impact have been limited.

At the national level, the Chinese state charged the Women's Federation with promoting 'gender mainstreaming'. In principle, this meant the Women's Federation would ensure that gender equality was addressed in the structure, staffing, budgets and policies of all state organizations, and that men and women would be treated equally and equitably in all legislation and policy. However, the Women's Federation possessed neither the political and administrative clout nor the resources to mainstream gender equality even within government organizations, and its activities in the state arena largely focused on box-ticking and the training of and reporting on exemplary women leaders. Similarly, its calls for gender-sensitivity and warnings about the potentially adverse gender impacts of legislation and policy on rural women have frequently fallen on deaf ears. The eclipse of rural women's interests in recent property laws illustrates the latter point. The authors of the 2002 Rural Land Contract Law ignored submissions from not only the Women's Federation, but also the Ministry of Agriculture Research Office and Academy of Social Sciences, advising that the law allows the readjustment of contract land periodically so as to provide land shares to women, most of whom move to their husbands' home at marriage and, by custom, can no longer farm land in their natal villages. Suggestions that household land contracts be signed by all farming adults so as to protect women's rights were rejected by policy elites committed to the economically liberal goals of strengthening contractors' rights and promoting the market circulation of farmland, and the gender-conservative goal of preserving unitary 'household-based' agriculture. For the same reason, women's advocates' criticisms of provisions in the 2007 Property Law were set aside, and the Law consequently allowed land contract signatories, the vast majority of whom are male, to sell and, in some areas, mortgage their use-rights without gaining their spouses' consent (Liaw 2008: 251). Not surprisingly, researchers have subsequently found that women are disproportionately represented among the growing population of 'landless villagers' (He Lirong 2008; Wang Zhuqing 2007; Yang, Li and Yinsheng Xi 2006; Zhang, Linxiu et al. 2008).

Expanding the numbers of women's NGOs and international NGOs (INGOs) working to reduce gender equalities through 'participatory' approaches and Gender and Development (GAD) programmes initially seemed to provide organizational and methodological alternatives to the state's instrumentalization of women in rural development. Ross (this volume) argues that these organizations have strengthened awareness of women's rights of association and citizenship and nurtured female leadership. Certainly, most of the agencies have included gender equality in their project goals, and several of the most prominent international organizations, including the Ford Foundation, Oxfam, the Global Fund for Women and UNIFEM, have funded projects and programmes that specifically target gender inequalities in rural areas. Moreover, many have involved local branches of the Women's Federation in project implementation in order not only to secure state approval and access to rural sites, but also to better 'mainstream' gender equality goals and resources. Finally, the incorporation of 'participatory' and GAD discourses[4] in donor-funded projects implicitly challenged the state's construction of rural women as 'low quality', vulnerable subjects in need of protection and guidance from outside development agents.

Ironically, however, many donor-funded projects align neatly with the state's vision of why and how rural women are to be developed. The most common goals of NGO and INGO projects targeting gender inequalities are to bring about improvements in three key areas: women's income generation (through skills training and micro-credit); reproductive and maternal and child health; and girls' education. Nowhere is the interface between INGO projects and the state's vision closer than in gender education interventions. As Ross shows in Chapter 6, the Spring Bud programme to educate rural girls dovetails with state education policies that define women as 'mediators of modernization', because improvements in their personal competence are viewed as the key to reducing poverty, improving the population's 'quality', and strengthening the nation. And for all the rhetorical emphasis placed on gender, it is by no means clear that donor-aided GAD projects contest either the organizational cultures or the institutions through which gender inequalities are reproduced in the course of rural development. On the contrary, Yang's case study in Chapter 9 shows that donor-funded projects often provide revenue for

County Women's Federations, even though 'their cooperation tends to be contingent on the project containing easily achievable, economically quantifiable targets and no political risk'. Nor do donor-funded gender equality projects necessarily contest even the most powerful norms under-pinning unequal gender relations. Jacka (2010) has noted elsewhere, for example, that GAD-inspired community development programmes run by the Shaanxi NGO, WestWomen, make little effort to alter assumptions about gender divisions of labour. Instead, they tend to exploit women's labour in the traditionally 'female' areas of health and family welfare, while leaving men's dominance of formal village political institutions undiminished. This raises the possibility that one of the most significant practical effects of NGO and INGO projects has been to serve, rather than to counter, the state's and Women's Federation's instrumentalization of women in rural development.

Feminist scholars and development practitioners in China have tried to build on globally-inspired 'participatory' and GAD discourses to improve and, in some cases, challenge the state's and Women's Federation's approaches to gender and development. Yet, as Zhao explains in Chapter 7 (see also Ye, Jingzhong 2008), partly because of the attraction of interna-tional donor funding and the consequent power of donor agencies to shape project agendas, there has been little sustained critique of these discourses within China. Instead, NGO activists tend to assume that GAD and 'par-ticipatory development' approaches are superior to those taken by the state and the Women's Federation, and fail to see the congruence between them. To be sure, some, including Gao Xiaoxian (2005), have recom-mended that GAD concepts and terminology should be 'indigenized'. But there has been little investigation into the political economy of knowledge production – the structures, political processes and sets of power relations at the international, national and local levels that shape how the keywords 'development', 'participation' and 'empowerment' are defined and har-nessed to strategic agendas in China. Few analysts have acknowledged that, although some terms central to global development-speak, including 'development' and 'equality', have a long, potent history in the politics of rural China, others, including 'participation', 'agency' and 'empower-ment', are new and, to most rural people, are meaningless or carry con-notations very different from those associated with the concepts in other places. Finally, Chinese critiques of rural development interventions tend to focus on technical obstacles, or the limited ability of 'traditionally-minded' women to capitalize on programmes aimed at enhancing their 'quality', 'participation' or 'empowerment'. Comparatively little attention has been paid to the dispositions of different rural women with respect to 'development', or the ways in which they experience, appropriate and use for their own purposes, deflect or are affected by, rural development agencies, institutions and resources.

Thus, the central questions that this volume seeks to address are, who are the 'rural women' that simultaneously have been elided in China's 'new' approach to rural development, and are discursively constructed and mobilized in development policies, discourses and projects in contemporary China? What kinds of women-subjects, enmeshed in what multiplicity of political, social and gender relations, are engaging in rural development? And what rights and visions of development are invoked in their engagements? In responding to these questions, the following chapters reveal that despite their scripting as backward, 'vulnerable', and instrumentally 'empowered' mediators of national modernity, rural women are using the knowledges, expectations, organizational and institutional tools and resources produced by and for development, for purposes not always intended, and with sometimes unpredictable consequences for both local development outcomes and gender relations.

CHAPTER OUTLINE

Our organization of chapters reverses the perspective of much of the existing literature on women, gender and rural development in China, which either presents an analysis of the *impacts* of rural development *on* women and gender relations (see, for example, Han and Su 2006; World Bank 2006), or explores top-down strategies to transform gender relations by increasing women's participation in rural development (Chen, Lanyan 2008). Unwittingly, this literature reproduces the problematic assumptions that women in 'underdeveloped' communities are the passive recipients or victims of other people's visions of development, or, alternately, those who, with proper guidance, might become virtuous instruments of national development-as-equality. We aim to make a modest contribution to destabilizing the hierarchies of knowledge, power and agency inherent in that conceptual structuring by literally putting rural women first. Thus, Part I explores the agency of women in the context of land developments, intra-household distributions of labour and leisure, and public cultural performances; Part II examines interactions between state and NGO development policies relating to population policy, land rights and education, and social institutions; and Part III focuses on the roles played by NGOs, overseas-funded projects and global discourses in the 'empowerment' of women in rural China.

Part I: Women Shaping Development

Urban–rural integration is one of the strategic goals of China's 'new' approach to rural development. In Chapter 1, Sargeson and Song draw on a comparative study of three sites to analyse women's agency in villages' determination of citizenship and distribution of benefits from urban land development. In their research sites, the authors report, men vastly outnumbered women in village rule-making bodies and, consequently, decided on villagers' citizenship and eligibility to share in compensation for land loss. And, in each site, the rules flouted constitutional guarantees of gender equality, prompting excluded women to challenge the rules.

How women claimed equal citizenship in these urbanizing communities, and with what degree of success, was shaped by local structures and institutions of political authority. In Changsha, Hunan Province, the centralized, top-down management of land development meant women were relatively successful in contesting gender discrimination in compensation distribution, and in securing commitments from government to provide social protections for expropriated villagers. This represented an example of what one might term a 'virtuous cycle', involving the actions of a developmental state, women's active participation in the deliberative life of the community, and citizens' realization of entitlements as members of an inclusive, 'modern' nation. In contrast, around the outskirts of the provincial capital of Fujian, Fuzhou, women were marginalized not only from village organizations and decision making, but also from local state agencies and remediation policies and practices. This closed off opportunities for 'Fuzhou women to exercise the types of autonomous, rightful agency demonstrated by women in Changsha' (Chapter 1, p. 44) prompting them instead to emphasize their membership of, and align their entitlement claims with, androcentric villages and households. Compared to the other sites, in Fuzhou not only did women lose most in terms of their livelihoods, entitlements and potential agency as national citizens, but their exclusion increased community inequalities and undermined 'social harmony' in the course of land development. The authors show, therefore, that the ways in which questions of gender and citizenship are dealt with at the local level are central to the efficacy of urban–rural integration as a developmentalist strategy.

In Chapter 2, Huang draws on fieldwork in Lianhe, a village in Hubei Province, to examine generational shifts in the gender distribution of leisure. Her findings offer a fascinating corrective to both the Marxist and liberal feminist development discourses propagated by the Chinese state and Women's Federation, and contribute to more recent feminist literature showing the complexity of interrelations between intra-household gender relations and relations of production. In Lianhe, economic development has reduced the labour intensity of agricultural and domestic work, and increased the time and money that villagers are able to spend on leisure. This leads Huang to ask: 'How has the rise of leisure affected the linkage between 'labour' and 'gender equality' in leisure within households? Huang reports that while elderly women in Lianhe had little conception of 'leisure', and did not begrudge the disproportionate time and money their husbands spent on leisure, younger generations of women demanded that their husbands share leisure resources more equally. The author explains older women's 'self-sacrifice' and younger women's 'selective self-sacrifice', as a consequence of women's changing participation in paid employment, and corresponding changes in responsibility for unpaid domestic work within households. The self-sacrifice narrative of the oldest generation of women was a self-serving discursive strategy aimed at highlighting their unpaid contribution to the family, thus enhancing their security. Younger generations of women, in contrast, argued that their monetary contributions towards the household entitled them to rest and 'play'. Moreover, they were aware that their husbands' relative power in the family would decline with age as their income contributions diminished. When women age and no longer are employed, however, their domestic work and childcare still provide them with a measure of influence in the family. Younger women, therefore, did not feel the same need to sacrifice their leisure for their husbands, but did devote time and money to their children.

Yet even in households in which women earned a relatively large cash income, greater gender equality in leisure distribution was by no means assured. In such cases, husbands sometimes felt their status as males was threatened, and sought to shore up their 'face' by demanding a greater share of leisure resources. Some women were reluctant to press their case for fear of domestic violence, and because women's 'assertiveness' was blamed by community members for causing family disharmony. Hence, Huang concludes, husband–wife arguments over the distribution of leisure resources among the younger generations are the result of complex links between changing labour patterns associated with economic development, perceptions of the relation between paid labour and leisure, and norms of fairness and gender-appropriate behaviours in the village.

Chapter 3 shifts our attention to the agency of ethnic minority women in state-sponsored 'cultural development'. Often involving significant changes to lifestyles, authority structures and gender relations in China's ethnic minority communities, such cultural development projects are generally motivated by a range of desires of both state and non-state actors, for the economic benefits of cultural tourism, the recognition and conservation of local cultures, and the participation by non-Han populations in a strong, 'modern' state. Ingram and five Kam co-authors, discuss what cultural development and 'taking the stage' in song performances mean to women in a Southern Kam community in Guizhou Province.

Although historically, women and men equally were recognized as 'song experts' in Kam villages, in the state's 'development' of Kam musical culture since 2000, women have been excluded from the design of cultural policy and management of staged performances. However, because many men and young women have left the community for work or study, song performances have increasingly relied on the participation of older Kam women. For all this, the authors do not depict the Kam singers as mere victims of state efforts to exoticize, essentialize and exploit them. Rather, they argue that Kam women actively support, collaborate in, and benefit from the staged song performances. Indeed, women derive considerable economic, cultural and social capital from participating in the performances, and this has led to changes in Kam women's positioning within their households and the community. In particular, the singers make money and gain opportunities to travel. Performances enhance their self-confidence and provide new models of Kam femininity for young women, as well as changing the attitudes of their husbands and other men towards them. Hence, Ingram (as main author) concludes, 'state sponsorship [of the development of Kam song performances] . . . has provided women with a legitimate foundation from which they can act to develop their own culture and cultural practices in ways that are appropriate for their own communities, and has been a legitimate source to draw upon to validate actions that challenge gendered cultural norms' (Chapter 3, p. 89).

Part II: Tangled Ties: Policies, Institutions and Discourses

In Chapter 6, Ross refers to Stromquist's characterization of gender issues as 'wicked problems', 'complex, interrelated, and less amenable to technical or scientific solutions since they depend primarily on value preferences' (Chapter 6, p. 144). In Part II, we take a look at some of the complex interrelations – the tangled ties – between development policies, global, national and local constructions of gender, and donor-funded projects, and rural social institutions, including virilocal marriage,[5] patriarchal kinship and inheritance practices, and son preference.

The first two chapters focus on the gender dimensions of what has been a core element in the post-Mao Chinese state's strategy for development; control over reproduction. In the late 1970s, concerned that population growth was threatening economic development, Chinese state leaders introduced stringent limits on reproduction. These measures rolled into what became known as the 'one-child' policy, which greatly reduced population growth, but also produced contradictory social effects. On the one hand, many girls benefited from the state's emphasis on raising fewer 'quality' children, and their parents' greater investment in their health and education. On the other hand, the population measures indirectly exacerbated gender inequalities and discrimination against women (Greenhalgh and Winckler 2005: 245–284). In particular, many women were pressured by government to have late-term abortions and some of those who gave birth to girls were subjected to domestic violence or divorce. The infanticide of baby girls and sex-selective abortions produced a growing sex ratio at birth. To try to resolve these problems, Bossen argues in Chapter 4 that the state population policy itself became gendered, as local governments effectively converted the 'one-child' policy into a 1.5 child policy that permitted rural families with one daughter to try for a son, and provided 'compensatory' awards to couples with daughters. Despite these changes, distortions in the sex ratio continued to grow, and this, rather than aggregate population growth, began to be viewed as an impediment to 'people-led development' and the creation of an 'harmonious society'. At the same time, however, China's population planners argued that their policies were not the sole cause of the problem, because similarly skewed sex ratios were evident in India, and, until very recently, South Korea. Instead, China's sex ratio was attributed to rural people's 'needs' and traditional preference for sons.

Clearly, however, a tradition of 'son preference' does not explain the significant regional variations in sex ratios across China's countryside. Bossen accounts for these variations by examining intersections between three variables: the ways in which land and housing rights are allocated in villages; lineage solidarity; and villagers' tolerance for uxorilocal marriage. Drawing on a comparative study of Huang Tu, Henan Province, and Song Gou, Yunnan Province, she argues that variations in the strength of patriliny and virilocality exert a strong effect on household reproductive choices and consequent sex ratios. In Huang Tu, where there were dominant lineages, and neither uxorilocal marriages nor inheritance of property by daughters was tolerated, the incentive to have sons was particularly strong. Sex ratios correspondingly were highly skewed. In Song Gou, in contrast, there was no dominant lineage, uxorilocal marriages were tolerated, and sex ratios were normal. But until 2000, land had been readjusted to accommodate changes in household size in Huang Tu, whereas Song Gou had not readjusted land since the 1980s. Bossen therefore suggests that the strength of patriliny and virilocality may have a greater impact on sex ratios than villages' land adjustment policies.

In Chapter 5, Eklund examines the issue of son preference from the perspective of the state's Care for Girls Campaign. This Campaign has sought to overcome son preference by means of awareness-raising and preferential policies for families with daughters. Eklund argues that the Campaign is underpinned by a state narrative that attributes the phenomenon of son preference primarily to the material needs, 'feudal' cultural traditions and discriminatory actions of villagers. Reflecting this, the awareness-raising components of the Campaign promote reproductive behaviour free from son preference as 'modern', 'scientific' and 'civilized'. Campaign posters and slogans seek to portray a positive, 'modern' role for daughters, while financial incentives enable parents to invest in the 'quality' of daughters. Eklund argues, however, that the Campaign's aim is undermined, both by contradictions among the Campaign's messages, and disparities between Campaign messages and villagers' needs and gender norms. As an example of the former problem, family planning posters highlight stereotypically 'female' traits of daughters, such as being pretty and caring, implicitly suggesting that other, perhaps more important things, such as economic security, are best provided by sons. Drawing on fieldwork in Anhui Province, Eklund refutes the proposition that the importance of male agricultural labour contributes to son preference in villages. Male manual labour has become far less significant in agriculture over the last few years, due to industrialization and mechanization, and the large-scale outmigration of men. Consequently, narratives focusing on rural households' need for male agricultural labour as the reason for son preferences simply serve to entrench public perceptions of rural 'backwardness'. Also missing from the state narrative is an acknowledgement of the role of population policies in valorizing sons over daughters. For example, when population policies were amended in the late 1980s to allow rural families with only one daughter to have a second child, this effectively reinforced the understanding that sons are more valuable than daughters. Similarly, the provision of compensatory benefits to families with daughters, but not to those with sons, contradicts the message of equal value.

How is gender socialization shaped by developments in rural education? In Chapter 6, Ross examines an 'affirmative action' project that sought to improve the years and quality of schooling received by rural girls. Ross shows that the developmentalist discourse propagated top-down by state education policy, and bottom-up external education programmes supported by NGOs and donor agencies, is closely tied to China's integration into global markets. Educated girls in this essentialist, instrumental discourse, become the 'mothers of development', the means of reducing rural poverty, improving the population's health and quality, and achieving national 'modernity'. Hence, the schools in which the Spring Bud programme was implemented functioned as civilizing places that both emphasized rural 'underdevelopment', and fed parents' and daughters' desire for, and anxiety about entry into higher education as an escape from rurality. Yet in these civilizing places, biological essentialism and gender stereotypes continued to construct a 'gender trap within the market solution' of girls' schooling. Ross concludes that although state education policies and programmes like Spring Bud have indeed contributed to major improvements in girls' educational enrolment and attainment, the developmentalist assumptions informing educational interventions undermine the value of education to girls and women. Told that they have equal rights with men in all spheres of life, girls nevertheless learn that they are inferior to boys with regard to some of the most sought-after skills and occupations. Meanwhile, their status as 'backward peasants' is reinforced, both through increasingly available technologies of communication, such as television and the internet, and through state policies that privilege the urban.

Part III: The Global, the Local and the Project

A corollary of China's integration with global regimes has been the increasing circulation within China of global development discourses, institutions and funding, as well as a proliferation of non-state development agencies. In Part III, we ask: through what avenues and processes have global development concepts and strategies, and the greater participation of non-state actors and new technologies, shaped understandings and practices relating to gender and development in rural China? What are the consequences of this for development actors, rural women, and gender relations in China's countryside?

Zhao Jie, a leading women's activist and head of the Gender and Participation Research Centre of the Yunnan Academy of Social Sciences (GPRC), critically interrogates how global GAD discourses and projects have affected her own participation in development projects in rural Yunnan in Chapter 7. Zhao suggests that development interventions in general, and GAD projects in particular, are underpinned by a self-serving, neo-colonial discourse that continually reproduces power inequalities, and freeze-frames rural women in Yunnan as stereotypical subjects of development that are both culturally diverse and uniformly 'backward'. Meanwhile, Yunnan women's own expressions of their interests are marginalized, and the social, structural inequalities which shape patterns of disadvantage and need remain unchallenged.

In order to effectively promote gender equity and social justice, Zhao writes, development practitioners in China need to interrogate their presumptions, interests and positions, and make better use of existing structures to improve the possibilities for rural women to represent their own needs in development. In the second half of her chapter, she reports on two projects through which she and fellow members of the GPRC have tried to do this. The first focuses on the potential for village governments to represent and realize local women's interests, but recognizes that, to date, members of village governments have generally lacked the gender awareness, skills and resources to achieve that potential. The project therefore makes use of existing Party and government grassroots training resources to increase awareness among Party School leaders and teachers about gender concerns, and state policies and laws regarding gender equality, and to instruct village leaders on methods of gender analysis and the incorporation of gender equality into local policy. The second project involves training female leaders of minority ethnic associations in gender analysis, participatory governance, gender-sensitive development planning and other areas, so that they can lead the way in promoting gender-equitable, sustainable development in their communities in the future.

Wesoky offers a different perspective on rural women's interaction with global feminist and development discourses in Chapter 8. As she notes in the first part of her chapter, 'empowerment' has become a key goal of the projects that Chinese women's NGOs run with funding and guidance from overseas development agencies. How does rural women's 'empowerment' work when the discourses and resources of globalized feminism encounter authoritarian, gendered local-level power structures? In responding to this question, Wesoky's chapter draws on the stories of two rural Chinese women in Hebei whose lives have been shaped through their engagement with the leading overseas-funded NGO, Nongjianü. The first woman, Li, was trained by Nongjianü, and then stood for election and became head of the local Village Committee. The second woman, Xu, worked as the principal of a training school in Beijing founded by Nongjianü, then returned to her village to set up an NGO committed to suicide prevention and rural women's health support. In challenging local-level power dynamics, both women met with strong local resistance. Nevertheless, they claimed to have been empowered through their engagement with Nongjianü and their subsequent work, and to have improved the lives of other village women.

Wesoky identifies three main avenues through which globalization has affected the activities of local activists like Li and Xu, and local gender power dynamics. The first is local–global communications and media, which now connect even poor, otherwise isolated Chinese villages into extensive social and political networks. As Wesoky shows, this can have both positive and negative ramifications for women who challenge local power relations. Media coverage unfavourable to local officials invites repression. At the same time, however, the exposure of repression might gain sympathy from a broader audience and legitimate women's activities. Second, globalization has broadened the agenda of NGOs, and put pressure on existing state organizations and the Women's Federation to democratize and address new concerns. Finally, globalization has presented new challenges to local discourses about gender and power. Through their exposure to global concepts and norms about gender equality and women's 'empowerment', activists like Li, for example, gain the skills and confidence to contest local assumptions that women are unfit to exercise political power in the village.

In the concluding chapter, Yang presents a less positive account of global–local interactions intended to 'empower' rural Chinese women. Yang's case study examines a donor-aided project in north-western Inner Mongolia, which included as project goals gender equity in land rights, community participation and the 'empowerment' of local women. Through three vivid, ethnographic snapshots of project activities, Yang shows how the gender participatory outcomes of the Grassland Management Project (GMP) were shaped by a complex mix of political and operational constraints, and local cultural and institutional limitations to participatory thinking and practice. In some cases, measures to increase women's participation and ensure gender equity introduced during the project directly conflicted with existing practices relating, for example, to the distribution of land-use rights. In others, they were stymied by the discriminatory attitudes of male power holders. And throughout the project, participation and equity were repeatedly undermined by the bureaucratic work practices of project officials and their failure to devote sufficient resources to changing gender norms.

Nonetheless, Yang notes that, through the GMP, women in the project sites gained a new awareness of their rights to land. Furthermore, like Sargeson and Song, Ingram and co-authors, and Wesoky, Yang rejects the representation prevalent in the literature on China's rural development, that rural women are merely passive recipients, victims or instruments of the state's or global visions of development. Certainly, the project failed to increase 'participation' in the specific ways that the project designers originally envisaged; however, Yang's study also points to high levels of agency among local women, sometimes expressed in their 'incorrect' deployment of project resources, as, for example their expenditure of microcredit on family medical expenses rather than pig raising. And in yet other cases, women's agency was expressed precisely in a refusal to respond to hectoring from project workers, or by women literally walking away from 'participatory development' activities.

In sum, the nine chapters that comprise this volume present valuable case studies of gender relations and women's varying involvement in development across China, from Inner Mongolia in the north, to Guizhou in the south. Taken together, they provide important empirical evidence of the contingent construction of the subject 'rural woman', and the centrality of gendered power relations in shaping both 'development' and the agency exercised by differently positioned women in rural development.

NOTES

1. The Women's Federation is a 'mass organization'. As such, it is officially separate from the state (that is, the Communist Party and the government). However, the state funds the Women's Federation, appoints its leadership and determines its policies. For this reason, the Women's Federation is sometimes referred to as a 'government-organized NGO' or GONGO (see Ross, this volume).
2. The *hukou*, or household registration, system was introduced in the late 1950s. Chinese citizens are registered at birth as holding either rural, agricultural or urban, non-agricultural *hukou*. It is very difficult to transfer from a rural to an urban *hukou*. Thus, the majority of rural migrants residing in cities have only temporary resident status rather than local, urban *hukou*. As such, and despite the state's efforts to reform the situation, they face discrimination, exploitation and a number of restrictions on their rights as citizens. For further detail, see Wang, Fei-Ling (2005).
3. For an introduction to, and critique of, Women in Development (WID) and Gender and Development (GAD) discourse, see Razavi and Miller (1995). See also, Yang, this volume and Zhao, this volume.
4. See note 3 above.
5. The majority of marriages in rural China are 'virilocal', by which is meant that the woman moves to her husband's home at marriage. In some rural areas, however, uxorilocal marriages, in which the man moves to his wife's home, have become more common in recent years. For further discussion, see Bossen, this volume.

PART I

Women shaping development

1. Gender, citizenship and agency in land development

Sally Sargeson and Song Yu

The changing agency of women is one of the main mediators of economic and social change, and its determination as well as consequences closely relate to many of the central features of the development process. (Sen 1999: 202)

INTRODUCTION

Urban expansion is one of the defining features of development in contemporary China. The level of urbanization increased from 17.9 per cent in 1978 to almost 50 per cent in 2010. By 2050, with the anticipated inclusion of another few hundreds of millions of people in urban areas, the government plans that the urban residential population will comprise 65 per cent of the total population (Lin, George 2009: 204; *People's Daily* 22 December 2010). To date, urban expansion has been facilitated by governments' expropriation, development and leasing of rural land. These transactions have generated revenue for municipal and sub-municipal governments, attracted investment, spurred economic growth and created jobs (Po 2008). Yet in most regions of China, village collectives, prohibited from acting as principals in land markets and unable even to negotiate land prices with expropriating governments, have received comparatively modest compensation payments for the loss of their land to development (Zhou Feizhou 2007). In October 2008, China's leadership signalled that governments' rights to expropriate land progressively would be curtailed, while village collective organizations within the boundaries of municipal construction plans would be allowed to transact land and retain, invest and distribute profits from land development (CCP 2008). This decision foreshadowed a significant devolution of decision making and control over profits from land development to village collective organizations.

In this context, the question of who is a village citizen, a full member of the village collective, assumes profound importance. For, while village citizens will be entitled to participate in and benefit from land development, non-citizens will not. The stakes for women are particularly high. The way in which the question of village women's citizenship is addressed could either reverse or exacerbate gender inequalities in civil, political and social entitlement associated with the rural reforms undertaken in the last decades of the 20th century (see e.g. Li et al. 2006; Liaw 2008; Guo Xiajuan et al. 2009).

Some scholars of Chinese politics have recently turned to theories of participatory citizenship to argue that, in the long term, villagers' defence of their rights to property and self-government might produce a more accountable, inclusive polity (He 2005; O'Brien and Li 2006). We are concerned that this focus on what is represented as villagers' collective defence of their common, local citizenship rights overlooks gender discrimination in village citizenship, and obfuscates the significance of women's efforts to achieve inclusion as citizens for development processes in both rural and urbanizing areas. Here, we aim to render explicit how villages manipulate gender as a criterion of citizenship, how gendered citizenship mediates women's agency, and how, under certain conditions, activism by women is expanding citizens' entitlements in the course of land development.

The chapter begins by exploring literature theorizing links between citizenship, entitlements and gender differentiated agency. In the following empirical sections, we draw on our research into women's experiences of land developments in three municipalities in eastern, central and western China to show that villages' gender-specific citizenship criteria affect women's entitlements to participate in and benefit from land development, and their capacity to act as citizens. Variations between the models of land development emerging in different municipalities partly reflect the extent to which women in those sites have succeeded in securing government support for their claims to inclusion and equal entitlement, and for an expansion of the citizenship rights of all expropriated people. The conclusion reflects on our finding that women's entitlements and agency mediate economic and social changes in communities experiencing land development.

GENDER-DIFFERENTIATED CITIZENSHIP ENTITLEMENTS AND WOMEN'S AGENCY

The significance of citizenship as a means to, and indicator of, modern, liberal democratic development is implicit in the definitions of citizenship offered by two disparate theoretical approaches. Liberal scholars define citizenship largely in terms of citizens' rights to have rights. In Marshall's influential formulation, those rights include civil rights, such as the entitlement not to be excluded unjustly from the polity, the right to legal protection and judicial process, to own and use property and to enter contracts; political rights to contribute to the deliberations of, or assume office in the community; and social rights to the community's public goods and to a life that is considered decent by prevailing standards (Marshall 1963). In contrast, republican theorists typically interpret citizenship as active participation in the deliberative life of the community. By participating in debates over community conceptions of the common good, criteria determining citizens' status and entitlements, and rules regulating relations among citizens and between citizens and non-citizens, people shape the composition of their community, its development goals and strategies, and their own role within the community's democracy.

As Sassen remarks, assumptions of autonomous subjectivity and agency underpin these definitions of citizenship (2007: 439). From both theoretical perspectives, differentiated, unequal citizenship entitlements are explicable (and become ethically acceptable) as historical legacies of interactions among holders of various bundles of rights in polities constituted at varying levels of geo-political scale (Somers 1994: 76), and as discursive, legal and political resources that autonomous rights-aspirants strategically draw upon in contesting the boundaries of citizenship. Indeed, assumptions about agentic citizenship underpin the emphasis on individual rights, democratic procedures, civil society and market transactions that are central to the modern liberal models of governance and development propagated by international development organizations and states (Meyer and Jepperson 2000). Consequently, the abstract figure of an autonomous, strategic, rightful citizen-agent is a powerful heuristic in policies, programmes and projects promoting participatory community self-governance and individual self-development.

Yet even proponents of participatory citizenship acknowledge that participation in community affairs is enabled or precluded by pre-existing definitions of citizenship status and rights (Gaige 2008). In Lister's words, 'Citizenship as participation represents an expression of human agency in the political arena . . . citizenship as rights enables people to act as agents' (1997: 37). What is required for unequally entitled citizens and non-citizens to participate more actively in the deliberative life of the community? Kabeer (2002, 2005) points to three minimum conditions conducive to expanded participation. First, to act as citizens, people need to believe that citizenship status does bestow rights. They need information about achievable criteria determining citizenship, and confidence in the procedures through which this rights-bearing status can be secured. And they must be able to speak out and reject rules, norms or practices producing discriminatory exclusion. Thus, a second condition is that governing authorities must endorse citizenship and enforce institutions enabling people to claim just entitlement. Third, people must be able to engage in collective and individual actions to claim citizenship. Conversely, Kabeer cautions, people who lack information and confidence in either the strength of citizenship rights or the procedures through which citizenship claims are determined, or are impeded from speaking out because of their political marginalization, institutional positioning as dependents of patrons or families, or poverty, will be constrained from expressing precisely the types of rightful agency that are theorized as being immanent in citizenship and which have been translated into participatory development agendas (Kabeer 2002: 15).

The caution is of particular relevance for research into women's entitlement and agency as citizens. For, as Kabeer remarks:

> when women's subordinate status within the community is incorporated into constitutional definitions of citizenship, the possibility that they can look to alternative sources of authority and legitimacy, such as the state, public policy, or the legal system, to assert rights which they are denied within their own communities . . . is effectively closed off. (2002: 30)

Alternatively, when national constitutions endorsing gender equality in citizenship rights contradict community rules stipulating female gender as a criterion of unequal citizenship, women have incentives and alternative institutional resources that might be deployed to claim full citizenship, but face substantial impediments to acting locally as citizens. Throughout history, and in national and sub-national communities across the globe, changing formulations of citizenship status and entitlement bear witness to women's efforts to negotiate such exclusions and contradictions (Augustine-Adams 2002; Kaufman and Williams 2004; Siim 2000; Voet 1998; Werbner and Yuval-Davis 1999).

China's modern history offers a case in point. Edwards (2008) and Choe (2003), for example, show that urban feminists' arguments that women's subordinate status, particularly in rural areas, impeded the country from achieving nationalist and revolutionary goals, led to the adoption by China's governments of laws de-linking women's nationality from their husbands', and guaranteeing women equal civil, political, economic and social rights. However, the introduction in 1958 of the residential registration (*hukou*) system bifurcated citizenship into urban and rural residential statuses, and made both categories of residents entitled only in their place of registration to different bundles of rights and resources (Liu, Serena 2007; Solinger 1999). Research by Judge (2002), Woo (2002) and Li (1995) has shown that among the urban and rural citizenry, gender ideology, often couched in biologically essentialist terms, continued to justify and perpetuate women's different treatment as a 'special' category of citizens. Thus, although rural women constitutionally enjoyed equal rights as citizens of the nation, they experienced a subordinate status and entitlement in village communities that, in turn, had only local, partial rights.

Recent research in rural China has enhanced our understanding of how villagers' 'rightful resistance' might lead to the emergence of a more inclusive, accountable and equitable polity. In an influential series of publications, O'Brien and Li have argued that, by citing national laws, policies and leaders' pronouncements and capitalizing on the structural fragmentation of the state, villagers are pressing officials to respect their legal rights (Li and O'Brien 2008; O'Brien 1996, 2002; O'Brien and Li 2006). Like Kabeer, they posit that villagers' activism is enabled by their confidence in the legitimacy of their entitlements. But they further argue that these active expressions of citizenship are made possible by the 'un-fragmented' structure of village polities and protest leaders' facility in mobilizing villagers to uphold their common rights. For example, they cite Hunan activists' assertion that they 'are undertaking to defend the citizenship rights (*baohu gongmin quan*) of all villagers' (O'Brien and Li 2006). A key demand of activists is that local governments respect villagers' rights, enshrined in the Organic Law of Village Committees, to elect leaders and Village Committees, convene Village Assemblies to vote on important matters,[1] and manage village resources and community affairs. He Baogang argues that villagers' experience of asserting their rights to self-govern has 'turned peasants into modern citizens, as villagers empower themselves by using democratic institutions and procedures to defend their interests' (He 2005: 216–217).

However, we are concerned that the analytical focus on the political efficacy of villagers' collective rights defence against bureaucratic wrongs deflects attention from the significance of struggles amongst villagers over who is included, and who excluded from the community. Gender constitutes a common axis of unequal membership and entitlement. Indeed, studies of village citizenship acknowledge women's low representation in Village Committees and Assemblies, and the greater likelihood that men will acquire qualities associated with protest leadership, including further education, organizational experience and what O'Brien and Li refer to as 'moral' authority (2006: 135). He Baogang concedes that village assemblies often violate what he refers to as 'the minority rights of women' by voting to exclude 'married-out women' (He 2005: 216). Yet, nowhere in this literature is women's contestation of their exclusion from village polities considered as an example of participatory action that might have broader consequences for villagers' civil, political and social entitlements.

To appreciate the importance of women's participation in changing citizenship, it is necessary to explore ideological and institutional

*Table 1.1   Characteristics of Survey 2 respondents (*N = 208*)*

% aged 20 to 40 years	49.3
% currently married	93.2
% uneducated or with primary education	43.7
% with experience of migrant work before expropriation	8
% with experience as member of village, team or workplace committee before expropriation	5

constructions of gender-specific village citizenship, and how those constructions inspire, enable or constrain women in acting as citizens. To
address these tasks, we draw on findings from research conducted between
2007 and 2009 in a total of six districts and counties in the municipalities of
Fuzhou, in the coastal province Fujian, Changsha, in central Hunan province, and Yuxi, in Yunnan.[2] Half the sites were free-standing settlements
a few kilometres from built-up areas where villagers had farmed inten-
sively before their land was expropriated for the construction of development zones, commercial housing and infrastructure. The other sites were
'villages-in-cities', surrounded by medium density suburbs.

Field research combined qualitative and quantitative methods. All
principal interviewees and survey respondents were women aged 20–60
whose villages' land had been expropriated between 2000 and 2007. In
the six research sites, lengthy interviews were held with 92 women, all of
whom had been registered as residents of the villages from which land
was taken. Ten of those women were interviewed twice. Two surveys were
conducted. The first was implemented by women in local Community and
Village Committees among a non-random sample of 842 respondents in
all six sites. A second detailed, spatially randomized sample survey of 208
respondents was conducted independently by local female postgraduate
students under the direction of the authors in two of the sites, in Fuzhou's
Minhou County and Changsha County.[3] In this chapter, we quote from
interviews in each site, but for the sake of consistency cite statistical data
from Survey 2 only. Summary demographic and personal characteristics
of respondents in Survey 2 (which mirrored the characteristics of interviewees) are given in Table 1.1.

INSTITUTIONALIZING GENDER AS A CRITERION OF VILLAGE CITIZENSHIP

Rural marriage customs partially explain the androcentric construction of
village citizenship. Judd identifies women's virilocal marriage – in which

women move to their husband's home when they wed – as the key cultural practice ensuring 'the residentially structured predominance of agnatically related men in territorially based communities' (1994: 58–59). The cultural embeddedness of men's sedentary marriage and women's marital migration is implicit in the gendered lexicon of the verb to marry: men 'bring in a daughter-in law/wife' (*tao xifu/ laopo*), while women 'marry out' (*jiachu qu*) or 'marry in' (*jiaguo lai*). The persistence of virilocal marriage is sustained by normative pressures. Men who marry uxorilocally – moving to their wife's home – often face pity or ridicule. Shaking her head when asked if she could recall any cases of uxorilocal marriage in her village, one interviewee explained, 'We've got this saying, "Better to live in a toilet than at your wife's mother's home!"' (Fuzhou interviewee 21, 5 December 2008). Usually, only poorer men will countenance an uxorilocal union, so women marrying uxorilocally tend to receive less valuable wedding gifts (Zhang 2008). For this reason, many women also prefer to follow the orthodox, virilocal, marriage custom.

Potent though marital customs are in influencing the agnocentric formation of village populations, they are not rules defining who is categorized and entitled as a village citizen. How and by whom rules are determined affect the content of the rules. In our research sites, village citizenship rules were decided by the Communist Party Secretary, Party branch, village or team leaders,[4] the Village Committee, and Village Assembly. In the site in which rule-making procedures were most inclusive, equal and transparent, a village on the perimeter of Yuxi, votes on membership and other important matters were cast in secret ballots:

> Under village rules, it's the villagers who decide . . . With difficult issues, we vote on it. They hand out voting slips, and you write on them whether you agree or disagree. In this way, it's a completely local rule, its nothing to do with laws . . . Women get the same say as men. The majority decide.

But even here, where procedures for voting were gender-equal, the composition of the rule-making bodies was not. Although all villages complied with the stipulation in the Organic Law to include 'an appropriate number of women' on Village Committees, and women members could participate in Village Assemblies, the single feature common to the rule-making bodies in all sites was that men vastly outnumbered women. No Party Secretaries or village leaders were women, and few Committees included more than one woman. Village Assemblies predominantly comprised male household heads, because wives typically attended only if their husbands were away. Women classed as non-citizens were excluded. Consequently, rules on village citizenship were largely decided by men.

In all sites, the rules that villages applied before their land was expropriated flouted constitutional guarantees of gender equality, and stipulated different criteria for men's and women's citizenship. Men's citizenship was determined by patrilineal birthright, *hukou* and their household's fulfilment of villagers' obligations. No limit was placed on the number of sons in each household who could become citizens, bring in wives and form new households. Women's status was determined by their birth, *hukou* and household's fulfilment of obligations only until they married. After marriage, it was contingent on their husband's citizenship. Women who married village men thereby retained their citizenship. Those who married non-local men were categorized as 'married out', irrespective of their place of post-marital residence and *hukou*, and their local civil, political and social entitlements were rescinded. As a woman newly elected to a Village Committee in Yuxi explained, 'When a woman marries, she has to present her marriage licence, and from the date of the licence her *hukou* is removed from the team. If she can't move her *hukou* – say, into the city – the team retains it, but it's empty, devoid of any benefits whatsoever' (Yuxi interviewee 15, 3 May 2008). Only in households without sons could one daughter – conceptualized and institutionally treated as a proxy son – marry uxorilocally and retain her village citizenship. Women courageous enough to question the institutionalization of virilocality were scolded: 'If you complain that it isn't fair they curse you, insisting, "It's right for girls to marry out and sons to bring in families and make their living here. Isn't that so!"' (Yuxi interviewee 23, 13 December 2008).

In each site, village rules also placed conditions on the citizenship of in-marrying women. As we found in Changsha, a minimum requirement for their naturalization as citizens involved their registration as village residents, usually as members of their husbands' household. The most stringent requirements were placed on long-distance marriage migrants, who in some sites had to complete a three-year probationary period of marriage or give birth to a child before they could be naturalized. Naturalized women enjoyed membership entitlements only for the duration of their marriage, as a divorcee in Yuxi found:

I moved my *hukou* to my husband's village and farmed there for the eight years I was married. My *hukou* is still there. But when I gave birth to a daughter, my husband said I'd have a rough time. He wanted a son. He became unbearable, abusive, saying filthy things. We got divorced and he remarried. I separated my *hukou* from his. But with divorce, if the powerful won't budge, the weak get nothing. When I divorced, they stripped me of everything. I asked for a room in the house, but they wouldn't let us stay there. I tried to get a one-child certificate for my daughter so she could get into school under the preferential policy. But the village cadre refused to handle it. Earlier, I'd asked the old team leader for some land, and he'd said I could get some in the next readjustment. But the readjustment wasn't made until after my divorce. By then the old leader had died, so I got no land. When the land was expropriated I got no compensation. So after the divorce, I had no home, no land and not even the right to vote! I'm not eligible for anything. I can't attend meetings. They wouldn't even let me join the Women's Day festivities! I asked, 'Am I considered to be a man or a woman?' and they said, 'You're not a resident!' So I pulled out my *hukou* booklet and showed them, and they asked how I'd managed to stay registered there. They keep telling me to find another husband . . . There are three of us divorcees in the village now. One of the others is my ex-husband's second wife. She had a daughter too.

Village organizations have harnessed democratic institutions to legitimate their conversion of virilocal marital custom into gender-specific citizenship criteria. The androcentric structuring of village polities and households is being preserved by making women's citizenship contingent on their affiliation with village men. This has important distributive consequences for women's entitlements, livelihood autonomy and agency as citizens – consequences that become particularly apparent when land is expropriated for development.

WOMEN'S ENTITLEMENT TO LAND AND LIVELIHOODS

Cross-national surveys show that women predominate among landless villagers, and many women become landless when they marry or divorce (He Lirong 2008; Judd 2007; Yang and Xi 2006). Women's landlessness is more pronounced in areas such as our research sites, where limited availability and high demand for construction land inflate land values (Zhang et al. 2008). Among our survey respondents and interviewees, we found that before expropriation, most women lost their entitlement to land in their natal village when they married out. In contrast, landlessness among unwed youths of both sexes occurred because villages had not reallocated contract land since their birth. Rules on marital naturalization meant that some in-married women had received a portion of land when their husbands' village reallocated contract land. In Survey 2, 57.8 per cent of Fuzhou respondents and 69.9 per cent of Changsha respondents had been allocated a portion of contract land prior to expropriation, though less than one-fifth were registered on land contracts. Some women who had lost access to land in their natal village and not been allocated a portion of land in the village into which they married nonetheless farmed land contracted by their husbands' household. But regardless of whether in-married women had been allocated a portion of land, they lost that land if they divorced.

Although most women's land entitlements are contingent on their marital status, women rely more heavily on farming for their livelihoods than men. A cross-national survey found that the percentage of women whose main occupation was farming was 17.4 percentage points higher than for men, and in 20.7 per cent of households women undertook all the farming (Quanguo Fulian and Guojia Tongjiju 2001; see also Zhen 2008). Moreover, compared to male farmers, a larger component of female farmers' income derives from agriculture. Gender variations in villagers' participation in, and reliance on farming increase during middle age (Chen and Fu 2009). In peri-urban areas, village men typically continue to work off farm until their mid- to late fifties, whereas women's lower education and gendered age discrimination by employers begin to reduce their job prospects at around the age of 40, forcing many to rely more on agricultural production for their livelihoods.

Village women's reliance on farming[5] as a source of livelihood entails not just their generation of cash income, but also a capacity to contribute to household consumption and resilience. Certainly, among our informants, a few specialized farmers in close proximity to markets had earned substantial incomes; but two-thirds of the women who described themselves as farmers said that they did not earn an individual income. To some extent, this reflected households' interdependent (though unequal) production, budgeting and consumption. Simultaneously, however, it signified that women worked on property that was conceptualized and registered as men's patrimony. For example, some women who performed most of the farm work described themselves as 'just helping' husbands who worked off-farm. But even those women said that their 'help' had been critical in cushioning their households against the effects of price inflation and periodic unemployment. Thus, although farmers had not necessarily earned an individual income, they had not considered themselves to be dependent on their families.

To track changes in women's sources of livelihood, we asked respondents to Survey 2 to describe and rank their three principal sources of personal livelihood in the year prior to land expropriation, and again after expropriation in 2008. As shown in Table 1.2, before expropriation, farming was the principal source of livelihood for 45.9 per cent of respondents. Regional variations reflected the availability locally of jobs that employers considered appropriate for women. Hence, the percentage of respondents primarily reliant on farming varied from 41 per cent in the hinterland of Fuzhou, where electronics, sports goods, clothing and footwear factories proliferated, to 51 per cent around Changsha, where heavy and high-tech industry predominated. Age variations also were significant, with 70 per cent of those aged 40 or over primarily reliant on farming, and

Table 1.2   Women's most important source of personal livelihood (% respondents)

	Prior to expropriation	2008
Farming	45.9	3.9
Wage work	25.1	22.7
Husbands' or children's income	19.3	48.8
Business	3.4	7.2
Other own income	3.4	1.4
Rent	2.9	7.7
Own savings, share dividends	0	1.4
Own pension	0	1.1
Public welfare (*dibao*)	0	3.4
Own compensation from land expropriation	0	2.4
Total	100	100

Source: Survey 2.

only 14 per cent listing wages, savings, rent, business or other forms of work as their main sources of livelihood before expropriation.

Land expropriation deprived most women farmers of their livelihood, making them more dependent on family support. The proportion of Survey 2 respondents who worked 15 or more hours per week, including in farming, declined from three-quarters before expropriation, to just over one-third in 2008, while the percentage primarily reliant on income earned by husbands and children soared 29.5 percentage points, to 48.8 per cent. Tracking changes in the ranking of all three main sources of livelihood, we found that after expropriation around half of all respondents relied more heavily on their families.

Women's increased dependence on their families after expropriation of the land was involuntary. Many complained it had led to lower household living standards, a decline in their ability to capitalize on new economic opportunities, and a diminution of the sense of self-worth they gained from contributing to their household. Many said they felt 'useless'. Older women, in particular, had lost confidence in their ability to stand up for their rights, much less negotiate disagreements in their household and neighbourhood.

A key factor contributing to women's increased dependence on families was that they were less likely than men to receive compensation for the expropriation of land. In restitution for land taking, village collective organizations received a compensation fund from the governments responsible for the expropriation.[6] Receipt of this sum of money created an incentive for all village citizens to try to maximize their own and their households' share of compensation by minimizing the number of eligible beneficiaries within the village. Gender-specific village citizenship rules were applied to achieve this goal. In breach of the Law on the Protection of Women's Rights and Interests, women registered as village residents but deemed to be non-citizens because of their marital status were ruled ineligible to receive compensation.[7] Moreover, because most villages distributed all compensation to household heads, the great majority of whom were male, even eligible women allocated a share of compensation said that they had to negotiate with their husbands over how the compensation money would be spent.

On the other hand, women's loss of livelihood, the exclusion of many from compensation distribution and their increased dependence on families created an incentive for women to contest distributive outcomes by appealing to state authorities either to increase the payment of compensation to villages, or make villages distribute the compensation according to gender-equal criteria. Struggles between villagers differently entitled to compensation by village citizenship criteria were conditioned by, and further propelled changes in spatial governance in the three municipalities, as the following discussion will make clear.

WOMEN'S CITIZENSHIP ENTITLEMENTS AND AGENCY IN THREE PERI-URBAN SITES

How best to assist villagers affected by land development has become an urgent problem for governments across rural China. In each of our research sites, municipal and sub-municipal governments adopted different policy approaches to expropriated villagers' compensation, resettlement, residential registration and complaints, the political and administrative reorganization of villages, and the provision of public goods. Regionally distinctive policy approaches affected the extent to which women were successful in claiming equal citizenship entitlement. To varying degrees, women's 'rightful resistance' spurred governments to adopt those approaches.

Changsha

The management of expropriation around Changsha represented a triumph of unified, comprehensive and, in general, legally compliant governance. All expropriations had been authorized by appropriate agencies. All villages were demolished, and the city invested heavily in constructing the development zones and transport corridors that supplanted them and which were intended to attract foreign and domestic investment in high-tech industry. Following a period of subsidized residence in temporary relocation barracks, the expropriated villagers moved into identical rows of privately purchased, new multi-story houses situated in large, purpose-built urban communities. All were re-registered as urban residents. Village Committees were disbanded and replaced by urban Community Committees. Eight per cent of the land in the communities was allocated to the construction of businesses collectively owned by the residents. Villagers' protests against the terms of expropriation were comparatively mild, and most governments followed due process in responding to the protests.

The transformation of Changsha villages into urban communities had far-reaching consequences for Changsha women's civil entitlements. As urban residents, they became subject to more stringent family planning restrictions, reproductive monitoring and fines for births that failed to comply with the state family planning policy. Yet the great majority of survey respondents and interviewees said they were less concerned about family planning restrictions than about unemployment and welfare provision. Conversely, most appreciated what they viewed as the safer, cleaner environment, better clinics and schools, and stronger property rights provided in the urban communities.

According to a range of indicators, Changsha women's property rights were strengthened. This was evident, first, in the extent to which women had been informed about and participated in community decisions relating to compensation distribution.[8] More than 80 per cent of interviewees and respondents to Survey 2 said that their Village Assembly decided on the criteria of eligibility for compensation, half had attended those Assemblies, and all had been informed of what criteria were applied. Second, 72 per cent of women personally received compensation for loss of the portions of land that previously had been allocated to them. Third, 37.5 per cent of Survey 2 respondents said compensation was paid to them directly, rather than to their household heads. Finally, after their relocation, 85 per cent of survey respondents had their names registered on leases of new house sites, and the percentage registered on house titles grew from 11.5 to 26 per cent.

The property entitlements achieved by Changsha women were secured through a sequential process of claim-making by women, and systematic regulatory reforms undertaken by local authorities. Among Changsha respondents to Survey 2, 21 per cent reported that they had complained to government, the Women's Federation, the media or courts over inadequate compensation or villages' application of gender-specific rules that denied them a share of compensation. The cascading institutional consequences of women's protests were outlined by a District Women's Federation official, who told us that prior to 2006, petitions from rural women against infringements of their property rights had constituted around one-third of all petitions lodged with local authorities.[9] To stem the tide of complaints, the Federation provided legal aid to women contesting village infringements of their property, the district government then prohibited Village Committees from discriminating against women residents on the basis of their marital status, and its Land Bureau began registering the names of all eligible household members on the leases of new house sites. Across town in Changsha County, women's activism had triggered a similar chain of events:

> Early on, married-out women [that is, those who had married out, but retained their *hukou* in the village] and their kids weren't eligible for compensation. It was only after the women complained to the town government that they got some. And women whose husbands married in. Afterwards, everyone whose *hukou* was there got a full share of compensation.

Finally, in 2007 the municipal government directed that all residents whose *hukou* was in the village at the time of land expropriation were eligible for compensation, and Village Committees must hold 2 per cent of the compensation fund in reserve to pay reparations to any resident unjustly excluded. The application of a gender-neutral, *hukou*-based criterion for compensation eligibility dramatically increased the percentage of women receiving compensation, though some villages sought to preserve distributive disparities by creating gender-differentiated age categories of compensation beneficiaries.[10]

Changsha women's political representation also increased after land development. Whereas women comprised less than 20 per cent of Village Committee members, they made up around two-thirds of urban Community Committee members. It would be inappropriate to interpret the 'feminization' of grassroots governing organizations as a signal that women's participation in the exercise of political power had increased. On the contrary, it reflected the fact that, as the operational arm of street-level government offices, urban Committees enjoyed less autonomy, authority and revenue than Village Committees, and staff salaries were below the average urban wage.

Women's inability to exert more influence over social policy through the Community Committees caused widespread dissatisfaction. As one respondent wrote on her questionnaire, 'We ordinary people want a say, to have real power, and expect the higher authorities to listen to us, care for us, provide us with job opportunities and long-term subsidies'.[11]

Unemployment was a key concern: 69 per cent of Changsha interviewees and survey respondents had no paid employment in 2008. Household incomes consequently were low, and almost half the respondents reported that their households' debt had grown. Community officials confirmed anecdotal reports that debt stress was precipitating domestic conflict.

In response to these concerns, local authorities provided expropriated people with free vocational training courses and employment advice. However, the effectiveness of the courses in ameliorating women's unemployment was limited by the 50-year age limit on enrolment, which precluded retraining of the age cohort that predominated amongst the jobless. Authorities also subsidized residents' contributions to urban commercial insurance schemes. As a result, although Changsha respondents' had lower per capita average incomes than their Fuzhou counterparts, their rate of participation in commercial insurance schemes was higher, with 13 per cent holding old age insurance, and 18 per cent, medical insurance. The remainder had the limited coverage provided by rural cooperative medical insurance. Finally, as welfare provider of last resort, local governments provided urban minimum income guarantees (*dibao*) to all households who fell below the local poverty line. By 2008, *dibao* had become the primary source of livelihood for 6.7 per cent of respondents in Changsha. Consequently, although unemployment among the Changsha respondents was considerably higher than the Fuzhou sample, because they had access to social insurance and *dibao*, only 43 per cent of respondents in Changsha were primarily reliant on family support, as compared to 54.4 per cent in Fuzhou.

Women in Changsha who received *dibao* also were noticeably more assertive about their social entitlements than women in Fuzhou who depended on their families for support. Their assertiveness was illustrated in December 2008, when district and county-level governments attempted to rein in their welfare expenditure by instructing Community Committees to apply more restrictive, asset-based criteria to determine eligibility for *dibao*. Dozens of households that had purchased air-conditioners to cope with the summer heat during their sojourn in relocation barracks suddenly lost their principal income source. The response from women was immediate: 'We've rebelled! We padlocked the Community Committee's office, and we are demanding that if they cancel our *dibao*, then the higher level government has to pay us a land-use fee. So now a group of us has gone off to the county government to raise hell!' (Changsha interviewee 32, 12 December 2008). Public notices announcing which households' *dibao* payments had been terminated or reduced were ripped up and the notice boards defaced.

Events around Changsha provide evidence of the indivisibility of women's citizenship and agency in land development. Governments' provision of information, enforcement of equal rights legislation and provision of public goods increased the scope of women's citizenship entitlements, but those conditions were created partly in response to women's opposition to villages' gender-specific citizenship rules and their demands for civil and social rights. In struggling to enhance their own entitlements, women contributed to the application of a gender-neutral, residentially-based criterion of citizenship, and an expansion of all residents' ability to participate in and benefit from land development. In contrast, the entitlements and agency of women affected by land developments near Yuxi and Fuzhou continued to be relationally circumscribed by villages' gender-specific formulations of citizenship.

Yuxi

Between 2003 and 2007, repeated land taking, some unlawfully approved by the office of the Yunnan Governor, Xu Rongkai, transferred hundreds of hectares of land to Yuxi municipal departments and the local corporate giant, Hongta, for commercial developments. Complaints about inadequate and unequal compensation outnumbered all other grievances in the 12464 petitions received by the city government in 2006 (*Yuxi nianjian 2007*).[12] When local authorities failed to address villagers' complaints, petitioners such as Granny Li (a pseudonym) appealed to higher levels of government to protect the rights of androcentric communities and patrilineal households:

> They said they'd only give us a little money because the land would be used to build a university. But instead they built villas, more than a thousand Hongta corporation villas! So the money was never given to us at all, for more than 200 *mu*[13] of our land! . . . We've spoken out. Lots of us. Originally, we complained here [to the municipal government]. Then we went to the province. I myself went to the provincial government in Kunming. Kunming wouldn't handle it. Eventually, we pooled money and sent representatives to Beijing. They were received by the petitioning office and told that they'd resolve the problem. But later we were told it would be fixed by the local authorities, and of course they've done nothing whatever to sort it out! It's been more than two years since they went to Beijing. My son's son was just a tiny baby then, and I carried him on my back through countless government doors! All I wanted was to pass something, some kind of a livelihood on to him!

Responding to escalating protests and media exposés of corrupt land transactions, the central government dispatched a discipline inspection team to Kunming, Governor Xu resigned and officials at various levels of government in Yuxi were demoted or transferred (Xu and Li 2006). In this politically fraught environment, Yuxi governments adopted policies intended to moderate rural unrest and avoid further censure from higher authorities. First, they increased surveillance and detained activists in communities where land was being developed. Second, in villages where average per capita land holdings fell below 0.2 *mu*, they changed villagers' residential registration to urban, converted Village Committees into urban Community Committees and took any residual land. The citizenship status and entitlements of expropriated people therefore differed according to whether their settlements had remained villages or had become urban communities. Finally, governments increased payment of compensation to village collective organizations. With more money at stake, conflicts over gender-specific citizenship entitlements intensified.

Women's low representation in Village Committees meant they had limited access to information about land developments, and little say in deciding on the rules governing compensation distribution. In all villages, married out women and female divorcees initially were denied compensation. The amounts of compensation to which village citizens were entitled were made proportionate to the length of time they resided in the village between the dates when notice of expropriation was served and compensation was distributed – thereby limiting the amounts payable to newly arrived brides. In all but a few villages, the compensation was paid into the bank accounts of household heads.

Women's responses to these compensation rules tended to correlate with their status as either naturalized, and therefore contingently entitled citizen, or out-married, divorced or newly in-married non-citizen. Women such as Granny Li, who as long-standing citizens were entitled to compensation, defended both their villages' rights to set their own rules on citizenship and women's mandatory marital expatriation as an appropriate way to restrict the distribution of benefits among community members. To avoid being categorized as out-married and losing their entitlements, increasing numbers of young women opted to live in de facto relationships or refused to notify Committees of their marriages. But women already deemed to be out-married and thereby denied a share of compensation rejected villages' right to link their entitlements to their marital status, insisting that national laws endorsing women's rights to choose their place of post-marital residence, own and contract property, and receive equal benefits should trump village rules. In some communities, including Granny Li's, after persistent petitioning and protests, excluded women succeeded in getting governments or courts to overturn villages' marital expatriation rules (Yuxi official 1, 15 December 2008). Many local agencies, anxious to appease restive Village organizations and keen to avoid scrutiny from higher levels of the state, refused to intercede. Their failure to enforce national law infuriated one former farmer, denied restitution because of her marriage to an urban resident:[14]

> I went to the city government. They said they'd sort it out. I told them, 'This is entirely a problem of the village cadres!' They said, 'But village cadres are all chosen by the villagers.' So I said, 'Don't you care if the village cadres are rotten?' Then I went to the court, but they looked at my material and said it was a government matter and they couldn't handle it . . .

> [Song Yu: Wouldn't the Women's Federation help?]

> The Federation help? Don't even bother going! They said 'Situations like yours, there's nothing to be done, there are thousands like you in Yuxi now and we haven't the capacity to handle it.' Although the Constitution states that men and women are equal, here we aren't, we women are victims! The 1998 Land Law stipulated that there would be no change in land contracts for 30 years. I signed my land contract in 1998. It's still valid for another 20 years. But they took my land and sold it, then gave me no money! They have infringed the Rural Land Contract Law, the Law Protecting Women's Rights, the 2007 Property Law. How can village rules, a vote by the team, infringe the Constitution, and government not do anything about it?

Local authorities attempted to moderate the resulting intra-community conflicts by encouraging women's appointment to newly created Community Committees, and making social entitlements more inclusive. As in Changsha, women therefore outnumbered men in the grassroots urban committees. To address the 50 per cent unemployment rate among expropriated women, governments provided vocational courses transmitting 'women's skills' (hairdressing, cosmetics, word processing, domestic cleaning), and paid cash incentives to women who enrolled (Yuxi Fenghuang Jiedao Banshichu 2006; Yuxi official 1, 15 December 2008). But like Changsha, an age limit was set on enrolment because 'after 45 it's terribly difficult for them to find work, because no-one wants them' (Yuxi official 2, 15 December 2008). Workshops were held to instruct the former 'peasants' in a feminized urban civics that centred on performances of loyalty to the state, participation in neighbourhood beautification, and modern techniques of home management and parenting.

Welfare measures also became more inclusive. Yuxi villages explicitly linked entitlement to collective property to patrilineal welfare provision. In households containing adult sons, only the sons could apply for contract land and house sites, and Village Committee approval of their applications was conditional on their agreement to support their parents. Eligibility for rural *dibao* was restricted to disabled and elderly village citizens without adult offspring. Out-marrying women's shares in collective enterprises were rescinded, while in-marrying women were issued shares once they were naturalized. In recent years, however, petitions from out-married and divorced women had resulted in ad hoc interventions by governments and, much to the consternation of villagers, some had won rights to house sites and rural *dibao* (Yuxi official 2, 15 December 2008). Tighter national regulations on shareholding prohibited villages from rescinding and issuing shares to accommodate women's marital migration, though this caused less disquiet among villagers because they viewed shares as an inducement for in-marrying women to fulfil their filial responsibilities: 'Daughters-in-law, if they don't look after the old folk really well then their parents-in-law won't bequeath them their shares. So actually this solved our problems of old people's support. Now the elderly are really well cared for and their status has improved'.

In 2008, in response to ongoing complaints about gender and rural–urban disparities in welfare, the Yuxi municipal government introduced an inclusive pension scheme. Expropriated residents aged 60 and over became entitled to draw on a fund accumulated from contributions by expropriating district and county-level governments, village collectives and residents (Yuxi Shi 2008). Women's pension rights remained vulnerable to infringement because their citizenship status and entitlement to participate had to be confirmed by Village and Community Committees.

Around Yuxi, women's citizenship entitlements were variegated and in flux. This regional and temporal diversity was partly a consequence of activism by women to win state backing for their claims to entitlement, either as relationally defined village citizens or as constitutionally defined citizens of the nation. Though Yuxi villages continued to apply gender-specific citizenship rules, governments' transformation of villages into urban communities and women's struggles against their exclusion combined to reduce the salience of marital expatriation rules and increase the significance of national laws and policies in determining expropriated people's entitlements not only to compensation, but also to other civil, political and social goods. In this respect, Yuxi represents an intermediate case, between the encompassing model of residence-based citizenship being created in peri-urban communities around Changsha and the gender exclusivity of Fuzhou villages.

Fuzhou

Around Fuzhou, ad hoc, often unauthorized land taking by district and county governments had left many villages encircled by urban development, without incorporating them into municipal administration, planning codes or budgets for service provision. Land around free-standing villages had been expropriated by provincial and municipal authorities to construct port infrastructure and a massive, joint-venture auto-parts manufacturing zone. Yet despite the involvement of higher level governments, those villages were no better serviced. Although rural incomes around Fuzhou were higher than in the other two municipalities, the embezzlement of compensation funds by local authorities and village leaders meant that Fuzhou villagers received less in compensation for loss of their land than in the other two municipalities (see also Zhao Yan 2004). We were told everywhere that villagers had protested against infringements of their rights, but the protests had been brutally repressed and activists imprisoned. Of particular relevance for women was the fact that governments left village political organizations and villagers' *hukou* unchanged. Women's citizenship therefore continued to be determined by rule-making bodies that in structure and operation mirrored the single patrilineages that populated villages, and which precluded women's participation.

In around half the research sites, villages had never held an Assembly to discuss land developments and compensation issues. Even in villages in which Assemblies had convened, few women attended. One-third of the survey respondents were not informed what criteria decided villagers' eligibility for compensation. In most villages, married-out women and divorcees whose *hukou* remained in the villages automatically were ruled ineligible for compensation. In some, unmarried daughters received half the amount of compensation given to unmarried sons, and women married-in from remote locations received less than wives from nearby. Whereas in Changsha, 37.5 per cent of women were compensated directly by the village collective, only 3.9 per cent of Fuzhou respondents said they were compensated directly and 71.8 per cent said that all compensation was paid into their household heads' bank accounts. As a result, only 59 per cent of women who had been allocated a portion of contract land received restitution for loss of the land. More than a quarter of respondents and interviewees said that their property rights weakened as a consequence of land expropriation.

Governments' failure to respect (much less, enforce) villagers' rights, and women's marginalization from village rule-making bodies meant few Fuzhou women exercised the types of autonomous, rightful agency demonstrated by women in Changsha. Rather, most identified their interests with those of their androcentric villages and households, and acted as caring wives and mothers of citizens when agitating for higher compensation. Outside the gates of building sites, women demanded that the enterprises being constructed on their former land preferentially hire village youngsters. Some confronted village leaders and, emphasizing the neediness of ageing farmers and parents without sons, demanded that they distribute more of the compensation fund to villagers. A few had attempted to negotiate the scheduling and terms of expropriation with demolition contractors and local authorities. But in all these actions, women's gender and their status as villagers precluded recognition of their rights:

> I had a few *mu* of sweet potatoes that were almost mature, just needed another couple of weeks. We begged them not to bulldoze the land until we had harvested. When they cut off the water and power, we carried water from the irrigation channels. But then they called in thugs who detained and threatened us. We women were terrified! Then they bulldozed the land, buried our crops, tools, sheds, everything. We went to Mawei Labour Bureau to complain but no-one paid us any attention. As soon as they saw we were villagers, they put their heads down and walked away. They wouldn't let us all in, so we selected a few representatives, mostly women, a few men. But when we got in they just said, 'this is a municipal regulation, there's nothing you can do'.

Similarly, women categorized by their villages as non-citizens, who sought support from authorities for their claims to an individual share of compensation, confronted deep-seated beliefs about that doubly 'backward' category, rural women. In the first half of 2004, rural women's appeals against infringement of their rights to land and housing had accounted for 62.5 per cent of complaints received by the Fujian Women's Federation (He Fuping 2004). The Women's Federation responded by creating a legal hotline and providing ad hoc support for claims relating to the most egregious cases, but insisted there was no reason to register village women's rights in property: 'Generally rural property is all registered under men's names. It isn't significant. Registering men's names isn't particularly feudal . . . Rural women aren't interested in who has title to the property'.[15]

Economic changes precipitated by land development exacerbated intra-community wealth inequalities associated with age, education and gender-specific citizenship. Younger, better-educated women in well-off households seized on new employment and business opportunities and invested in rental accommodation for migrant workers. But many middle-aged and older women said their age and lack of skills prevented them from finding employment, while the unemployed and those who had missed out on receiving compensation could not afford to invest in the expansion and upgrading of their houses to attract renters. In total, 55 per cent of survey respondents were unemployed. For many, household budgeting became a daily struggle: 'Even with careful management it's hard. We have to scrimp on food. We've nothing. We're really in a mess. There's no work, we got nothing for the land because it was eaten up by the officials. With the price of rice increasing we can hardly afford to eat!'

Fuzhou governments were slow to implement social protection measures to moderate the impacts of women's lost livelihoods and growing
wealth differentials. Between 2001 and 2008, Fuzhou municipality repeatedly announced that it had expanded the scope of its employment, training and urban *dibao* schemes to include all expropriated villagers (Fujian
sheng minzhengting 2006; Fuzhou shi n.d.). Yet 98 per cent of our survey
respondents said they had received no government assistance finding
work or securing training. Only a couple of the poorest widows received
urban *dibao*, while others told us it was unobtainable: 'There's nothing
like that [social welfare], they don't care. As long as the insiders get their
cut, they don't care if we live or die'. In wealthy areas, villages and district
governments co-contributed to small pensions for village citizens who had
reached locally determined retirement ages, but women's pension eligibility was determined by their marital status. Commercial insurance coverage was limited to the wealthy: only 8 per cent of survey respondents held
old age insurance and 6 per cent, medical insurance. The remainder had
rural cooperative medical insurance. Without land, jobs or adequate social
protection, the percentage of respondents dependent on their families for
support more than doubled, from 26 per cent prior to land expropriation,
to 54.4 per cent in 2008.

Sites around Fuzhou illustrated the adverse consequences for women's
agency of villages' application of gender-specific citizenship rules during
the course of land development. Excluded women's ability to act *as* citizens was circumscribed by non-interventionist governments, androcentric
village organizations and gender-unequal formulations of village citizenship that limited women's entitlements and increased their dependence on
families.

CONCLUSION

Questions of women's citizenship have been overlooked by both the archi-
tects of China's recent decision to devolve control over profits from land
development to village collective organizations, and scholars speculating
about the possibility that self-governing villagers' defence of their common
rights will expand participatory citizenship in China's polity. This occlu-
sion is troubling, for, as we have shown, village polities are by no means
inclusive and the citizenship criteria they adopt are not gender-equal. On
the contrary, village organizations predominantly populated by men are
adopting gender-specific citizenship rules that make women's status and
entitlements contingent on their affiliation with village men.

Villages' utilization of gender-specific citizenship rules adversely affects women's capacity to participate in and benefit from land development. Application of those rules to compensation distribution denies recompense to many women, undermining their ability to seize on new livelihood opportunities by investing in retraining, business, rental property or social insurance. The consequent increase in women's dependency on their families is reflected in lower household living standards, and a significant decrease in women's sense of personal efficacy and agency. Although we examined only three, not necessarily representative, cases of municipal land development, our findings suggest that villages' application of gender-specific rules on citizenship might also exacerbate risks for entire communities in the urban perimeter. Where women's marital expatriation was enforced, as in Fuzhou, women's dependence, intra-community wealth inequalities and village–state conflicts were most pronounced. In contrast, in Changsha where citizenship rested on the gender-neutral criterion of residential registration, although unemployment was high and incomes were comparatively low, women's dependence on family, intra-community wealth inequalities and conflicts were less extreme.

Our research supports Kabeer's argument that women's active citizenship is enabled when they feel confident in the legitimacy and strength of their entitlements. In Changsha and in some communities in Yuxi, where state authorities upheld women's constitutional rights, complied with due process and provided social protections, women displayed greater confidence in acting *as* citizens and deploying national laws to overturn discriminatory village rules. Conversely, in Fuzhou, where village political power was 'un-fragmented' and coterminous with lineages, and state authorities closed off alternative institutional channels, women's capacity to engage in rightful citizenship was limited. How women rallied to defend their entitlements differed from O'Brien and Li's (2006) observation that village activists defend the rights of all villagers against official wrongs. Instead, women's claims and the targets of their activism reflected their different positioning as either relationally defined, contingently entitled citizens of androcentric villages, or as people excluded from village membership. The first group sought to force officials to respect the local self-governance and property rights of village communities and households, sometimes at the expense of excluding women neighbours. The second claimed the civil, political and social rights of citizens of the nation and appealed to officials to force androcentric villages and households to respect the equal, individual rights of all.

Finally, we have shown that the agency of differently entitled women is central to some of the economic and social changes propelling urban development in China. As both expropriated citizens and as women excluded from village citizenship, women simultaneously act as agents and subjects in municipalities' formulation of citizenship and social policy. In so doing, women are influencing the design of the bundles of entitlements which underpin the participatory agency of all people caught up in land development, and which distinguish China's rapidly expanding urban centres.

NOTES

1. The Village Assembly is a meeting of a simple majority of adult village members or representatives of two-thirds of village households.
2. Research was funded by Ford Foundation Grant No. 1075-0591 and Leverhulme Foundation Research Fellowship No. 2006/0381. We are grateful to colleagues at Fujian Agriculture and Forestry University, Hunan Agricultural University, Yunnan Agricultural University, the three provinces' Academies of Social Sciences, and local authorities for their assistance in facilitating field research.
3. The sample selection method is explained in World Bank (2005, Appendices: 55).
4. Villages are political-administrative entities made up of several teams. Teams, also called small groups, are resource-managing hamlets or groups of neighbouring households.
5. Farming included crop cultivation and animal husbandry.
6. The Land Administration Law, amended in 1999 (Zhonghua Renmin Gonghe Guo 1999) states that compensation for expropriated land should be paid to the rural collective economic organization representing collective owners, so it can provide for their future livelihood. Resettlement compensation should go to the organization arranging villagers' relocation, re-employment and social protection. Compensation for fixed assets, businesses and crops is to be paid to individual owners. In most of our research sites, the first two payments were combined into a one-off monetary payment to the Village Committee. In some areas, local governments retained part of the second payment and provided villagers with a combination of urban *hukou*, re-housing, vocational training or social insurance.
7. Articles 32 and 33 of the Law on the Protection of Women's Rights and Interests, amended in 2005 (Zhonghua Renmin Gonghe Guo 2005), stipulate that 'Women shall enjoy equal rights with men in . . . distribution of the earnings of the collective economic organizations, and use of the compensation for expropriated or requisitioned land'; and 'No organization or individual shall infringe women's rights and interests in rural collective economic organizations on the pretext of their being single, married, divorced or widowed'.
8. Knowledge about one's property is a precondition for the exercise of property rights (see Ogletree and de Silva-de Alwis 2004).
9. Interview, Women's Federation, 10 December 2008, Changsha.
10. These categories are explained in Sargeson and Song (2010: 42).
11. Survey Questionnaire 2/46, Changsha.
12. Data on petitioners' sex are unavailable.
13. 1 mu = .0667 hectares.
14. To restrict urban population growth, villagers married to urban residents have been prohibited from moving their residential registration to their spouse's place of registration.
15. Interview, Women's Federation, 9 December 2008, Fuzhou.

2. Labour, leisure, gender and generation: the organization of '*wan*' and the notion of 'gender equality' in contemporary rural China

Yuqin Huang

INTRODUCTION

Since the early 20th century, the relationship between 'labour,' 'gender equality' and 'development' has been a central concern for both policy makers and scholars interested in the situation of women. Following Engels and liberal development economists, the Chinese Communist Party (CCP) and some scholars have endorsed rural Chinese women's participation in the labour force as a means of achieving greater gender equality, as well as contributing to economic development in villages. However, others insist that women's participation in the labour force does not guarantee gender equality, as it cannot overcome women's inferior position in gendered divisions of labour, their lower incomes and lack of access to and control over income within the household, or their 'double burden' of work in both the paid labour force and in unpaid domestic work. They suggest that a materialist understanding of gender and development, such as that adopted by the CCP, does not pay enough attention to family and other social relations women are involved in, and neglects the complex connections between the material side of women's lives and cultural practices (Jacka 1997; Wolf 1985).

This research aims to contribute to this reassessment of materialist models and strategies of development by introducing the household distribution of leisure resources as a lens through which to envisage the complex relationship between labour, development and gender equality. In the post-Mao reform era, a series of structural and technological changes increased leisure time for many people in rural China. Economic reforms also have increased the amount of money that villagers are able to spend on leisure. This raises a series of questions. How has time and money for leisure been distributed within rural households? What dynamics of power relations between women and men and between different generations within households can be observed in relation to the distribution of leisure? And how has the rise of leisure affected the linkage between 'labour' and 'gender equality'?

In this chapter, I aim to answer these questions by examining the disparate experiences of three generations of rural Chinese women with regard to the intra-household distribution of leisure resources. I suggest that, despite their common active involvement in labour, rural Chinese women are differently positioned in the household distribution of leisure resources. Women's share in time and money for leisure is determined, to some extent, by their participation in labour (including both cash-generating and unpaid labour). At the same time, it is also the result of family dynamics and socio-cultural norms, institutions and practices, particularly the rural population's own understanding of how development should make their lives less arduous, their perception of 'labour' and their understandings of notions of fairness and female assertiveness. In developing this argument, I explore the links between changes in the labour–leisure relationship, differently positioned rural women's experience of these changes and their understanding of, and agency in, these changes.

The analysis draws upon data collected in a village called Lianhe[1] in Jingmen Prefecture, Hubei Province, central China. It starts with a brief introduction to Lianhe Village and its residents, followed by an examination of the changing relationship between labour and leisure since the introduction of economic reforms, the local rural population's understanding of this change and an outline of previous research on rural women's leisure. It then moves on to the empirical data about how spare time and money are distributed across gender and generation in Lianhe, and the power relations involved. Finally, it focuses on women's changing self-identity, observed through the lens of husband–wife relations regarding leisure resource distribution, and the understandings of husband–wife fairness and gender equality held by men and women.

THE SETTING AND THE PEOPLE

The information used in this study comes from eight months of ethnographic fieldwork, undertaken primarily in Lianhe Village, from September 2005 to May 2006.[2] Lianhe was then composed of eight teams, comprising about 450 households with some 1600 residents.[3] It is mainly a farming village with about 2200 *mu*[4] of farmland. Rice is the main and the most important agricultural product, which makes planting rice in May and harvesting rice in September the two busiest seasons for the villagers. After rice, cotton, rape and wheat are planted as well, but not as commonly as rice. And the labour for planting and harvesting them is much less intensive than for rice. For their livelihoods villagers largely rely on farming, migrant jobs in cities, or a mixture of farming and skilled, manual or seasonal casual jobs in nearby towns to which they commute. As I explain later, who does which job is closely linked to gender, age, marital status and family circumstances, and this affects individuals' share in the distribution of leisure time and money.

The villagers observed in this study are roughly categorized into three generations.[5] The members of each generational grouping share certain demographic features, which distinguish them from the other generations. Members of the oldest generation were born before 1949. As a result of poor healthcare conditions in the early 20th century, they have relatively few siblings. However, improvements in rural women's reproductive health and infant survival rates, resulting from the training of midwives and improved medical care after 1949, mean that they have a relatively large number of children (Davin 1975). The middle generation was born in the post-1949-revolutionary baby boom. It has a large number of siblings but a small number of children due to the enforcement of family planning policy since the 1970s. The youngest generation was born in the 1970s or 1980s, and has a limited number of both siblings and children, due to the family planning policy and couples' reproductive choices.

Differences in family structures, individuals' education and economic opportunity mean that each generation is characterized by different work patterns and intra-household divisions of labour. Generally speaking, women and men in the oldest generation have been farming for most of their lives. The relative poverty of the collective era, combined with the task of marrying off a large number of children, has left many of them destitute in their old age (Guo Yuhua 2001; Yan 2003). The majority of elderly couples live on their own, and only widowers and a few widows live with married sons and their families.[6] The middle generation is a 'divided generation' (including an 'older' and a 'younger group') because of what Redlich (1976) describes as the interaction of 'historical generations' and 'biological generations'. On the one hand, the large number of siblings resulting from improvements in life expectancy and the lack of birth control in the pre-1970s era has caused considerable age differences between siblings. On the other hand, and most importantly, economic reforms since the late 1970s have endowed the 'younger group', who were in their formative years at that time, with opportunities for better education and non-agricultural occupational training, which the 'older group' missed out on. Because of this disparity, the majority of both women and men in the 'older group' now rely primarily on farming, with wives also taking on unpaid domestic work for the whole family and husbands occasionally doing odd manual jobs in nearby towns. This means that there is little difference in the cash incomes earned by husbands and wives. In contrast, in the 'younger group', most husbands are engaged in non-farming occupations in nearby towns and even far away cities, and they therefore generate much higher cash incomes than their wives. Like their counterparts in the 'older group', wives in this group take care of unpaid domestic work and farming, which generates much less cash income than non-farming occupations. Aside from some people in the 'older group' who live in 'cooperative families',[7] most members of both the 'older' and 'younger' groups in the middle generation live in nuclear families. Finally, in the youngest generation, most people live in cooperative families and the majority of both husbands and wives are engaged in non-farming occupations in towns and cities (see Table 2.1).

THE CHANGING RELATIONSHIP BETWEEN LABOUR AND LEISURE ('*WAN*')

When speaking of leisure, the villagers in Lianhe use the term '*wan*', which is similar in meaning to 'leisure' in English, but has broader connotations. For most purposes, '*wan*' is a verb. It can mean 'to play' games, such as Mah-jong or cards, which usually involve a dedicated expenditure of money and time.[8] It can also refer to 'resting' or 'being served', when visiting relatives or friends.

Large amounts of spare time available for '*wan*' did not appear until the post-Mao reform era. Hanying, a woman in her early 70s, sighs with emotion when remarking, 'How happily the people of today are playing!' For Hanying, 'the people of today' refers to women and men in the two younger generations. She predicts that 'They are going to live several decades longer than our generation', since, besides enjoying better food and healthcare, they do not have to spend so much time labouring and have more time to relax. It is widely accepted among villagers in Lianhe that they have much more leisure time now.

A key reason why villagers enjoy more leisure is that much less labour time is required in agricultural production, especially compared to the collective era. Greater flexibility resulting from the dismantling of the collective and the return to household farming in the early 1980s is one factor

Table 2.1 Three generations: basic demographic features

Generations / Demographic features	Birth date	Number of children (on average)	Current family structure	Household division of labour between wife and husband		Cash income disparity between wife and husband
				wife	husband	
The oldest generation	1930s–1940s	6–7	Empty-nest family; or living with adult children's family when widowed	Farming; domestic work	Farming	No significant difference
The middle generation — The 'older' group	1950s	2	Nuclear family or cooperative family with their married children	Farming; domestic work	Farming; occasional manual jobs	No significant difference
The 'younger' group	1960s–early 1970s	2		Farming; domestic work	Non-farming occupations; occasional farming	Husbands earn much more than wives
The youngest generation	Late 1970–1980s	1–2	Cooperative family or stem family	Non-farming occupations	Non-farming occupations	Either might bring in more cash income or no significant difference

53

accounting for the reduction in labour time, but several others also are significant. First, less farm land per capita is available due to the growing population and the increasing demand for land for infrastructure and residential and industrial use. In addition, the adoption of such agricultural techniques as using pesticides and herbicides, and the mechanization of sowing and harvesting, has saved time and effort. Some of the changes in agricultural production have implications for the labour input required of women. For example, as most weeding is done by women, the use of herbicides has saved rural women a good deal of time.

Certain institutional and technological changes also have been particularly favourable to rural women. Domestic work and childcare have become much less demanding because of the smaller size of families resulting from the family planning policy, villagers' reproductive decisions and the increased prevalence of nuclear households. These changes have spared rural women and given them more free time. Importantly, rural women also have benefitted from improvements in home appliances. For example, the reduction of family size has coincided with widespread adoption of coal stoves, which allow one person to cook for three to four people, in contrast to the traditional firewood hearth which usually required attention from two people and a large amount of firewood. This change not only saves on labour, but also saves time previously spent in collecting firewood. Another change, which took place just a couple of years ago in Lianhe Village where there is no running water, is the popularization of wells dug near homes by hired machines rather than the use of natural ponds that often were located some distance from villagers' houses and which supplied water for cattle and irrigation as well as household use. This again has greatly reduced the time women spent fetching water. Other electrical appliances, such as rice cookers, washing machines (although not adopted widely), and so on, also reduced women's labour time. Finally, the expanding production and sale of mass-produced apparel and footwear has freed rural women from making clothes, socks and shoes for the family.

It is hard to estimate the amount of labour time villagers, especially women, have saved as a consequence of those changes.[9] But at least it is clear that the traditional image of a farming life, as defined by the phrase 'to start labouring at sunrise and not stop until sunset' (*richu er zuo, riluo er xi*), no longer applies. During my stay at Lianhe, from early October 2005 when harvesting rice had just finished to early May 2006 when planting rice was about to start, for only about one week in late October when rape was being planted were residents in Lianhe somewhat busy, working for around seven to eight hours each day. Then they rested, by playing Mah-jong or cards in the village grocery store or at someone's home, chatting under the sun, visiting relatives or watching TV. Even during the two busy seasons of planting rice in May and harvesting rice in September, according to the villagers, although they had to work around 10 hours each day, these periods only lasted for at most one month each. This has meant most villagers have plenty of spare time.

In other words, the relationship between labour and leisure in the village has changed. The villagers do not have to squeeze odd times from the middle of labouring to '*wan*' any longer, and most have relatively clear-cut periods of time for labour and leisure respectively. This change, as demonstrated by the quote from Hanying above, is welcomed by the villagers in Lianhe. To some extent, villagers' appreciation of increased leisure time is indicative of their understanding of what a better life is like, that is, what they desire is not to participate more in production but to have a comfortable and easy life without toilsome labour. The rise in leisure and the villagers' understanding of this change have affected the distribution of leisure resources and power relations both within and outside the household. Before moving on to elaborate these by drawing on findings from Lianhe, I will give a brief introduction to existing research on gender and leisure.

THEORETICAL PERSPECTIVES ON RURAL CHINESE WOMEN'S LEISURE

In conventional sociological studies, 'leisure', understood as 'not-work time', exists only in relation to time left over after paid employment. This framework obscures time spent in various labouring activities, including women's time spent in housework and unpaid care, unremunerated agricultural production, unemployment and retirement, all of which fall outside paid employment (Bittman and Wajcman 2000). Feminist perspectives on leisure attempt to 'rescue' women from the shadows of the paid employment framework and explore gender differences in leisure experiences (Adam 1995). In the feminist literature, 'leisure' has been conceptualized in terms of 'time budgets' and 'activities' (Henderson 1990), and the gender division of leisure has been assessed in terms of such variables as leisure time, the use of time, leisure spending, leisure place (out of home or at home), and patterns of leisure activities. Many feminist studies focus on the gender division of leisure in dual-earner families. These studies report different findings, with some saying that women have similar amounts of leisure time to men (Shelton 1992) and others maintaining that the former have less than the latter (Tian 2004). In general, researchers all agree that women's experience of leisure is distinctive: their leisure time is interrupted and fragmented by multiple activities, both paid and unpaid, which makes it less leisurely than men's. Men are more likely to enjoy 'pure leisure', which is uncontaminated by being combined with work activities. Women are said to have less leisure time alone or with adults, and are more likely to spend their leisure time with children. Differences between women are also explored. A woman's position in the life cycle is seen as an important factor. Single women are more likely to enjoy leisure time than married women, and women with young children will have a tougher time than women who are childless or who have grown-up children (Bittman and Wajcman 2000; Deem 1988; Shelton 1992). Finally, women's leisure is much more likely to take place in the home than men's, especially during the working week (Deem 1988).

Most literature on leisure has focused on the leisure of people in industrial economies, and the leisure of rural women has been neglected. Little is known about historical changes in the availability of leisure time for these women. As for Chinese rural women, their leisure suffers a 'double neglect' in the scholarship as, on the one hand, the study of leisure is marginalized in gender studies scholarship and, on the other, what little literature exists on women's leisure is mainly about urban women (Tian 2004: 26). In the available literature on rural Chinese women's leisure, a feminist perspective also is adopted, and attention centres on gender inequalities in amounts of leisure time and patterns of leisure activities. Women are shown to be in a relatively weak position with respect to men in terms of these indices (Tian 2004). But an International Fund for Agricultural Development (IFAD) report reminds us that women's time-use patterns in China vary by region, age and education (IFAD 1995).

To sum up, relatively little has been written about leisure in the lives of the rural Chinese population, especially women, and what has been written suffers from several limitations. First, there has been no examination of historical changes in rural people's access to time for leisure. Second, although some research has focused on gender disparities in leisure patterns, and time and money spent on leisure, few have mentioned women's and men's views about the distribution of leisure resources. Finally, although differences in leisure experiences between genders, and between urban women and rural women, have received some attention, disparities in the distribution and understandings of leisure across generations have not been studied. An exploration of the links between power relations and the distribution of leisure resources between generations, especially between disparate generations of women, is missing from the current scholarship. Below, I address these issues.

TIME, MONEY, GENDER AND GENERATION: THE ORGANIZATION OF '*WAN*' IN LIANHE

This section presents empirical data from Lianhe. It starts with an exploration of the organization of '*wan*' across age and gender, and then moves on to examine the power relations involved in distributing leisure.

Age and Gender Divisions in '*Wan*'

What do the villagers in Lianhe do in their spare time? This section answers the question by examining the leisure experiences of differently positioned rural women and men. It also suggests that by adopting a generational perspective as well as a gender perspective, some conclusions drawn in the existing literature, for example that women's leisure time is broken and non-pure, can be revised.

As mentioned above, in Lianhe '*wan*', as a word having similar but broader connotations to 'leisure', refers to several kinds of activities or statuses, such as 'playing', 'resting' or 'being served'. But what the villagers do when they think they are '*wan*'-ing, and how the different meanings of '*wan*' are referenced, depends on available resources, gender, age, marital status, stage of life cycle, and family structure.

The resources and activities for '*wan*' differ between the generations. This affects how each generation understands '*wan*'. There are very few entertainment facilities in the county in which Lianhe is situated. A cinema in the county town is about a half-hour cycling distance away, but, aside from some young people who go there on dates, most villagers are not willing to pay the price of a cinema ticket. Internet bars in the county town have become fashionable among teenagers in the past two years. Television is a popular source of entertainment, but because few people from the oldest generation have their own TV, they watch it only when their adult children's family are watching. The lower economic status of the oldest generation also makes money-consuming leisure activities out of the question.

For the oldest generation, '*wan*' more commonly means sitting and resting, or being served. Even when sitting and resting, elderly women usually continue working, for example, by husking peanuts or cotton. Thus, the 'non-pure' leisure time of women proposed by previous research applies to elderly rural women in Lianhe. Besides resting and chatting, elderly villagers, particularly women, visit their siblings. Some also go to the Buddhist temple once or twice a month. Married-out daughters usually invite their elderly parents to stay with their families for some time each year, especially after the Chinese New Year when they are less likely to be working and have some good food left over from the festival. However even when they stay at their siblings' or daughters' homes, elderly people, especially women, still try to help with domestic work or even farming. Arguably, in fact, they have no sense of 'leisure'.

In contrast to the oldest generation, the middle and youngest generations are able to engage in a broader range of leisure activities. Playing Mah-jong is particularly popular, and a Mah-jong set is an essential item in almost every household. Besides eating,[10] the main activity when visiting relatives is playing Mah-jong. Watching TV substitutes when playing Mah-jong is not feasible. In this sense, '*wan*' is more related to 'playing' (Mah-jong) and spending money for the younger generations. Compared to the oldest generation, women from the two younger generations therefore are more likely to enjoy pure leisure time.

But not everyone from the two younger generations enjoys equal or even similar opportunities for '*wan*'. The second point developed in this section is that who spends most time and money in '*wan*' depends on gender, age, marital status, family structure and so on. Generally speaking, evidence from the organization of '*wan*' gathered in the grocery stores of Lianhe Village suggests that the youngest generation enjoys more unbroken leisure time than the middle generation.

In recent years, the pattern of 'a grocery store in each team' has become increasingly common, and this provides villagers with a social centre.[11] The emergence of grocery stores is correlated with villagers' improved economic situation and the smaller number of children per household. This means that extra money is available for children's snacks, and these are the main products stocked in this sort of store. Besides snacks, cigarettes, alcohol, cooking ingredients and basic toiletries are also sold by village grocery stores. Since stores usually are situated beside the main village road or at intersections, they also provide a site for the everyday social life of villagers. Information and gossip spreads from here. People gather at the store to play Mah-jong or cards, and the store profits by providing boiled drinking water and charging each person half a yuan per day.

From the end of October, when the villagers finish planting rape, to the beginning of the following May, when people start planting rice, the Lianhe grocery store is crammed almost every day. A typical day in the village starts with some women or men sending children to the primary school by bicycle or motorbike, and others feeding and watering their cattle. After finishing breakfast, at about 10 o'clock some adults start heading for the grocery store. Among the early comers are men of all ages and young women who are temporarily unemployed or having a day off work. More middle-aged and old men can be seen than young men, as most of the latter have taken non-farming jobs. The women who appear

Figure 2.1   Grocery store in Team Two, Lianhe Village: the centre of villagers' leisure lives. The villagers are playing Mah-jong, with onlookers standing or sitting around. This happens inside the store when it is cold outside. (Photo by Yuqin Huang.)

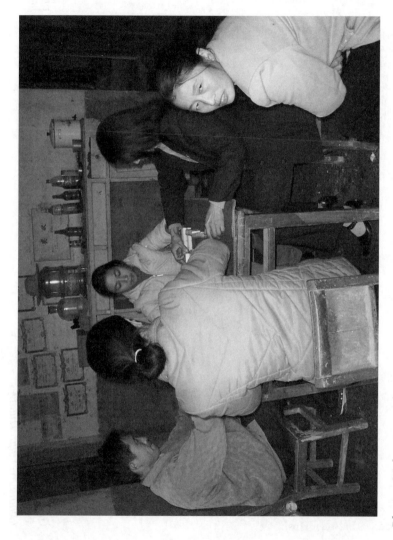

Figure 2.2   Playing Mah-jong at a house in Lianhe Village. (Photo by Yuqin Huang.)

at the grocery store in the morning are those of the youngest generation, most of whom are from a cooperative family and whose mothers (-in-law) take responsibility for domestic work and childcare, and some unmarried women who live with their parents. Later in the morning more people come, including middle-aged women from the second generation who have just finished washing the dishes and doing the household's laundry. Some of these late comers are the mothers (-in-law) of the young women who arrived early. In a room with an area of about 12 square meters, three tables allow 15 people to play Mah-jong,[12] while the rest watch. Normally the latecomers, that is, the middle-aged women, have to leave earlier to cook lunch for the family. The men and women from the youngest generation typically do not stop playing until they are informed that lunch is ready. Most return after lunch. Some leave to collect their children from school at about four in the afternoon, and the remainder stay until dinner time. Occasionally, the game resumes in the evenings, but only when the weather is warm because no heating is available.

The broken leisure time of women described in previous research is not the case for women of all generations in Lianhe. Although it is an accurate descriptor of the leisure time of the two older generations, it is inapplicable for most of the youngest ones who are from cooperative families and whose mothers (-in-law) perform most domestic work and childcare. The unbroken leisure time of both men and the younger generation of women is enjoyed at the expense of reducing the leisure time of the older generations of women. Furthermore, in contrast to the conclusion drawn by existing research that women with small children enjoy less and poorer quality leisure time than women with grown-up children, in Lianhe young women with small children enjoy much more and better quality leisure time than their middle-aged mothers (-in-law) who care for both their grandchildren and adult children.

To sum up, compared to the elderly, the two younger generations have access to more money for leisure. As for leisure time, young men possibly have less than old and middle-aged men, due to their non-farming occupations. However, young women from cooperative families certainly have more leisure time than their elderly or middle-aged counterparts, and are more likely to enjoy 'pure' leisure time than those from a nuclear family.

From Self-sacrifice to Selective Self-sacrifice: The Distribution of Leisure Resources between Husbands and Wives

Stories recounted to me by women in Lianhe provide insights into the distribution of time and money in '*wan*' between husbands and wives and the perceptions of this distribution among women in different generations.

Story one: Hanying

Hanying was born in 1933. When I asked her about her relationship with her husband, she claimed that they had been quietly married for 50 years before he died in 2000. They hardly argued with each other, and her husband never hit her. Her husband drank, was a heavy smoker, and sometimes played a little Mah-jong. Hanying said she had never complained about these activities, and she concluded this was the secret behind their 50 years of peaceful marriage. When her daughters-in-law accused their husbands of spending too much time drinking, smoking or playing, she lectured them to be satisfied, as their husbands only 'wan', without committing any serious wrongs. As for their husbands' expenditure on smoking and drinking, she thought she herself had set a good example for them:

> One day, my youngest daughter-in-law was blaming my youngest son as he smoked and coughed. I told her my story. When my husband, her father-in-law, was unwell and going to die, one day he ran out of his cigarettes and wanted to buy some in the grocery store. Although it was just five minutes' walk for us, it was hard for him, as he was already weak at that time. I then said, 'Let me buy them for you.' I never complained about his smoking or playing. Indeed, we lived quietly together for 50 years!

Story two: Suoxiu

Suoxiu was 50 years old in 2006. She was well respected in the village, as both her children went to university. However, Suoxiu said that at one time she had experienced severe hardship to support her children's higher education. The biggest problem was that her husband, who had a position as a local cadre in the village, always used 'work' as an excuse to play, while it was really Suoxiu who had done the hard work for their family. To earn the tuition fees for her younger child, for example, she even went to Zhejiang Province from 2001 to 2003 to work in a factory manufacturing cheap jewellery, while her husband stayed at home. Suoxiu told me the following, when I interviewed her in April, 2006. By that time both her children had finished university and could support themselves.

> I will not be like that any longer: only he [her husband] 'wan' while I do not. I absolutely will not. Before, he played Mah-jong a lot, but I did not. I just looked on sometimes, as my children were still in university. But now I think why should he have played while I did not? I think it is unfair. He earned money, and I earned too! I did not earn less than him! Before, I compromised for my children's sake. I had no choice then, as my children were in university. He did not think about them, but I had to. But since my children started working, I said I will play as much as him, and use as much money as him!

Story three: Pingfang
Pingfang was 39 years old when I met her in 2006.

Q: Do you communicate a lot with your husband?
A: Not really. He is normally quiet. The other day, I complained to him that when he's at home, he plays Mah-jong or watches TV, and never talks to me much.
Q: Do you argue with each other?
A: You can say that again! He likes playing Mah-jong, but we are not very well-off, and my oldest daughter is about to enter university, so I want to save some money for her. But he plays a lot of Mah-jong and sometimes I argue with him. I remember the other day, when I argued with him in the grocery store, his older brother, who lives in the same village, stood up, trying to hit me.
Q: Why?
A: At that time, my husband was doing indoor painting and decoration in Jingmen Prefecture, without coming back to help plant rape. I did the whole thing by myself, carrying fertilizer, watering the seedlings. I've had haemor-rhoids since I gave birth to my oldest daughter and so could not carry much. Anyway, in the end, I managed it. The day he came back was my birthday, which he totally forgot. He said nothing, going straight to the grocery store to play Mah-jong. I was very angry. His sister and brother-in-law happened to visit us that day and so I asked my husband to buy some meat from the market, but he was very reluctant to move. I knew he must be losing money. I was so angry that I grabbed some pieces of the Mah-jong and threw them onto the ground. His oldest brother was there playing too. He suddenly stood up, shout-ing at me: 'Your husband was working outside to support the family and has just come back, and you go and scatter all his Mah-jong?!' Then he tried to hit me, but was stopped by others. I was so furious that I yelled back: 'It is none of your business! I was arguing with my husband, not you!' Why was I so angry? My husband did not bring one penny back, and I was in an awkward economic situation at home. I even borrowed two hundred yuan from my sister. But he went straight to play Mah-jong, caring about nothing. That was why I was so angry. I did not speak to my husband after that until he coaxed me. [Laughing] You see, we do argue a lot, and every time it is related to playing Mah-jong.

In the stories of most women from the oldest generation, one can see them giving their husband and children great advantages in terms of time and money to spend on leisure. Their words emphasized their self-sacrifice of their interests, so their husbands and children could satisfy themselves. But this is no longer the case for the younger generations. Instead, as in Suoxiu's and Pingfang's stories, women from the younger generations report that their arguments with their husbands mostly relate to playing. And in most cases, it is because the wife is attempting to limit the money and time her husband spends on playing. It would be easy to construe this as gender essentialism. But it is suggested by both the women and men of Lianhe that, although younger women also play Mah-jong, they are more cautious about the time and money they spend on it out of concern for their children's education, which in turn is related to their aspirations for their children to enjoy an easier life as a result of 'self-development'. On the other hand, women in the two younger generations also claim an equal (or at least similar) amount of time and money as their husbands to spend on leisure. In other words, they are willing to sacrifice their interests for the sake of their children, but not for their husband, and so engage in what I call 'selective self-sacrifice'. Furthermore, when I asked the younger generations about their opinions on ceding advantages to husbands in terms of leisure, they usually deemed this to be 'foolish' behaviour, whereas women like Hanying, in the oldest generation, considered it a virtue.

Agarwal argues that wives in South Asia and Africa also 'see their interests as congruent to those of their dependent children and potentially antagonistic to those of their husbands' (Agarwal 1997: 27). The question to ask here is: why is 'selective self-sacrifice' practised among the two younger generations but not among the oldest generation of women in Lianhe? I suggest that changes in the structure of power relations within rural Chinese households over the past several decades have contributed to these inter-generational differences. In accordance with the norms governing family life between the 1950s and 1980s, the oldest generation of women, whether they were in an extended family or a nuclear family, were normally at the bottom of the power pyramid after marriage, so their husband's, parents-in-law's and children's interests were prioritized above their own. In contrast, among the younger generations, parents-in-law's interests have slipped off the radar of women's consideration, and after placing their children's interests at the fore, the women claim equality, or compete with their husbands. The self-sacrifice narrative of the oldest generation of women reflects their insecure position in the power relations pyramid and in resource control and income distribution within the household. From a functionalist perspective, it could be interpreted as a self-serving discursive strategy to remind their family of what they have done for them, and therefore enhance their security in the family. But the younger generations' congruence of interests with their dependent children constitutes an investment which will bring them returns after their children become independent. In addition, when their children marry, many members of the younger generations will live with them in a cooperative family, where the women's role in domestic work and child care will guarantee them security. In contrast, their husbands' relative power will decline as they relinquish control of household property and their income contributions decline due to old age (Huang 2009).[13] This explains why women in the younger generations can afford to confront their husbands over leisure distribution.

How do husbands react to changing power relations and emerging competition from their wives over leisure resources? The following stories offer answers to these questions. Hualing, who was born in 1972 and is the eldest among three daughters in her family, married uxorilocally so she could support her parents in the future.[14] Her husband, Baoxin, comes from the same village. Baoxin is the youngest of four sons.[15] His parents managed to finance the marriage of their older three sons, but because they could not afford to bring in a wife for Baoxin,[16] he agreed to move to Hualing's home. Hualing and her parents, according to some villagers, were very cautious with money. After their marriage, Baoxin did odd jobs in the town, but it was always his wife or father-in-law who collected his wages, giving him only a small amount to spend. Most of the time he had very little money in his pocket, as Hualing was afraid that 'He would become bad with lots of money'. In order to make enough money to allow him to join the other men of his age in playing Mah-jong, Baoxin resorted to gleaning rice from the fields alongside old women. After a couple of years of marriage, he asked for a divorce, as he felt that he had completely lost face among his fellow villagers since he had little control in finance and family matters. His parents also became involved as they thought Hualing's treatment of their son had humiliated their family. The conflict between the two families resulted in enduring enmity. Baoxin went to Shenzhen to work and stayed there for several years. The eventual divorce of Hualing and Baoxin was the first in Lianhe in several decades. Yet although the outcome of their marriage was almost unprecedented, it was not unexpected: villagers viewed households in which a husband married in as being particularly susceptible to serious disputes concerning leisure. I argue that this is because a woman who marries uxorilocally identifies herself with a position normally held by a husband, and she consequently attempts to exercise power and control resources in the household. This leads to conflict with husbands who wish to be treated as 'ordinary', that is, powerful and able to spend time and money in leisure pursuits. Otherwise the husbands risk losing face and dignity among their peers. This type of marital dispute also is more common among members of the youngest generation in cooperative families in which a middle-aged father or father-in-law is reluctant to give up his authority. The complexity of changing power relations between husband and wife and between generations in such families leads to disputes over leisure.

Another story of conflict also involved a couple in which the wife attempted to limit the money and time her husband devoted to leisure. One day, when the husband lost all the money he had in his pocket playing Mah-jong in the grocery store, he asked his wife who was standing nearby for money so he could continue playing. His wife refused. He abused her, and she responded by hitting him in the face. The husband tried to strike back, but was stopped by the other villagers. He then rushed home. When his wife returned home some time later, she found him dead, hanged from a beam of the house.

Disputes, divorce and even the suicide of husbands, signify the extent to which men link their control over time and money for playing with their masculine identity and dignity, and face as husbands. Particularly when men's control over leisure is challenged by their wives in public, husbands risk being mocked or pitied by their fellow male villagers. The two stories of extreme reactions recounted above show how reluctant husbands are to relinquish power, much less accept their wives' competition with them over family leisure resources.

The discussion thus far has centred on the demographic and social factors mediating intra-household gender distributions of leisure resources. Yet there remain questions about the grounds on which claims to leisure are made or resisted. What are behind the younger wives' claims and their husbands' reactions? Do these contestations over leisure have any implications for gender equality between husband and wife, and between men and women more generally? What are the rural husbands' and wives' own understandings of these contestations? These questions are explored in the next section.

Between Labour and Leisure: Rural Husbands' and Wives' Understanding of Husband–Wife Fairness and Gender Equality

Husband–wife relations have been changing across the different generations in Lianhe. As illustrated in Hanying's story, most women from the oldest generation reported that they enjoy peaceful and harmonious husband–wife relations. In contrast, almost every woman from the younger generations that I talked with mentioned quarrelling with their husbands.

As I have shown, although much more time and money is available for leisure among these two younger generations, many husband–wife arguments centre on the distribution of those leisure resources. I suggest that this tension is the result of the complex relation between villagers' labour and leisure, their perception of this relation and the prevailing social expectation in the local community that women should not be assertive in relation to their own interests. This expectation further affects their understanding of husband–wife fairness and general gender equality. All women from the two younger generations engage in income-generating labour. However due to macro-economic shifts and the generations' different educational backgrounds and family structures after marriage, women's labour activities and the proportion of household income they bring in compared to their husbands varies. Generally speaking, as mentioned above, in the older middle-aged group, there is no significant gap between the cash earnings of wives and husbands. Consequently, the wives think that they deserve a share of leisure resources comparable with their husbands'. This is demonstrated by Suoxiu's remark that 'He earned money, and I earned too! I did not earn less than him!' In contrast, wives in the younger group of the middle generation normally make a smaller contribution to the family's cash income than their husbands, as husbands continue working off-farm while the wives are constrained by domestic demands, farming and gender-age discrimination in labour markets. This in turn makes it more likely that their husbands will feel that they deserve comparatively more time and money for leisure. But since these middle-aged women also work hard for their families (especially through farming and unpaid domestic work), they are reluctant to let their husbands have what they consider to be a disproportionately large share of leisure. When they attempt to limit their husbands' leisure, disputes arise, as we saw in Pingfang's story. Among couples belonging to the youngest generation, sometimes the husband makes a bigger cash contribution to the family, and sometimes the wife does. Like middle-aged women, young wives strive for an equal share of time and money for leisure, but because of their position in the cooperative family and the 'self-sacrifice' of mothers or mothers-in-law, there is less conjugal tension over leisure distribution among the youngest generation.

Despite their different circumstances, the two younger generations of women both claim that leisure should be fairly distributed between husbands and wives and they share a similar sense of what is a 'fair' intra-household distribution of leisure resources. The logic behind their appeals is the same; that is, they earn money by their labour in the same way as their husbands, so they deserve a certain share of leisure resources. They see income-earning labour as causally related to, and morally justifying, leisure. In the stories recounted above, when Suoxiu asked herself 'why he should have played while I did not?' she reasoned, 'he earned money, and I earned too! I did not earn less than him!' It was for this reason that her husband's playing was 'unfair'. Men in the younger two generations appear to view the relationship between income-earning labour and leisure in the same way. Thus, in the story above, Pingfang's husband's older brother yelled at her when she tried to stop her husband from playing more Mah-jong, saying 'Your husband was working outside to support the family and has just come back, and you go and scatter all his Mah-jong?!' By implication, since Pingfang's husband was performing the role of 'bread-winner', he deserved time and money for playing Mah-jong.

But the criterion of 'deservedness' is only cash income brought about by labour. That is to say, it is money rather than labour itself, which is valued. Domestic work, subsistence farming and care work done by women do not count in either men's or women's understandings of husband–wife fairness in the distribution of leisure resources. Women may complain about their role in such work, but they do not use it as grounds for claiming leisure resources. It is for this reason that when Pingfang's husband's older brother shouted at her, she did not counter with something like 'I work for the family too'. The truth is she did work very hard. But according to her, what infuriated her was not that her work was not recognized, but that 'My husband did not bring one penny back home!' The logic behind this is not 'I deserve leisure', but rather, 'because you brought no money home you do not deserve leisure'.

However, first, this monetary 'fairness' measure did not motivate women to participate more actively in paid work. On the contrary, Lianhe women envy those who do not have to work but have money to play. Though they apply the 'fairness' measure to challenge unfair distributions of leisure, they would prefer to 'reap without sowing'. While many men no doubt have similar preferences, to some extent, this may also reflect rural women's frustration with gender inequalities in both intra- and extra-household divisions of labour and the gender wage gap. It is partly a reaction to women's 'unfair' treatment in the complex relation between labour and leisure. Certainly, farming, domestic work and child care consume a great deal of their energy and time. Second, even when they think they deserve a fair share of the household's leisure resources as a result of their cash income contribution, women may be reluctant to compete or make an appeal on these grounds, because this may be seen as contravening the social norm that women should not show 'assertiveness' (cf. Agarwal 1997: 17). Indeed, women's 'assertiveness' is often blamed by the local community, especially by men and older women, for causing negative reactions from husbands, including such tragic outcomes as suicide. Thus, Hanying's lecture to her daughter-in-law, cited above, hints that it is women's assertiveness and criticism, rather than the behaviour of neglectful or spendthrift husbands, that causes disharmony in the family.

Of course, the ways in which power relations and tensions between different understandings of husband-wife fairness play out in everyday interactions vary from one rural household to another, and are moderated by different personalities and degrees of conjugal affection. A rural man whose wife claims an equal share in the couple's leisure resources might continue to show respect to her, but conclude that other women who do the same thing are strong-willed and unreasonable. In Pingfang's story, for example, although Pingfang's husband said nothing in response to her outburst and tried to coax her afterwards, his older brother stood up to chide her, and even tried to beat her when she answered him back. His reaction might have differed if the outburst had come from his own wife. But if the relation between the couple is not based on affection, it is likely that the husband will react against his wife's claim for an equal share, and this may result in domestic violence.

CONCLUSION

Using leisure as a lens, this research explores the links between changes in gendered labour patterns and differently positioned rural women's experience of development, and the ways in which younger women's exercise of agency contributes towards social change. In so doing, it contributes to a reassessment of the explanatory value of materialist models of gender inequality and development strategies based on the assumption that women's participation in paid work will lead to improvements in gender equality.

Recent improvements in agricultural technology, together with a series of institutional changes in the rural economy and demographic shifts, have resulted in less time required for labour and a rise in leisure resources for rural women as well as men. They also have meant that different generations of rural women have markedly different histories of, and expectations for work and leisure. This is not to suggest that rural women's changing experiences can be fitted into a crude materialist model of development. Clearly, women's participation in the labour force does not always result in improvements in gender equality, as, apart from their role in paid labour, the allocation of unpaid social reproduction tasks, family dynamics and other social relations and norms play a part in shaping gender roles and relations. However, observations of the shift that has occurred from the self-sacrifice of women in the oldest generation in Lianhe to the selective self-sacrifice of those in the younger generations, and the cash-income measure that villagers use to assess 'fairness' in intra-household distributions of leisure, offer evidence that a bigger role in income-generating labour can somewhat empower women. Younger wives generating cash incomes feel justified in opposing gender-unequal divisions of leisure with their husbands. Behind the younger generations' aspirations of 'reaping without sowing', though, one can see that women are not highly motivated to participate in paid labour. Their attitude may reflect their own experiences of the discriminatory terms under which women work, and their dissatisfaction with materialist models and strategies of development.

NOTES

1. Lianhe as the name of the village and the names of the villagers mentioned in this research are pseudonyms.
2. The fieldwork focused on the transformation of the gendered organization of labour and leisure from the 1920s to 2006.
3. This number refers to those with household registration (*hukou*) in the village.
4. 1 mu = 0.0667 hectares.
5. My utilization of generational categories is intended to assist analytically, and does not imply that there is a clear-cut division between different 'generations'.
6. The great majority of widows choose to live independently while almost all widowers are living with an adult child's family in Lianhe. For more details see Huang, Yuqin (2009).
7. I have coined the term 'cooperative family' based on my observations in Lianhe Village. It is a family form which is similar to but different from both the nuclear family and stem family. In this type of family, the old couple lives with the nuclear family of the young married couple, eating with them but keeping a different budget. There is a cooperative relation between the two generations, with the older couple taking care of domestic work and farming, setting the young couple free for more profitable non-farming occupations. For more details see Huang, Yuqin (2009).
8. Normally, only a small amount of money will be involved in playing Mah-jong or cards, so they are more like leisure activities than serious gambling.
9. In some cases, it might take rural women more time to fulfil certain domestic tasks now due to increased expectations (also see Jacka 1997: 114). For example, they may spend more time in cooking as food is expected to be more delicate. But generally speaking, the amount of time saved outweighs any such increases.
10. Normally, food is cooked by women, and women also wash up afterwards. Men often drink while women are catering for the household.
11. Lianhe has at least eight grocery stores scattered in eight teams.
12. One table with five players is the new way to play Mah-jong which has been developed in recent years in Lianhe. The fifth player waits and watches while the other four are playing, and then replaces the loser when a run has finished.
13. Although husbands in both the oldest and middle-aged generations experience the same decline in power as their resource control and income contribution decrease, the oldest generation often stay in an empty-nest family with their wives rather than in a cooperative family as the middle-aged generation do. This results in different household power relations at old age for these two generations. Husband–wife relations becomes the key relationship in empty-nest families, while in addition to husband–wife relations, intergenerational relations are also important in cooperative families (see Huang, Yuqin 2009).
14. Uxorilocal marriage involves the groom's post-marital residence in the bride's household or, sometimes, village.
15. His oldest brother was adopted by his parents to 'introduce' more siblings as they were childless for some years after their marriage.
16. In Lianhe, when parents 'bring in' a wife for their son(s), they are expected to provide the newly-weds with a house or at least a furnished room, furniture and wedding clothes, as well as present gifts for the brides' parents. Parents of the bride can spend much less for their daughter's wedding without incurring fellow villagers' criticism. I was told by several parents that they 'married the daughter out to her in-law's home without dowry or hosting banquets'.

3. Taking the stage: rural Kam women and contemporary Kam 'cultural development'[1]

Catherine Ingram, with Wu Jialing, Wu Meifang, Wu Meixiang, Wu Pinxian and Wu Xuegui (Kam singers and song experts)[2]

INTRODUCTION

Today, in many of the rural communities of China's 55 officially recognized *shaoshu minzu* ('minorities'),[3] major social and economic changes have seen women assume key roles in the transmission of local culture. Concurrently, many rural minority women are increasingly required to take a prominent role in state-sponsored cultural projects that are promoted as 'cultural development' – projects that are now one of the major influences on the cultures of China's minority peoples.[4] How rural minority women negotiate these new roles and, in certain respects, responsibilities, is crucial to the present and future socio-cultural situation of their communities, yet has previously received only incidental scholarly attention.[5]

This chapter directly addresses this lacuna by examining the views and experiences of Kam (in Chinese, *Dong*) women living in rural areas of south-eastern Guizhou Province – particularly in Sheeam, one Southern Kam region (see Figure 3.1).[6] Within the last decade, so-called 'cultural development' (hereafter given without quotation marks) has intensified markedly, and has focused upon staged Kam song performances featuring rural Kam women's singing. This development process has been stimulated and directed by various factors, including increased state promotion of Kam culture and of the economic benefits of cultural tourism,[7] the associated recognition of several Kam musical traditions as National-Level Intangible Cultural Heritage (one was also inscribed on UNESCO's 2009 Representative List),[8] and the ongoing political importance of controlling the development of minority culture to ensure appropriate categorization and integration of such groups within the socialist state (Davis 2005:

*Figure 3.1   Map of Guizhou, Hunan and Guangxi showing Liping County
(shaded) and other main counties of Kam residence. (Map by
Wu Jiaping.)*

17–23; Rees 2000: 10–27; 2002: 442; Sifabu Faxue Jiaocai Bianjibu 1996:
398; Tuohy 2001: 121). This chapter traces the effects of Kam women's
participation in and response to such development, illustrating the ways in
which Kam women understand their participation in this process to have
brought positive change to their lives.

In this discussion, I (Catherine Ingram, main author) have utilized
musical ethnographic inquiry and a feminist-oriented analysis of socio-
cultural and gender construction.[9] My Kam co-authors created their
own narratives and analyses of their own and their peers' experiences,
and together we edited these contributions into their present form.[10] I
am responsible for the framing discussion, which is based on the views of

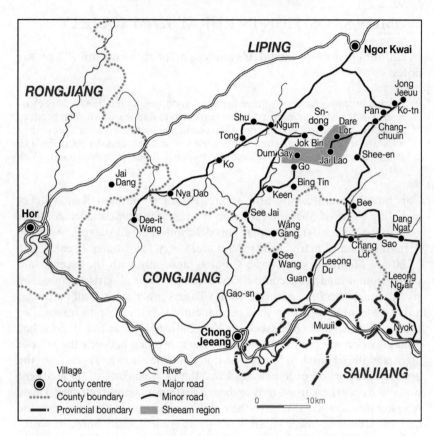

Figure 3.2　Map showing the location of Sheeam in Liping County (shaded), and its position in relation to nearby Kam villages and county centres. Names of county centres and villages are given in Kam. (Map by Wu Jiaping.)

many Kam women and men, as well as on data and understandings developed during 20 months' research in Kam villages between 2004 and 2009.

The chapter begins by outlining women's position in rural Kam society and providing further background to recent cultural development in rural Kam areas. It then describes and analyses Kam women's reception of, responses to, and individual experience of cultural development, and how such development affects their agency. The conclusion focuses on what 'taking the stage' has meant in the lives of Kam women – discussing the benefits Kam women have gained through participating in this process, and illustrating the links between rural women, gender and state-directed development.

WOMEN'S POSITION IN RURAL KAM SOCIETY

In anthropologist Yen Fang-tzu's analysis of a Southern Kam village, she notes:

> Despite the importance of women in [Kam] myth, gender relations . . . are characterised by male dominance. Men are expected to find a wife who can produce a child that will carry on the line of the patrilineal family. Women's prescribed roles are to accept unmarried and married men's courting, to participate in arranged marriage, and to accept the responsibilities of motherhood. (Yen 2007: 56–57)

This broad generalization also applies to other Southern Kam villages including those of Sheeam, although my research reveals more complex gender and power dynamics than this description might suggest.

In Sheeam and many nearby rural areas very few women over the age of 30 are literate in even basic Chinese, and only with the recent state promotion of nine years compulsory education have all girls attended the six full years of primary school. Kam villagers practise virilocal marriage, although a young wife only lives permanently at her husband's house after the birth of her first child (see also Yen 2007: 66). Since the 1990s it has gradually become typical for young Sheeam women between the ages of approximately 13 and 30 to work or study outside Sheeam. Aside from the growing proportion of female students, the vast majority of these absent women are workers in eastern seaboard restaurants and factories. Those who are mothers usually leave their child or children in the village in the care of parents-in-law.[11] Apart from some student visits home at weekends, most absent women make only occasional visits home for holidays or to help with rice planting and harvesting.[12]

Public positions of power are almost exclusively the domain of men. Although evidence indicates that some rural Kam women are attempting to change this situation, such changes are not yet acceptable to the majority of men. For example, male power brokers recently rejected an application from a female villager to stand for election to the Village Committee in a non-female-specific role (that is, not as the Head of the Women's Committee), with the rhetorical question: 'Isn't there a man who can do the job?' Nevertheless, many Sheeam women are extroverted and forthright in asserting their views in certain situations, such as amongst female friends and relatives, and sometimes even when directly addressing and criticizing men.

Gender power relations within families in Sheeam are not uniform. While in some families women assume an equal or even dominant role in the management of the family's finances and domestic affairs, in others the men hold ultimate responsibility for these and other decisions, including for the movements of family members into or out of the village for work or study, and even regarding women's participation in song performances.[13] According to Kam women in their 20s and 30s, the pattern of power-sharing within families is becoming increasingly equitable – a factor they attribute to changing social conventions, women's greater economic independence, and their increasing access to education. Although Sheeam women maintain that most middle-aged and older Kam women (the age cohort now most involved in staged Kam song performances) still rarely refute men's decisions, they acknowledge that these women may neverthe-less attempt to influence men's decisions in various ways.

Regardless of their age, all married rural Kam women are expected to take care of and obey parents-in-law, fulfil clan social obligations, manage or greatly contribute to all domestic and many agricultural tasks (or contribute financially if working away from the village), and give birth to and care for children. Their onerous domestic responsibilities and the dif-ficulties of living with parents-in-law are common topics of women's dis-cussion. On several occasions I heard older women encouraging younger ones to postpone their marriage for as long as possible, in order to delay the end of their relatively free girlhood. The years before marriage are idealized in numerous Kam songs, since they represent the period during which women are valued for their beauty and free from the burdens of adulthood.[14] For example:

> [K.][15] In your father and mother's home you can do as you like
> One day [you] get married and go to their [that is, your husband's] home
> [If you] still want to be [free of responsibilities] as in your youth
> They will say you want to marry someone else.[16]

Understanding women's position in contemporary Kam rural society is necessary for realizing the significance of changes brought about through women's experiences of, and responses to, cultural development. As dis-cussed below, Kam women themselves see the indirect effects of their new role in cultural development to be an expansion of their agency and confi-dence in both private and public spheres.

CULTURAL DEVELOPMENT IN RURAL KAM AREAS

The state-sponsored changes to Kam culture promoted in official dis-course as a form of Kam cultural development are not viewed by all Kam people as creating 'developed' forms of their own culture. This variance in attitudes recalls observations regarding the use of the term 'development' within the global commercialization of cultural heritage. As Miriam Sahlfeld notes:

> Taking the term 'development' literally, presupposes a speaker's attitude that 'developedness,' progress and being developed is 'good' and desirable and that achieving little or none of this is 'bad' and needs to be improved. The term as used by representatives of the industrialized nations therefore has always had a slightly condescending connotation that all who are not developed should develop. (Sahlfeld 2008: 256)

The words Chinese scholars and officials (groups which include some Kam elites) commonly use to describe Kam cultural development include terms evident in national policy discourse: *fazhan* (develop, expand, grow), *kaifa* (develop, open-up, exploit) and *hongyang* (carry forward, develop, enhance). These terms suggest desirable changes, creating a sense of dualism that implicitly positions a lack of such change in a negative light. However, because not all Kam people describe these changes in the same way, and because of the subjectivity and power discrepancy implicitly associated with this term, use of the word 'development' within this chapter is both positioned and conditional.

State-sponsored development of Kam musical culture began in the 1950s, and has primarily focused on the creation of staged Kam song performances. Although natural, constant musical change and customary forms of musical creation are processes of change accepted within Kam culture, the conscious process of state-sponsored developmental change falls outside these parameters. Instigated and orchestrated by representatives of various levels of the Chinese state and, occasionally, by Kam elites, state-sponsored development has moved through a number of phases (see also Yang Xiuzhao 2003).

In the 1950s and 1960s rural Kam women and men, including several from Sheeam, were recruited into professional performance troupes as short-term performers. These groups gave performances in various county, prefectural, provincial and even national centres, and occasionally in larger rural townships. The performers were skilled in local musical traditions before entering professional troupes, and directors of the staged performances drew heavily upon that local knowledge. Almost all the professional performers during this period returned to rural life after several months or years of employment (Pu and Zhang 2003; Ya 2003; Yang Guoren 2003).

In the 1980s and 1990s, after restrictions on traditional musical performance enforced during the Cultural Revolution were lifted, professional

Kam song troupes once again recruited members and resumed giving Kam song performances. Many of the performers entered the troupes without prior knowledge of, or experience in, local musical traditions, and were employed in long-term positions (see also Harris 2004: 7–12). This may have contributed to the growing distinction between local and staged Kam musical performance. From the 1980s, state development also focused on the production of Kam song teaching materials, the scheduling of song classes in schools in Kam regions, and professional performance training in tertiary institutes (Pu Hong 1991; Wu Pei'an 2003; Yang Dianhu 2003; Yang Xiao 2000; Yang Zongfu 2000).[17] While some scholars claim that these initiatives are designed to 'preserve' Kam song, this can only be achieved if students learn songs from their local repertoire. However, printed teaching materials are not regionally specific, thus aside from instances where village 'song experts' teach songs from their local repertoire to children of their home region, the classes and materials have mainly served to promote staged song performances rather than local traditional activities.

Since around 2000, state professional troupes have been increasingly engaged in nationally broadcast performances and overseas engagements (see *Guonei tuanti* 2008; Liping Xianwei Xuanchuanbu 2008), and several privately operated tourism-oriented Kam performance troupes have been established. Additionally, the scale of, and local involvement in, Kam staged performances also has increased markedly, and rural women have participated as occasional performers to an unprecedented degree.[18] Since most young women are absent for work or study, these performances have relied on the participation of the remaining older Kam women.

In recent years, Sheeam women in the 30–60 year-old age bracket have been involved in many such performances. For example, they participated in the three major Drum Tower Culture and Arts Festivals (2000, 2002, 2007) staged by Liping County and involving massed Kam song performances, and in a huge Liping Airport-Opening Arts Festival in 2005 that involved 10 000 people (including 200 women from Sheeam) singing Kam 'big song' (see Figure 3.3). Within the last decade these Sheeam women have also participated in numerous smaller festivals, performances and competitions. Although it is unclear why such large numbers of Sheeam singers have been invited to take part, it may well have occurred as a direct consequence of the revival of public singing within the village domain by married Sheeam women (discussed below); organizing officials would have known that many Sheeam women were still capable and confident singers.

Throughout all these phases, the songs performed as part of these developments have drawn upon a range of Kam song genres that are all sung in the Kam language, a Tai-Kadai language quite different from Chinese.[19]

Figure 3.3   Liping County centre, November 2005. The 200 women from Sheeam, with accompanying township officials, giving a staged performance at the 2005 Liping Airport-Opening Arts Festival. (Photo by Catherine Ingram.)

In staged performances, the songs are sometimes sung in their original village form, but are also frequently subjected to a process known in Chinese as *yishu jiagong* ('artistic processing'), whereby musical or lyrical elements are altered, occasionally quite radically, to produce 'Kam songs' considered appropriate for performance. The small range of Kam songs considered to provide suitable material for these performances comprises only a tiny fraction of the immense repertoire of Kam song, and according to many Kam song experts is not representative of the most important or meaningful songs.[20]

Two aspects of this process of development are of particular relevance to this discussion. First, such development is not controlled by the local cultural custodians, contravening a principle considered elsewhere as basic to indigenous cultural development (Janke 1999). Even amongst the few Kam elites holding some degree of power in orchestrating this official process of development, to my knowledge none have been women.[21] The gendered management of staged cultural production stands in marked contrast to local views regarding gender in cultural activities: within villages, Kam women and men have always had equally important roles in Kam musical performances, and are equally recognized as 'song experts' (in Kam, *sang ga*) able to teach songs. The fact that Kam cultural custodians are not offered a part in controlling the development process makes the various ways that Kam women assert agency in and through their participation particularly significant.

Second, the primary motivation for increasing the scope of Kam cultural development, and thus necessarily drawing on the participation of rural women, appears to be economic. This is confirmed in analyses by Chinese researchers, which implicitly and explicitly connect the initiation of staged performances involving rural Kam women and the promulgation of the Great Western Development strategy (*xibu da kaifa*),[22] both dating from 2000. Despite some mention of 'cultural preservation' as the purpose of Kam development (Fan 2003), the underlying objective appears to be to profit from cultural tourism featuring, and promoted through, staged song performance.[23] For example, in his preface to the collected papers from the first Symposium on Kam big song and the Ninth Annual Conference on Chinese Minority Music, held in Liping County in 2002, Yang Zhengquan explicitly refers to the role of Kam song in tourism:

[Ch.] In 2000, after receiving permission from the State Council to construct the Liping tourism route and airport, and proposing the 'tourism promoting the county' strategy, Guizhou Province named Liping [County] as the special 'Kam culture representative' tourism route. Thereafter, how to develop and enhance Kam culture in order for it to become a culture useful as a tourist resource became the topical subject of everyone's great interest. After planning and preparation, Liping organized the first Drum Tower Culture and Arts Festival. At its conclusion, despite the inclement weather, it can be said that we completed our objectives. Just after the Arts Festival finished we were contacted by China Central Television, and Kam big song was selected for entry into the 2002 Spring Festival Evening Party.[24] (Yang Zhengquan 2003b: 2)

Yang's understanding that the aim of cultural development is to bring economic benefits is a belief shared by many other researchers. Even those researchers who have advocated engaging in other music-related activities to promote Kam and other minority cultures invariably believe these activities should serve the demands of such ideas of cultural development. For example, in his opening remarks to the above-mentioned 2002 symposium and annual conference, the then Chairperson of the Chinese Minority Music Association[25] Fan Zuyin states:

> We must earnestly practice what we preach, and actively participate in work towards the protection and transmission of minority musical cultures . . . We must initiate provision of assistance to relevant local governments in their organization and development of minority musical cultures, with the aim of [developing] all kinds of musical arts activities (such as the 'Drum Tower Culture and Arts Festival' occurring along with this conference). (Fan Zuyin 2003: 5)

KAM WOMEN'S RECEPTION OF AND RESPONSE TO CULTURAL DEVELOPMENT

Owing to the power disparity between Kam women and state (including the Kam elite) orchestrators of Kam cultural development, women singers are unable to overtly refuse these forms of cultural development. Many Kam women are aware of the ways that the cultural development of staged Kam song performances essentializes and exoticizes Kam people, and know that Kam people's participation in staged song performances brings certain political and economic benefits to state agencies without always directly benefiting the Kam people involved. Some Kam women further believe that the process produces music of an inferior standard, although others see the new musical changes as positive. However, despite their awareness of the above-mentioned power imbalance and various aesthetic concerns, women still collaborate in the performances for other strategic reasons, such as to increase their own cultural, symbolic and economic capital within the local arena.[26] Women's participation not only assists them in acquiring these forms of capital, but it is also influencing gendered power relations within rural Kam communities. In many cases, simply the act of women's public participation exemplifies greater female agency.

Although the development process is generally supported by Kam women, some women have responded to certain types or instances of cultural development by seeking to control the terms of their participation, unwilling to passively accept changes to aspects of their own culture. On such occasions, resistance to non-negotiated collaboration appeared to remain Kam women's primary avenue for asserting agency and/or control over the process. Yet different women negotiated their participation in or response to development processes in different ways, as the following example demonstrates.

In 2008, six female Sheeam song experts and singers in their 50s and 60s formed a singing group to compete in the preliminary rounds of a nationally televised song competition. Since the invitation to compete was initiated by the local township government it would have been problematic had the women refused. Thus, the women had little control over their participation in the event. Fortunately, the women were willing participants, mainly because their group and another group of women in their 30s and 40s were the only groups from the whole of Sheeam invited to take part, according them considerable status. They also received support from both women and men, as the community wanted Sheeam to be represented in the competition.

For some of the women in the older group, their participation in the numerous rehearsals in the village, and their absence from home and domestic duties for the two days of dress rehearsal and final competition held in the county centre, seemed to be facilitated by an auxiliary demonstration of personal agency within their own domestic spheres. As outlined in the earlier description of married Kam women's role in village society, demonstration of such agency is highly significant because it challenges prescribed gender roles and relations, particularly for this age group.

As I was invited to sing in the older women's group, I heard how the members negotiated amongst themselves regarding the form of their performance in the competition. Despite the fact that we were competing in the *yuanshengtai* ('authentic') song division, competition results over past years indicated that the group would have to make various creative alterations to the songs for the performance to be rewarded in this supposedly 'authentic' category. Such changes were rarely accepted in the singing performances that occurred as part of traditional village celebrations. One younger singer who sat in on rehearsals suggested to the song experts and singers that they should just think of the changes as adding 'spice' to the performance – not too much, but just enough to make it interesting. This drew no response at all from the older women, clearly indicating that they did not agree. Although they did make some alterations to the sequencing and vocal delivery of the performance, they did not make any of the more radical melodic or structural musical changes that the younger singer had advocated.

I understood the older women to have two reasons for refusing the alterations. Although such changes are accepted in staged song performances, they render the performance aesthetically inferior in Kam cultural terms. In other words, from different standpoints these changes index either development or incompetence, and the older Kam women were anxious to avoid it being perceived as the latter. Furthermore, such changes are associated with the professional staged performances that many singers view negatively as having appropriated local song and devalued local singing competence and aesthetic principles. It is significant that these older Kam women preferred to uphold their traditional Kam aesthetic notions rather than apply others' aesthetic principles to their own culture. From the perspective of the younger singer, a member of the other Sheeam group competing, it was precisely because of the modernity indexed through these developments of Kam singing that it seemed appealing to participate in the performance. To her, the possibility of being perceived as culturally incompetent was less worrying than the possibility of being perceived as old-fashioned or 'backward'. The differing aesthetic responses of the older and the younger singers encapsulated different understandings of, and attitudes towards, the process of developing song forms for public presentation within the state-supported context.

However, it is notable that all the women seemed to positively appreciate the status acquired through the performance. This was one of many examples suggesting that regardless of women's mode of participation in the process, simply the act of participation was viewed by women as benefiting them within their own domestic and cultural spheres, influencing both their own immediate experience of gendered power relations and the course of those relations for themselves and others into the future.

KAM WOMEN'S VARYING EXPERIENCES OF CULTURAL DEVELOPMENT

Despite the economic motives propelling cultural development, the lack of agency that Kam culture-bearers have in response to developments proposed by state representatives and Kam elites, and the above-mentioned aesthetic conflicts, it is precisely because these developments have official recognition and support that they provide a strong basis for supporting changes in Kam women's lives. Nevertheless, there is no indication that such development is intended to bring the positive changes Kam women identify.

Below, my five co-authors narrate and analyse their own and their peers' experiences of participating in Kam cultural development. The accounts of these women, from three different generations, illustrate some of the many different ways that Kam cultural development has directly enhanced the lives of some rural Kam women by expanding their opportunities, confidence and resources. They illustrate one stage in a process that has proved critical in sustaining Kam culture, and has also been beneficial to many other Kam women. Aspects of these narratives could be understood as illustrative of women's limited agency – similar to the limits that affect the lives of other women (and, sometimes, men) both within and beyond China. However, I suggest that these narratives might better be understood as exemplifying various ways that rural Kam women have responded positively to and been influenced by cultural development, and have maximized their own agency, even without that being part of the explicit design of such developments.

1. Wu Meifang, Wu Pinxian and Wu Xuegui

(Wu Meifang, Wu Pinxian and Wu Xuegui are song experts aged in their mid-60s, and are amongst the most active Kam song teachers in Sheeam. They are all grandmothers, and two are widowed. All three women attended school for various lengths of time, and speak some Chinese (an unusual situation resulting mainly from their involvement in staged song performances during their youth). However, only Wu Pinxian, who worked for more than a decade in local government, is confident with written Chinese. All three women have participated in recent cultural development.)

In recent times the number of staged Kam song performances has greatly increased, and we have also been asked by people in the government here to go back on stage and sing. That's a big change, because previously older people like us would rarely go to sing in public. But amongst the three of us we have been to sing in a lot of different places in Guizhou province. For example, in 2003 we were part of the Sheeam singing group that performed at the Intangible Cultural Heritage meeting to prepare the [UNESCO] heritage application for big song, and we were also part of the Sheeam group that won first prize in the singing competition amongst 16 different Kam counties that was held in the Liping County centre. In 2006 we were invited to go to Sao [in Chinese, Zhaoxing] for several days to participate in performances of 'Four Generations of Kam Singers', and we also took part in the big singing festivals in Liping in 2005 and 2007 and other competitions and festivals in our county.

Nowadays Kam women have many chances to sing on stage, and lots of women in their 30s to 50s participate. Generally, we are the oldest. Women in their 40s and older don't get many chances to leave Sheeam, so it's a really important opportunity for them and it's one reason why they like to take part. For most people in our generation money is not important, we just want to participate because we like songs and we want to promote Kam songs. We also do it because it is fun to do things like that together with friends, and to go to see some other places. It's something different from the normal work we have to do here at home everyday.

Of course, it's a big change to sing songs on stage, and it brings other changes too. For example, with big song singing in our village in the past, singing groups used to just go to sing at New Year. As long as they sang together in a co-ordinated way it was fine. But when we sing on stage we have to pay more attention to other musical details about the performance to make it more interesting, pay attention to the feeling of our singing and the quality of the sound, not just if it is co-ordinated or not. That's something quite different from the past.

Most of the young people in our village must go off to study, or to find work, and before these performances most of them weren't interested in singing or they didn't have time to learn. But now more young people have learnt the songs we sing on stage. Also, now that we married people sing in public in the village, not only does no one dare to criticize us, but more young people are also getting involved, especially primary-school students. Now everyone likes to watch the groups of children sing at New Year! But they have to learn singing in the village to know our songs, because few of the songs we sing here are sung on stage or taught in school. Young people aren't interested in learning our most important songs because those songs are long and tiring to sing. But now some women in their 40s and 50s are learning those songs again, so that's another change. Some of the important songs these women are relearning can help them a lot, as they learn how to deal with different situations mentioned in the song lyrics, so it can help their thinking. Now that they go and sing with confidence you can see it is giving many of those women more self-confidence in other aspects of their lives too. For example, if others criticize them and say that they are stupid the women know that they don't need to listen. They gain confidence from the knowledge that they have a repertoire of songs, and that their singing is valued by people from outside our village who invite us to give performances.

2. Wu Meixiang

(Wu Meixiang, 36, has three children and is amongst the few women of her generation who completed six years of primary school. During her teens and 20s she gave many performances of Kam opera within Kam communities, and since around 2000 she has had a prominent singing role in staged Kam song performances.)

Because I have given performances on stage together with other Kam people, I have had a chance to travel to so many places: for example, to Zunyi in 2009 to sing at a competition and festival celebrating the 60th anniversary of the Participation Research Centre (PRC),[27] to Shanghai in 2008 to sing at the conservatorium, to Shenzhen in 2007 to sing in several festivals, and to Kaili in 2006 to take part in the 'Colourful Guizhou' singing competition. Those trips are really unforgettable! If I could have a chance to travel to Beijing to sing there, in the most important city in our country, it would really be a dream come true! Just like lots of my friends I've been to Guangdong and other places to work, but it's only by giving singing performances that we've had the chance to travel to so many different places, to travel by airplane, and to take a look around instead of spending all our time working here in the village.

Giving staged performances is really important for Sheeam because that's how people outside know about us, it's the road forward for us. Although so far we have only just begun to give performances in other places, this is the best way for us, as a poor area, to improve our lives in the future. So while a general education is very important for our children, it is also very important that we train children to sing songs so that they can represent Sheeam. This can help people know about Sheeam and how we sing, and hopefully that way our children can have a better future. It's not just to bring benefits for the people involved in singing – you can't get much for yourself from participating in these performances. It's to promote the development of our whole area.

So far it's true that most of the performances have been given by women, and especially by married women like myself. We really enjoy the opportunity to sing these songs and dress up in new clothes – it's fun for us, and that's why we like to take part. This kind of change is relatively recent, in the past we would never have dared to go and sing in public. But now, for some of us, our husbands even feel happy when we are chosen to take part in performances, and when we go to other places to sing we don't have to listen if they complain about staying home and doing our work looking after the family. According to Kam ways they cannot ever say their ideas about this to us directly, but we know from the kinds of comments they make that in their hearts they encourage us. For example, when a woman says to her husband that she has been invited go with friends to attend a singing festival, her husband might say a sentence or two pretending to complain that his wife always goes off to sing. But when the day comes that she has to leave, he will tell her to hurry up and get ready to go because her friends are waiting outside.

3.   Wu Jialing

(Wu Jialing, 16, recently completed three years of middle school. As a result of her middle school graduation exam results she was amongst the 30 per cent of young women of her generation offered places at senior middle school, and was one of only two young Sheeam women of her graduating cohort accepted to study at the key senior school in her county. She is also the first person in her family to ever attend senior middle school.)

I have always really enjoyed Kam singing. I started to learn singing when I was still a primary-school student, in grade three or four. My friends and I formed a singing group, and we sang at lots of occasions – especially at the different New Year evening concerts organized each year by various villages in Sheeam, and at the Women's Day festival in 2004. We only sang on stage, we rarely sang at other celebrations when people sing in our village. We learnt singing from my grandfather who is a song expert, and also from some other song experts in our village.

I finished primary school in the middle of 2006, and I knew I would have to leave the village to go to middle school. Most students from Sheeam go to middle school in our township centre – we stay at the school during the week, sleeping in dormitories with ten students in every room, and we walk two hours home each Friday night to spend the weekend back in our villages. Most of the girls in our singing group, along with several other Sheeam girls who are also good at singing, were offered middle-school scholarships. These scholarships gave us three years' free education and free board at the school, and we also received ten yuan each week to cover about half of the cost of meals.

As part of our scholarship, we were asked to represent our school by singing Kam songs when officials visited, or for competitions or festivals. We learnt quite a lot of new songs from our new teacher while we were at middle school. She is originally from Sheeam, but since she was about 18 she worked in Kaili, at the Prefectural Song and Dance Troupe. She has given a lot of performances in China, and in the 1980s she even went to Europe twice to give performances with a Kam singing group. When we were studying at school she sometimes came to teach us, but at other times we learnt songs from other teachers in the village as well.

Because we could sing Kam songs we received the scholarship from school. It was really helpful for us because it put less pressure on our family finances, so my parents were very happy. It meant that I didn't have to rely on my parents to pay for my education, that I could be independent and pay for my daily expenses through my own abilities.

At first when my friends and I sang Kam songs on stage we were so nervous we couldn't even smile, we didn't understand about how to be performers. But now we are more confident, and I don't get nervous at all any more. It's because I gave a lot of performances that I gradually became more confident, and I think it probably helped me to be more confident in the rest of my life, too.

THE RELATIONSHIP BETWEEN CULTURAL DEVELOPMENT AND RURAL KAM WOMEN'S AGENCY WITHIN AND BEYOND KAM VILLAGES

The preceding narratives demonstrate not only some of the ways that Sheeam women directly involved in cultural development have utilized this as an opportunity to exercise and enhance their own agency, but also the broader changes these women have witnessed in village gender roles and relations. This section summarizes three important aspects of the relationship between Kam cultural development and women's agency, as these pertain to the wider population of rural Kam women.

First, cultural development has directly challenged a traditional prohibition concerning married women's public performance of certain Kam song genres, especially the genre called big song which features most frequently in staged performances. Traditionally, after Kam women married and gave birth to their first child they were prohibited from publicly performing big song.[28] Once the relaxation of this prohibition became accepted for staged performances around the time of the large-scale Arts Festivals of 2000 and 2002, married Kam women in Sheeam also began to take up public performance of big song within Kam villages; such performances were widely accepted by late 2004.

This development in local tradition might be termed an 'indirect response' to state-sponsored cultural development, and is extremely significant. Previously, regular village performances of big song – the only Kam song genre formally taught by Kam song experts, and one of the most important means of recording and passing down Kam history, philosophy, social structures and other knowledge – had virtually ceased. Because education and labour migration took unmarried villagers away from home, the big song tradition was in danger of being lost. Although both women and men took part in staged Kam song performances during 2000–2002, in Sheeam only women broke the earlier prohibition and revived village big song singing. This singing eventually included participation from men, and won the support of the overwhelmingly male Village Committee. Through this process, married women in Sheeam and nearby areas became recognized as the primary custodians of Kam musical culture.[29]

Not all Kam women in Sheeam are directly involved in song perform-ances, even at New Year. However, the interest many women express in producing video compact disc (VCD) recordings of their performances, and the comments of my co-authors, strongly suggest that both state-sponsored and locally initiated cultural developments are enhancing Kam women's self-confidence. Even women not directly involved in any per-forming activities seemed to gain confidence from the role models offered by their female peers.

Second, since 2000 (especially since 2005) many married women singers from the area have been invited to take part in staged cultural produc-tions. As mentioned previously, in the most extensive of these productions 200 women from Sheeam were paid to perform in the 2005 Liping Airport-Opening Festival. For many, this experience brought them the largest single sum they had ever earned (126 yuan),[30] while the ten days they spent rehearsing and performing in the county centre was one of the longest periods during their adult lives that they had been freed from domestic duties. Moreover, attending the months of nightly rehearsals in the village, as well as the final performance, required many women to assert an agency within their own domestic spheres that they had never exercised before. Women were required to prioritize their participation in the performance over spending time on domestic tasks, and also needed to persuade others in their family to take on their many domestic and farming tasks in their absence. In many families, this process of negotiation began to radically alter family dynamics.

Sheeam women's participation in this 2005 festival was the most exten-sive of any Kam group. This was viewed as increasing the prestige and the cultural and symbolic capital of the region as a whole, a point that also appeared to influence many rural Kam men's attitudes towards women's singing. Some husbands began to take their wives' singing activities more seriously, and as Wu Meixiang notes, a few even gradually became active supporters of their wives' participation in village and staged perform-ances. This also influenced some men's attitudes towards prescribed Kam gender roles; some men began to speak of the women's performances as useful and important to the economy and cultural identity of their village, rather than as a leisure activity that took women away from more impor-tant domestic tasks.

Finally, the changes in Kam women's activities arising from this develop-ment process have exposed younger Kam women to new concepts of female Kam identity. They may be inspired and empowered not only by the model of active women in public facets of Kam village society, but also by the enhanced opportunities, resources and confidence associated with women's involvement in staged performance. These range from the renegotiation of domestic responsibilities to access to scholarship opportunities and new participatory roles in society, both within and beyond the village domain. Moreover, whereas previously only the few women able to speak fluent Chinese could engage in significant interactions with non-Kam, women's participation in the process of cultural development has afforded many middle-aged and older rural Kam women with a rare opportunity to directly interact with society outside Kam villages. On a few occasions, Sheeam women's interactions have also involved en masse resistance or insistence upon negotiating the terms of their collaboration in staged performances. Perhaps women's increased opportunity to simply have their voices heard, as occurs in staged performances, will further improve this situation.

CONCLUSION

Large numbers of rural Kam women have been central figures in recent developments of Kam culture, and the lives of many more women have been indirectly influenced by those developments. Broadly speaking, cultural development has brought greater opportunities for all women. The development of Kam song traditions into large-scale staged performances involving women from Sheeam and nearby areas has enabled the relaxation of the traditional prohibition against married women's participation, and consequently facilitated the ongoing transmission of important Kam song genres such as big song. This has positioned Kam women in key custodianship roles in the village context of the tradition, expanded other social and cultural roles available to women in the local domain, presented new, less restrictive models of Kam femininity for younger women, and enhanced many women's self-confidence.

The concurrent growth in state-sponsored cultural developments intended for display in the meta-local arena has had a twofold influence upon Kam women's sense of agency. This has occurred through women's participation in song performances, and also through women's negotiation of their participation/collaboration in the development process. Although the actions and attitudes of different women and of women of different ages have meant that individual women have different experiences of both participation and negotiation, in general women have acquired economic, cultural and symbolic capital, enhanced agency and a new position in gender relations through their participation. State sponsorship of Kam cultural development has been one vital aspect in these changes, providing Kam women with a legitimate foundation from which to develop their own culture and cultural practices, and enabling them to engage in and validate activities that challenge gendered cultural norms.

Despite these benefits, the recent development of Kam culture has been undertaken without appropriate consultation with Kam women and men, has altered Kam singing traditions, and has encouraged the commoditization of intangible song culture. Moreover, while cultural development has led to changes in Kam gender roles and women's agency, there is no indication that its design has been explicitly intended to benefit Kam women in these ways. It is only through the other vital aspect of this process – Kam women's utilization of such development to inform and support actions within their own lives – that many of the benefits of this process have become apparent. Thus, neither can cultural development be seen as an inherently beneficial process, nor can Kam women be seen as powerless in their participation within it. This situation illustrates that women cannot be assumed to lack agency in the development process, even when they choose or are required to participate in state directed 'modernization' activities which take no apparent account of rural women's position or specific needs. As the discussion in this chapter has demonstrated, it is precisely due to women's actions that Kam singing in Sheeam remains vibrant, and that Kam linguistic and cultural heritage continues to be transmitted.

Kam women's experiences within Kam cultural development illustrate the often marked differences between external power-holders' needs, aims and evaluations and those of different members of the local communities involved in rural development, and that careful research is required to understand what women themselves perceive to be the most important changes development brings within their own lives. In the case of rural women such as Kam minority women, many of whom do not speak the dominant Han (Chinese) language, the benefits they derive from cultural development may be particularly hidden from the view of non-Kam-speaking outsiders. Given the current evidence, there is no reason to doubt that as Kam women 'take to the stage' in the future, they will continue to develop strategies to increase the possibility of turning cultural development to the benefit of themselves, their peers, and their own communities. These strategies may bring further changes in women's position and role, further modifications to Kam cultural practices, and/ or a more significant underlying shift in the basic structure of local Kam culture and society and its position within a wider regional or national context. At the same time, women's actions will certainly be crucial to the continued transmission of Kam language and culture, and thus to the heritage and future of successive generations of Kam people.

NOTES

1. The Kam expression *cha tai* 'take/ascend the stage' – a literal translation of the Chinese *shang tai* – exemplifies the involvement of mainstream Chinese ideas of performance within Kam cultural presentation.
2. Many thanks to Tamara Jacka, Sally Sargeson, Cathy Falk, Adam Driver and Andrew Kipnis for thoughtful comments on earlier versions of this chapter.
3. The total 'minority' population is currently over 105 million; more than 91 per cent of China's population identify as the majority Han.
4. The most distinctive elements of minority cultures useful in state-supported activities are now primarily or only maintained within these rural communities, thus these women's involvement.
5. Hershatter, in a recent survey of English-language scholarship, acknowledges 'the Han-centred nature of most scholarship on Chinese women, without in any way assuming that this is a satisfactory or permanent situation' (2004: 992). Similarly, Kate Xiao Zhou comments that 'most analyses of rural China ignore women' (1996: 206). Schein's work (1996, 1999, 2000) is a notable exception, but as Schein (unlike all authors of the present study) did not become proficient in any local cultural traditions, important insights and collaborative opportunities were unavailable to her. Friedman (2006) discusses gender and state-directed representation, but not the state-sponsored development of cultural performances in non-Han and largely non-literate cultural communities. Some Chinese sources advocating cultural tourism (such as Liu Yong 2005) discuss minority women in cultural development, but are not seemingly based on long-term participatory investigation. As few researchers of Kam music are able to speak Kam, and very few are female, they rarely hear Kam women's own views.
6. Sheeam (in Chinese, *Sanlong*) is an agricultural area with an estimated population of 6000. Most of its 18 villages are located 30–40km by road from the centre of Liping County. Several Sheeam villages have been studied by Chinese researchers (see Zhongguo Kexueyuan Minzu Yanjiusuo Guizhou Shaoshu Minzu Shehui Lishi Diaochazu & Zhongguo Kexueyuan Guizhou Fenyuan Minzu Yanjiusuo 1963; Liu Feng and Long Yaohong 2004; Pan 2005; Yao and Shi 2005: 214–252). Southern and northern Kam-dialect-speaking communities differ significantly from each other in language and culture, but neither group is linguistically or culturally homogenous. Here, Kam words are transcribed using an English-language-based broad transcription system that I devised for transcribing the version of the southern Kam subdialect spoken in Sheeam (detailed in Ingram 2007, 2010).
7. See Dongzu Jianshi Bianxiezu and Dongzu Jianshi Xiudingben Bianxiezu 2008: 8–9; *Dongzu lüyou* 2009; Gao Lina 2007; Wu Dingguo 2005; Wu Xingwen 2008; Yang Zhengquan 2003a; *Zui gaodang* 2008.
8. Kam big song, pipa song, opera and '*nuo*' opera were recognized in 2006 as National-Level Intangible Cultural Heritage (see Zhou Heping 2006: 101–106, 510–502, 517–518). In 2009, Kam big song was inscribed (as 'Grand Song') on UNESCO's Representative List of the Intangible Cultural Heritage of Humanity (see UNESCO 2009).
9. In accordance with ethnomusicological research methodology I learnt to speak Kam and sing Kam songs, and participated in many Kam song performances.
10. These narratives were first communicated to me through telephone conversations in Kam; issues raised in this chapter were subsequently further discussed through letters and/or emails written in Chinese either by or for the women involved, and in telephone conversations. When I visited Sheeam briefly in October 2009 I took English versions of the final narratives for the authors' comments. Wu Jialing read her narrative in English and made several changes. Wu Jialing and I orally translated the second narrative into Kam for Wu Meixiang to approve, and I altered the narrative as Wu Meixiang suggested. I gave an oral translation in Kam of the first narrative for authors Wu Meifang, Wu Pinxian and Wu Xuegui, and subsequently also made the changes they requested.
11. Kam women are marrying and giving birth to their first child at increasingly younger

ages, a trend Kam people attribute to increased pre-marital contact between young people while working outside the village. Currently, many young women in Sheeam marry and give birth to their first child before the state-regulated age of 20. However, with the rapid rise in the number of female students continuing to senior secondary education, soon these trends may be reversed.

12. Some married women in this age group also return to the village for short periods prior to and following the birth of their children. The majority of males aged approximately 13–30 (and also many men in their 40s) spend most of their time working or studying outside the village.

13. Although there are no reliable data available on Kam women's role in domestic decision making, ethnographic observations suggest that Kate Xiao Zhou's (1996: 207–208) claim of relative equality in rural Han men's and women's decision making may hold in rural Kam communities in some contexts or generations. As Zhou comments, depending on the issue at hand, 'in children's mate selection, wedding preparations, birth, accounting, and management, women have more power than men' (1996: 208), and this may sometimes be true in Kam villages. Yet, as Judd (1990: 46) notes, in Han villages there may be 'often definite limitations of the woman's sense of agency'. Finally, recent increases in rural wealth may even renew discrimination against women (Beaver et al. 1995: 205).

14. The importance of song lyrics for understanding women's thoughts and perceptions has been discussed by Srivastava (1991), Naroditskaya (2000), Davis (2006) and McLaren (2008).

15. My English translations from Kam [K.] and Chinese [Ch.] are distinguished in this manner.

16. From the Sheeam big song *Bu no mair lao* (When there is a flood).

17. Use of Kam folksong in music education is not unique. For example, Miao writes that 'As far as folksong is concerned, the [Chinese] state is encouraging music education in schools, and protecting the heritage of traditional music, ensuring its survival and purity' (1991: 494).

18. The involvement of more rural women than men may be because more men than women are absent from work, or because men remaining in their village are usually in paid employment and thus have fewer opportunities to sing together or attend rehearsals. Male dominated control/direction of Kam cultural development, and women's greater involvement in contemporary song performance in village traditions, may also be influential factors, as may the feminization of minority representation through cultural performance (often interpreted by scholars as according lower status to such groups and objectifying women). However, it appears that within the Kam community the feminization of staged cultural performance is actually serving to increase women's status.

19. Despite centuries of unofficial borrowing of Chinese characters to notate the Kam language, and the promulgation of a romanized Kam orthography in 1958, Kam language (and song lyrics) are rarely notated.

20. Songs are selected by the male musical directors/composers employed by the local cultural bureau.

21. In 2008, the Chinese state began awarding women and men who had played significant roles in Kam musical culture (and paid application fees) with graded titles of 'cultural transmission person' (*wenhua chuanchengren*), and Wu Pinxian was awarded 'Kam Big Song Cultural Transmission Representative'. To date, these awardees have not been allocated any particular role within the process of development, and the awarding of these titles has not altered the state-sponsored developments described in this chapter.

22. This strategy was announced late 1999, to begin in 2000, and placed special emphasis on the economic development of provinces (including Guizhou) and autonomous regions in western China (see Goodman 2004; *Zhongguo xibu kaifa wang* 2009).

23. Advocated by many scholars as a strategy to assist in increasing the involvement of younger generations and thereby enhancing Kam song transmission, it cannot be said

to 'preserve' or 'protect' Kam musical culture. It involves only a fraction of the song repertoire (usually not the most significant songs which are crucial records of Kam history and philosophy), and frequently requires performance of songs in 'artistically processed' versions. Despite the focus on cultural development and 'protection' through staged song performances, the lack of any concurrent emphasis upon creating archives raises questions concerning the ultimate intention and the methodology of this development process. To my knowledge, the first and only archive of recorded Kam music is that which Kam people and I established with the Pacific and Regional Archive for Digital Sources in Endangered Cultures (www.paradisec.org.au).

24. This programme, broadcast annually, is viewed by an audience of hundreds of millions.
25. The Chinese Minority Music Association is an academic body whose members mainly comprise university- and government-affiliated scholars.
26. Following Bourdieu (1977, 1986), symbolic capital is understood as a non-relationship-specific form of honour or prestige, while cultural capital is knowledge or ability that can be used for material gain.
27. At this performance the Sheeam group included Wu Pinxian and Wu Xuegui. The group won first prize and Sheeam's largest ever prize money: 10 500 yuan.
28. Although it was acceptable for young married men to sing, older married men faced increasing derision over their participation, and eventually stopped.
29. Although both men and women continue to teach big song, now women are the most active performers and thus primary custodians. Recently, women have also assumed primary custodianship of other Kam song genres.
30. However, when in 2009 I recalled women's excitement at earning 126 yuan each in 2005, many denied having been impressed by the amount. Their altered recollection testifies to the changing economic situation over this four-year period.

PART II

Tangled ties: policies, institutions and discourses

4. Reproduction and real property in rural China: three decades of development and discrimination[1]

Laurel Bossen

During the past three decades of China's soaring economic development, two core aspects of state policy have had transformative effects on rural households. These are the imposition of state-imposed controls over reproduction and the shift from collective to privately managed agricultural production. The state controls over reproduction are widely known as the 'one-child-policy', even though the policy has not uniformly limited the population to one child per couple in rural areas. There has been a degree of flexibility so that in some provinces and counties parents have had to stop after one child if the first was a son, and in others they have been allowed two children regardless of the sex, and up to three if the first two were daughters. The population policy became 'gendered' in response to the persistent demand to have at least one son.[2]

In the transition to privately managed farming, the important change was the distribution of farmland under contract under the household responsibility system. Land did not become private property, but continued to belong to the village collectively. Contracted use-rights were, at first, of varying duration; in some communities they were adjusted every five years or so. Other communities made one-time distributions under long-term contracts without periodic readjustments. The initial distribution allocated land to households according to size. Although in some areas more land was distributed to men than women,[3] in many parts of China the village leaders allocated the same amount of land per capita to all members of a household, regardless of sex or age. More generally, the continuing practice of virilocal marriage meant that women had to leave behind the land allocated in their natal village, and were uncertain of their land rights' status in their marital village. In some cases, newly married women were allocated land in their marital village at the transfer of their residential registration (hereafter, *hukou*), or at the next readjustment of land. In other cases, women marrying into a village in which land was not

97

periodically redistributed were not allocated land. The implementation of the land policy thus was invisibly 'gendered'.

Together, these two government policies had a major influence in shaping China's rural development trajectory as population growth slowed and rural output rose. In the early period, controls on population movement and scarcity of urban housing meant that fewer women than men migrated to urban centres. Married women tended to remain in rural areas in order to secure their rights to house and farmland by working in their marital village (Bossen 1994). In the late 1990s and early 21st century, as jobs and housing possibilities for migrants in the cities expanded, more women joined the migrant stream (Gaetano and Jacka 2004; Jacka 2006b).

This chapter explores variations in the ways China's development policies regarding reproduction and rural property institutions have interacted with traditionally gendered institutions in rural China to generate different effects on gender relations. It is particularly concerned with understanding local differences in responses to family planning policies and in child sex ratios across rural China, and seeks to explain these in terms of variations in three key variables related to real property rights,[4] and in the ways in which these variables interact. These variables are: the implementation of land policy; lineage strength; and the incidence of uxorilocal marriage. The chapter addresses these issues through a comparison of two village case studies located in different provinces. The focus here is on agricultural communities; a different dynamic is often at work in peri-urban and industrialized locales.

There are many ways to examine gender relations. Changes in male–female inequality do not always move in the same direction or at the same time. China's education levels and employment options for women improved during the reform period. But alongside these changes has appeared the very disturbing trend of increased male–female sex ratios at birth. These reached very abnormal levels by the 2000 census, when the national child sex ratio (ages 0 to 4) rose to 120 (that is, 120 males per 100 females), compared to an average of 106 in developed populations (Attané and Guilmoto 2007; Banister 2004; Croll 2000; Greenhalgh and Winckler 2005; Li, Shuzhuo et al. 2007). If birth and child sex ratios rise above the level of around 106 males per 100 females, it signals that female infants and children are disadvantaged. China's birth and child sex ratios are now amongst the highest in the world, and the greatest 'female deficit' is in rural areas (Li, Shuzhuo et al. 2007: 28).

POPULATION POLICY AS DEVELOPMENT POLICY

When reforms began in the late 1970s, China's government viewed development (as did the West) primarily in economic terms and emphasized increasing income, wealth and modern technology. The government believed that rapid population growth posed a serious threat to development (Greenhalgh and Winckler 2005; White 2006: 1). Rather than wait for development to bring about smaller families, the government imposed strict limits on childbearing. The act of limiting families to one child for urban residents or two children for rural residents is seen as an important factor in China's sex ratio increase. In the first decades after the revolution, before the population policy was implemented, the ratio of males to females at birth was fairly normal (Banister 2004: 24). But once the policy was in force, the proportion of male births started to rise, and accounts of skewed sex ratios became increasingly common.

Reform and rapid development restored family farming in villages across China, introduced many new economic opportunities and technologies, and raised standards of living. Historically, female infanticide and abandonment have been interpreted as a product of poverty, pushing families to abandon less productive girls (Mungello 2008). As China became wealthier, it was surprising that families should still sacrifice daughters and favour of sons.

Broader concepts of development began to take hold in the 1990s, particularly the concept of 'human development' as put forth by the United Nations. Today, development refers not only to national income but also to a nation's ability to deliver health, education and opportunity to all its citizens. China has now become wealthy enough to address distributional issues, under its own Confucian-sounding rubric, 'harmonious development'.

As with the skewing of income or wealth, imbalanced sex ratios are taken as a sign that the government is not performing well by this new standard of development and is failing the sex whose proportion is significantly below expected levels, which in China means the female sex. Skewed sex ratios are related to other development issues such as the empowerment of women and their rights to life, citizenship and property (Croll 2000; Sen 2000).[5] The sex imbalance in rural areas reflects very strong and continued favouring of men and boys by family and patrilineal institutions. Practices producing the imbalance include the under-reporting and abandonment of female children, disproportionately high female child mortality and female infanticide. In the 1990s, ultrasound testing for early determination of female sex followed by abortion, a practice called female feticide, became more common (Attané and Guilmoto 2007; Li, Shuzhuo et al. 2007: 37). Childhood cohorts with clear male majorities, aware that boys are desired and have stronger entitlements, learn to see girls as less deserving and perpetuate discrimination. However, in China, fear of social instability arising from disaffected males who cannot find wives has garnered more government attention. Openly concerned about a surplus of 37 million males (Wang 2007), the government is seeking ways to address what could be called 'a dark side of the miracle'.

Many researchers have studied the impact of the population policies on families' reproductive decisions and birth and child sex ratios, endeavouring to verify the reality, severity and distribution of China's female deficit in time and space (Attané and Guilmoto, 2007; Banister 2004; Cai and Lavely 2007). These studies usually rely on government census sources and make adjustments for what Attané and Guilmoto call 'data failure', including distortions produced by the concealment of out-of-quota pregnancies and illegal activities such as infanticide or sex-selective abortion. Although these studies have found evidence that population policy has activated greater parental concern with reproductive outcomes, they suggest that the policy alone does not account for the priority given to sons.

CONSTANT SON PREFERENCE, VARIABLE SEX RATIOS?

A pervasive problem in understanding the underlying causes of China's sex imbalance lies in the tendency to generalize about patriarchy as a constant in Chinese history (see Li, Shuzhuo et al. 2007: 38). The reasoning is that China has an imbalance because patriarchy, patrilineality, and virilocality produce son preference. Another variant is that son preference is caused by the need for male labour, old age support and the continuation of the patrilineal family (Bossen 2007b). These explanations are almost stereotypic. They suggest that patriarchal and patrilineal institutions are customary and constant, without explaining how they operate in everyday life, or what strengthens or weakens them. If we want to understand the dynamics of rising or falling sex ratios, we need to examine the operation and strength of these institutions so that we can better measure their connections to the variables that we are trying to explain. Such an examination may not always be easy, but without it we face the problem of using a constant (patriarchy) to explain variation (in sex ratios), or of circularity – asserting that an independent variable correlates with the dependent variable (for example, when sex ratios are high, the patrilineal system is rigid, and when they are low, it must be weak). Is there independent evidence that patrilineal rigidity, that is, resistance to non-patrilineal family arrangements, corresponds to higher sex ratios? We need to know more about how to evaluate the rigidity of the patrilineal system, the conditions, policies, and practices contributing to its persistence, whether rigidity actually does correspond to higher sex ratios, and, ultimately, how gender inequalities can be reduced.

A number of studies have made important contributions to mapping out the variations in China's sex ratios over time and space. Researchers have documented changes in the percentages of missing females across the 20th century, and changes in the sex ratio at birth 1950–2000 (Li, Shuzhuo et al. 2007: 27, 34). Estimated percentages of missing females range from more than 23 per cent in 1935 to less than 2 per cent in 1960, rising again in the 1990s to over 6 per cent (Li, Shuzhuo et al. 2007: 34). Other researchers have mapped regional variations and changes in child sex ratios in China (Attané and Guilmoto 2007: 121, 125; Cai and Lavely 2007: 115, 117). Within and across provincial boundaries, they have identified 'hot spots' of high child sex ratios – clusters that are unevenly distributed across China. Why some areas have such high sex ratios and others much lower ones is not obvious. The 2000 census showed that child sex ratios had climbed above 130 in three provinces (Hainan, Jiangxi and Henan), and above 125 in five others (Anhui, Hubei, Guangdong, Guangxi, and Shaanxi). These provinces represent a considerable range in development indicators (Cai and Lavely 2007: 113; Population Census Office 1985, 2002).

If Chinese patrilineal inheritance and virilocal residence, male labour and family line produce son preference, we need to learn how and why they vary in these different times and places. As Cai and Lavely argue:

> Large variation in the child sex ratio across China, and the obvious regional clustering demonstrate the dangers of overgeneralization. While studies based on high levels of aggregation provide important insights on the general trend in sex ratio across the country, they mask the gravity of the problem in local areas, obscure the local environments as an important contextual factor, and could lead to erroneous interpretations and policy recommendations. This analysis calls attention to the importance of local ecology to the sex ratio phenomenon. (Cai and Lavely 2007: 120)

Understanding the local ecology and complex institutional dynamics of China's skewed sex ratios can benefit from taking a closer ethnographic look at village conditions. What produces these differences in sex ratios? Village studies help us to understand what strengthens or weakens patrilineal institutions, and how local gender cultures and practices affecting real property rights interact with national policies to produce different sex ratios. These practices include: lineage solidarity; allocation of land and housing rights; and acceptance of uxorilocal marriage. I am not aware of any of these being easy to observe in standard data sets. Because they are not easily measured does not mean that we can afford to ignore them.

Lineage solidarity is important for understanding women's rights to land and housing because patrilineal ideology and institutions might be enforced if lineages control village governing organizations. These are significant considerations for parents in deciding the importance of having at least one son or daughter, and whether to invest equally in sons and daughters. Where rural women's assets and the fruits of their labour come under the control of husbands or in-laws upon marriage, families have been reluctant to invest much in daughters. Framing the problem this way allows us to consider why having a son has been so essential to rural families. Lineage strength and solidarity in a village is related to numerical predominance. If a village has a mixture of surname groups, there is often a balance of power, and a greater tolerance for the property rights of those from other groups. Domination by a single lineage may be associated with intolerance for alternatives to patrilineal birth rights, and an unwillingness to allow any outsiders to establish rights to local resources.[6]

The post-Mao reforms transformed rural property rights from collective ownership and collective management to collective ownership and household management. The goal was to encourage farmers to allocate labour more efficiently, to produce more and accumulate wealth. Simultaneously, the government's ongoing population policy imposed drastic demographic changes upon families, demanding they become smaller in order to promote increasing wealth per capita. I suggest that households' responses to the population policy were linked to their concerns about claims to land and houses, not only to economic support from their sons in terms of income. Until government restrictions on urban migration and urban property ownership gradually loosened in the 1990s, villagers' security rested mainly on house and land rights in the village where they were registered.

Security in land rights is difficult to measure because village lands are collectively owned. Land-use rights are generally distributed to households.[7] Different villages allocate land at different frequencies and according to different principles and methods. Although village leaders say they are guided by their superiors, they have some discretion on whether they adjust land allocations according to population changes, or not. Local knowledge of landholding practices can help uncover how women's rights are determined, how women perceive their land rights, and what happens when there are no sons.

Women's rights to inherit village houses are indiscernible because they are typically merged with the rights of other household members.[8] It is difficult to discover if women have a secure share in these investments in either their natal or marital home.[9] Examples of families without sons, and cases of uxorilocal marriage, or of divorce, present situations in which women's property rights are tested and become more explicit. They thus can have a demonstration effect. Others who observe such cases draw lessons about their own possible choices. Thus, within the tradition of patrilineal inheritance, examination of local conditions affecting lineage, land and housing, and marriage can help us understand parental decisions about family composition and the dynamics of China's sex ratios.

Two village case studies, one in Henan and one in Yunnan, provide an opportunity to explore the way local conditions affect gender both in entitlements to real property and in reproduction. Neither of these villages represents conditions in their respective provinces, let alone rural China as a whole, with all its rich, complex variation. While provincial and regional differences influence the ways villages manage their affairs, there are also many variations within regions. For example, a wheat-growing village in Yunnan may resemble wheat-growing villages in Henan in terms of the gender division of labour. A multi-surname village in Henan may resemble multi-surname villages in Yunnan. Villages near towns may also share similarities due to off-farm opportunities. Historical differences, recent migration or ethnic pluralism may also come into play. Thus, village case studies can help reveal how responses to national land and birth control policies differ according to local conditions and cultural understandings and practices.

Henan province is located in north central China, the heartland of Han Chinese culture. Yunnan is located in the south-west, a mountainous province with a high proportion of ethnic minorities. Both village research sites have Han populations and operate within the general outlines of China's patrilineal heritage and national policies. However their local ecologies are quite different, reflecting variations to be found across China. Drawing on fieldwork conducted between 1988 and 2008, I discuss the similarities and differences between these villages in lineage concentration, property inheritance and ownership, and tolerance for uxorilocal marriages, and present data on child sex ratios from local interview samples conducted at different times. I consider the proposition that where there are higher measures of patrilineal rigidity, the sex ratio will be higher, and where patrilineal inheritance patterns are more flexible, sex ratios will be more equal.

HUANG TU OF HENAN PROVINCE AND SONG GOU OF YUNNAN PROVINCE[10]

Huang Tu (Yellow Earth) is a wheat-growing village with a population of about 3000, divided into teams that average less than 400 people each.

Huang Tu is a compact settlement sheltered by poplar trees, located on the flat, yellow soils of the north China plain. It is not close to any large city, but several regional markets and the county town can now be reached by car in less than an hour. I visited this village in 1988 when it was undergoing strict implementation of the population policy. At that time, the household responsibility system was less than a decade old, and the power of the state was still evident in everyday lives, symbolized by loudspeakers throughout the village that played morning music or made announcements. I have revisited the village at different intervals and witnessed massive changes in the standard of living, as technology improved, migration increased, family size decreased, and newer, larger houses were built. Wheat is the major crop. Manual labour and draft animals have been largely replaced by machinery in wheat growing. However Huang Tu also grows peanuts, a crop which still uses manual labour. In 1988 and again in 2008, I conducted sample surveys of households, covering about 5 per cent of the population spread across the different village subgroups. In 2008, Huang Tu residents were still predominantly farmers: 88 per cent of 153 male and female adults in the 2008 sample performed farm labour for more than one month per year. In all, 61 per cent of the villagers gave farm work as their primary occupation. The remaining 39 per cent also performed some off-farm work, such as running a small shop in the village, teaching, or transport and construction work. Of those with non-agricultural incomes, only 36 per cent were women.

Song Gou (Pine Glen), in central Yunnan, is a small village hamlet with just over 200 residents. It is actually one component team of a larger village, where other teams are settlements occupying separate farming niches nestled among the hills. Song Gou sits in a narrow valley between pine-covered hillsides. Its 43 households are Han, though the larger area is ethnically complex.[11] In the 1980s, to reach Song Gou from the nearest large town centre required travelling on dirt roads for about three-quarters of an hour by bicycle or horse cart and walking took considerably longer, but now cars can reach it in about 15 minutes. Other than Song Gou, larger villages closer to town have Han populations, but a hamlet of roughly ten households further from town identifies most of its residents as Yi, with some Han intermarriage. Many different minorities intermingle with Han in the market towns of central Yunnan, so Song Gou villagers are familiar with other cultures. In the 1980s, people grew wheat and potatoes as staples, and raised tobacco as a cash crop. In 2008 the villagers grew fresh vegetables such as cabbages as their cash crop. Tall tobacco roasting sheds stood as silent reminders of their former crop, while village men still smoked loose tobacco in Yunnan's trademark bamboo water pipes. In terms of local ecology and crop specialties, both tobacco and vegetable production use large amounts of female labour, much like rice production. In 2008, my survey of all 43 households showed that in all but one, men and women performed farm work for more than one month per year, and many stressed that they were busy farming between five and ten months of the year.[12] Several villagers also had part-time work selling insurance, in transport, or as shopkeepers. Some of the younger generation worked in town.

Huang Tu: Lineage Concentration

Lineages in Huang Tu are much more concentrated than it appears at first glance. This is a large village composed of multiple 'teams' or 'groups', each in charge of its own land area. The residential sections of each team are lined up side by side in a single large compound village; they share the school and use the various shops and periodic market in the village centre. The teams in this village each have a dominant lineage which accounts for 50 to 83 per cent of all households. Moreover, five teams are dominated by the same lineage. Lineage relationships are thus quite concentrated in Huang Tu. In addition, some Huang Tu lineages have kept written genealogies, and engage in lineage rituals and ceremonies. The village celebrates a local 'grandfather' god whose annual celebration is organized and rotated among the different descent groups in the village.

Land Holding, Adjustments, and House Rights

Since the early 1980s, individual households have had the right to contract the use of the village's agricultural land. Most villagers continue to practise virilocal residence and obtain contracts following patrilineal principles: if a man's father contracted land or owned a house in the village, he has the right to do so too. Women's rights to property in houses and land normally temporarily reside in their natal homes. They are expected to marry out, and at marriage they need to transfer their *hukou* to their husband's village in order to obtain land and shared house rights there, as wives if the couple occupies a new house, or as daughters-in-law if they live in a joint household. Just *when* these marital rights take effect is unclear but bearing a child undoubtedly strengthens a wife's claim. Under the contract system that was instituted in the early 1980s, team land was divided equally per capita without regard to age or sex, according to the number of residents registered in the village. The team then contracted land to households according to the number of members in each household. The amount of land was originally the same for everyone within a team. If a household had five members, they would get five portions of land. In

Huang Tu, every five years thereafter until 2000, the land allocated to each household was adjusted according to births, deaths, in-coming wives and out-marrying daughters. Teams whose population grew had less land to allocate per capita than those whose population was stable. Because of these readjustments, each woman who transferred her *hukou* into the village had a clear sense, once the land adjustments were made, that she brought to her in-law's family an entitlement to another person's share of land out of the general pool of land belonging to the team.

Since 2000 the readjustments have stopped. Originally in the 1980s, in order to encourage investment in land quality, the national authorities announced that the land contracts were good for 30 years, but many villages across China continued to make periodic adjustments (Kung 2000; Liaw 2008: 238). In 2003 with the passage of the Rural Land Contracting Law, the government re-emphasized the stability of use-rights to village land. Huang Tu has finally conformed to the national policy promoting long-term use-rights. As a result, incoming wives are no longer allocated land upon marrying into Huang Tu. Slightly more than half (11 out of 20) of the wives in my 2008 sample who married into Huang Tu after 2000 had not transferred their *hukou*, and claimed that they still 'had land' in their natal village. That is, their personal share of family land had not been returned to the pool of land in their natal village. The fact that so many women responded in this way suggests that they are aware of, and want to have, land rights, and associate the transfer of *hukou* with giving up land in one place and gaining it in another. What happens to the land in their natal village? Some women said that their parents or brothers use it, and gave examples of exchange, such as a share of the harvest. A daughter does her natal kin a favour by not transferring her residence and giving up her land; the use-rights remain with the natal household. Families with daughters temporarily end up with more land per capita after the daughters marry out. Married-in wives, however, are frequently without land, although they benefit with the household as a whole from land left behind by married-out daughters. Of 80 households, there were 17 wives who reported they had not been allocated land in Huang Tu.[13]

In contrast, the rights of men in Huang Tu, as elsewhere, are stable. When they marry, they can choose to keep their portion of land, whether they remain part of a joint household with their parents or separate to form a new household with their wife. Both men and women may be required to return land to their village team if they obtain urban household registration. Without urban registration, they may still acquire urban housing and decide they no longer want to farm the land and return it to the village team. Recently, there has been little incentive to give up land since farmers receive a subsidy rather than tax from the government, and can even hire others to farm it. However, even if village men give up their farm land, they claim they still have the right to apply for a house lot, and build a house within the village. Village men recognize this as their patrilineal birth right. Daughters do not have this right. At marriage, they are obliged to undertake a much riskier investment. The majority of women, unless they marry endogamously within the village of Huang Tu, transfer their residence to their husband's village, a community of strangers. They are obliged to invest their labour and incomes in a new household where others already have established rights to land. For a certain time after marriage, women may still have land rights at their parents' home if they have not transferred their *hukou*; this may offer them some security and sense of value.

Periodic readjustments to land according to household size give parents incentives to have more children, including sons and daughters. However, sons are better because they have a permanent birthright. Fines imposed on over-quota births have been contentious, but by paying the fine the parents can register the child. In recent years, as families gain more income from off-farm employment, they have been willing to pay these fines.

As the national government reforms agricultural land policy to conform to the demands of a market economy, it is not clear if rural women's individual property rights will be shored up, or left vulnerable to patrilineal village leadership and practice.

Needing a Son[14]

The belief that sons are necessary is often explained in terms of male labour contributions and patrilineal continuity. It is not always noted that patrilineal continuity is linked to the control of land under the village land contracting system. Parents of a son feel assured that they have a legitimate heir to claim and maintain their property as their abilities decline. They count on villages organized by patrilineal kinsmen to respect their rights. The capital fund that parents have accumulated over the course of their lifetime can be entrusted to a resident son as their fund manager. Legally speaking, both male and female children are obliged to support their parents. However, in practice, it is usually only sons who are given the resources to do so. Daughters are not usually granted the resources to support their parents, unless there are no sons. In their natal village, married daughters with brothers customarily lack the right to a parcel of land or a house plot to build on. Denied a patrimony, a daughter's primary choice for long-term security in a rural community is matrimony.[15] Through marriage and production of male heirs to her husband's family, lineage or community, a woman gains use-rights to land and home.

The rule of exogamy means that daughters must not stay around to claim an inheritance in competition with brothers. But some families lack sons.

Uxorilocal Marriage

The imbalance of son-only to daughter-only families is consistent with what I call the 'one-son minimum'. In Huang Tu, few families fail to get a son. This is connected with a lack of acceptance and very low incidence of uxorilocal marriage. Huang Tu villagers say that a family with daughters but no son can 'bring in' a son-in-law. A daughter, and only one daughter, can inherit if and only if there is no son. However this alternative is extremely rare, as if people assume it is doomed to failure. Relations between a mother and daughter-in-law are often strained, but there may also be strains between a father and son-in-law sharing the same compound. Further, according to the literature on uxorilocal marriage, the 'outsider' husband may be viewed with distrust as an illegitimate usurper of patrilineal resources (Jin et al. 2007; Zhang, Weiguo 2008). Villagers look down on him as a detached male without resources, else why would he be willing to marry out? Patrilineal groups are typically territorial. As a result, sons-in-law in uxorilocal marriages are rarely respected by family clans (Li, Xiaoyun et al. 2006).

In my 2008 sample in Huang Tu, out of 80 households, only one couple with children under 20 was likely to end up sonless. One of their two daughters, now in their late teens, may later choose uxorilocal marriage. Uxorilocal marriage was extremely rare. Out of roughly 120 marriages, I found only one couple that married uxorilocally. Liu and her husband, married in 2007, were both born in Huang Tu, but belong to different teams. The uxorilocal marriage option with residence in Liu's Team A was chosen because Liu has no brothers. Her husband has not transferred his *hukou* and retains land with his parents in Team D. By marrying uxorilocally, but within the village, Liu's husband retains the privilege of proximity to his family and kinsmen, and can still use his share of team land. Liu is the third daughter. Two older sisters married out, and the fourth daughter, unmarried, has a teaching job in the city and an urban *hukou*. Liu's husband contributed over 10000 yuan to the wife's family at engagement, and Liu's family built them a new three-room house worth over 30000 yuan, and provided a TV, washing machine and furniture. In this case, the parents transmitted real property to their daughter, but kept it in their own team's jurisdiction. One of Liu's older sisters married a man in Huang Tu's Team C, while the other after marriage moved to a nearby town. This sonless family thus has one daughter at home, and two others in the neighbourhood.

The strength of lineages in Huang Tu, inequalities in the land and housing rights of men and women, plus the fact that sonless families and uxorilocal marriage are extremely rare, indicate that achieving the one-son minimum is very important for parents in Huang Tu.

Song Gou: Lineages in a Minor Key

Song Gou villagers describe their valley as having been 'empty' until it was settled by their ancestors around 1870. While Song Gou looks like a 'natural village' based on patrilineal ties, it is actually composed of two primary lineages, plus some smaller surname groups. Together, the two main lineages account for 72 per cent of the population, but each lineage by itself is only half that, or roughly 35 per cent of the total. This produces a rough balance of power in the village between two family groups. While lineage concentration is not diluted enough to label it a multi-surname village, Song Gou is not dominated by one powerful surname group to the same extent as teams in Huang Tu. Moreover, villagers do not keep a written genealogy. Their small village temple has both male and female deities, including 'Earth Mother'.

Land Holdings Unadjusted

As in most of China, Song Gou land was de-collectivized and distributed to households on a per capita basis in the early 1980s. In this hilly area, plot desirability varies considerably depending on ease of access, shape, slope or flatness, and sunny or shady hillsides, to say nothing of soil quality. Plot allocations were conducted by estimating the grain yield of each plot. Each household was allocated several plots of different quality and in different places to reach a roughly equal productive potential per capita. Song Gou is different from most other villages that I have visited in Yunnan and Henan in that it has never re-divided the land since that date. This lack of change, combined with virilocal marriage, has meant that households with two sons have ended up with less land per capita from one generation to the next, as the sons have married and brought in wives. In the 1990s, a village leader who had two sons recognized this disadvantage when he remarked that his household would benefit if land were re-divided after his sons married, but there was nothing he could do about it. Others did not want to re-divide or readjust the land allotments, and the village head said that, in any case, the administrative village and county governments would not approve such a readjustment. In 2008, villagers still quoted the '30 years no change' policy to describe the duration of their contracts, although the policy continued to be ignored in other villages that adjusted land plots to accommodate population changes.

Interviews revealed considerable variation in quantities of land held per household and per capita, and in the extra quantities subcontracted from others. The prices for subcontracted land were also highly variable according to land quality and accessibility. Many households subcontracted extra land, but no one said they subcontracted land out to others.[16] One mentioned 'giving' land to a relative to farm, but in the accepted idiom of village reciprocity, that often means the relative 'gave back' a share of the harvest, or some other benefit.

Because Song Gou villagers assert that their village land contracts are indeed for 30 years, this village may undergo a new division of land and re-contracting when current contracts expire in 2012, but given the recent national-level announcement of new rural land policies, villagers are not certain if or how land will be re-allocated among households. If they contract land equally to households on the basis of family size, that will renew all residents' sense of land entitlement for another generation. If not, women's land rights at marriage will become less visible, possibly weakening their claims to this important form of property.

Fan, age 34, has not transferred her registration to Song Gou. She explains, 'I gave my share of land to my older brother to use, and my older brother gives me a little rice and money, so I still have not transferred my *hukou*'. Fan retains a sense of entitlement to land that was allocated to her in her natal village. Since her natal village has not re-allocated land, she feels that she still holds use-rights there. This perception is reinforced by the fact that, because she cannot acquire a share of land in her husband's village, there is no incentive to transfer her *hukou*.

Other women's accounts show the variation and lack of clarity in women's rights. Lin transferred her *hukou* to Song Gou in 1998 but claims to have land (not a house) in her natal village. Bao married a man from Song Gou, but has not transferred her *hukou* to the village because, first, she has both an urban *hukou* which is considered superior to rural registration, and urban housing, and, second, no land would be reallocated for her or her offspring even if she did transfer. Bao's family lives in town. Her son, an only child, inherited his mother's urban registration status but has his father's family name because his parents' marriage was not established in uxorilocal form. Although Bao's husband continues to farm and has a house in the village, his son is unlikely to become a farmer. While he may be able to inherit his father's house, his right to his father's farm land in the village is unclear. Chun married into Song Gou many years ago and was included in the land distribution. Her husband, son and daughter also got land but have since all transferred their registration to the county town. Chun remains registered in the village and thus the family still benefits from the four *mu*[17] of land formerly allocated to their four-member household. Many years ago she confided that she did not want to transfer her registration to urban status because as an illiterate woman she had few skills demanded by urban employers. She now lives in town with her husband but continues to manage the land with hired labour, and returns on weekends. Yang, after many years of marriage, remains registered as a resident in her natal village. She has no land of her own in Song Gou and has neither land nor house in her natal village. She and her husband were childless so they adopted a daughter.

Sonless Households

In 2008 in Song Gou, almost a quarter of families with children under the age of 20 had daughters, but no sons. Gao belongs to one of the two common surnames. He and his wife have two unmarried daughters who have completed high school. The daughters both work outside in big cities, with good jobs. The parents assert that daughters are 'the same' as sons, a politically correct claim that I heard frequently in Song Gou. The parents, in their forties, assert they are still young enough to do the farming, and do not need help. They have land for only three people, because their second daughter was not yet born when the land was divided 20 years ago. Both husband and wife work equally long hours in the fields in labour-intensive vegetable production, earning a good income. When asked, as a general rule, whether a daughter with no brothers can get a house site, they answered, 'Basically, she cannot'. They could think of no examples where it had happened. However the Village Committee does grant house sites to sons. Gao's house, said to be worth 100 000 yuan, was inherited from his parents. The village distributed the house plot to his parents, and they divided it among their sons. A large compound house was built in 1982, the year Gao was married. Gao's family shares it with a brother and his family. They last invested in repairs in 1987 when each family spent 10 000 yuan. Despite legislation granting daughters and sons equal inheritance rights, it is unclear whether in fact Gao's daughters can inherit the house, or if it will pass to his nephews.

Uxorilocal Marriage

In 2008, about 10 per cent of Song Gou households had been formed through uxorilocal marriages. This is not as high a rate of uxorilocal marriage as in Lu Village in west central Yunnan (Bossen 2002; Fei and Zhang 1990), but it is more common than in Huang Tu. Jin and his wife, both in their forties, have two daughters who completed high school. They do not belong to either of the two main lineages. The older daughter is a nurse in the town hospital, and her husband is a village doctor, running a private health station in the nearby village where the daughter's mother was born. They describe their older daughter's marriage as uxorilocal (*shangmen nüxu*). Their son-in-law is from west central Yunnan and did not transfer his *hukou* to Song Gou. Jin's daughter and son-in-law now live in town but are still registered in their home villages. The younger daughter is single and works as a salesperson in the county city.

Jin's family was allocated land for three people in the first division, so the younger daughter lacks land. Although they say there is no prejudice against families without sons, Jin's wife has had three pregnancies. The third ended in abortion because, they say, echoing government policy, 'two is enough'.

This household is interesting because of its pattern of investment. Unlike parents of sons, who typically avail themselves of the option to build a new house in the village for their son at marriage, these sonless parents assisted their uxorilocally married daughter to purchase a small one-story house in the nearby town. Jin and his wife gave 50 000 yuan, their son-in-law's family also gave 50 000, and the couple themselves spent 10 000. This is a clear sign of willingness to invest in daughters, but not within the village. The house in the town is convenient to the wife's hospital job, and to better schools for children. The option of buying houses in town provides sonless families with new ways of securely investing capital in a jurisdiction in which there seems to be less patrilineal prejudice against women as owners or co-owners.

Comparison

The comparison of these two villages in terms of their emphasis on lineage and patterns of agricultural and residential land allocation, inheritance and acceptance of uxorilocal marriage suggests that Huang Tu should have a stronger son preference. The strength of lineages militates against uxorilocal marriage as an option, and the lack of acceptance for such an alternative increases the demand for sons. It is hard to predict the effects of the two patterns of land distribution – once every five years until 2000, or once without further adjustment until the current 30-year contracts expire or the policy changes. In Huang Tu, adjustments may have given in-marrying women a sense of value because up to the year 2000 they brought a portion of land to their new households, with the extra land being drawn from the team. At the same time, this has dispossessed out-marrying local women who may or may not have received a portion of land in the village into which they married. In Song Gou, the lack of adjustments has meant that incoming wives never felt they were bringing extra land to their new households. However, raising more than one son means that future sons will have smaller per capita shares of land, and possibly not enough to support their new families.

We now turn to the evidence on child sex ratios for each village to see which conditions are associated with a shortage of daughters.

HUANG TU CHILD SEX RATIOS

Obtaining accurate information on sex ratios is as challenging at the local level as it is for those examining census data at the national level (Scharping 2007). Formal population records are no longer kept in Huang Tu village – this responsibility has migrated to higher levels. Locally, I obtained figures which were said to come from the 2007 report to the higher authorities. These yielded a population sex ratio of 146 for the whole village (a population of roughly 2750) suggesting there were three males for every two females. The sex ratio of 127 for the population age 20 and younger was not quite as skewed. I was not given a finer breakdown by sex and age. However, I learned informally that the actual population is considerably higher, perhaps as many as 3200, or about 450 more than officially reported. If this is true and if *all* the individuals who were not counted were female, then the population sex ratio would be close to normal. I present these 'false' findings merely to illustrate the problems with population data coming from the local level. Weiguo Zhang (2002) has discussed the problem of frequent cadre miscounting of the population.

Given the dubious quality of the official figures, I turn to several sets of household interviews that I have collected over the years. These focus on child sex ratios by cohort, which are unlikely to be affected differentially by migration.[18] In each case the sex ratio comes out well above the normal sex ratio of around 106.

The 1989 sample is based on interviews with 50 households evenly spread across the different teams within the village. The 2004 sample is from the household register of one team which I updated with members of that team (see Bossen 2007b). The 2008 sample is based on interviews in 80 households spread evenly across the different teams within the village. The 2008 survey asked married couples in total how many children they had who survived childhood. This produced a sex ratio of 124 for 193 offspring, some of whom were born before the family planning era and therefore not included in Table 4.1. Taken together, these independent

Table 4.1   Huang Tu child sex ratios over time

Sample	Birth years	Number of children	Sex ratio (M/100F)
1	1975–1989	73	152
2	1990–2004	97	126
3	1994–2008	93	145

Sources: Author's data. Sample 1 (1989) 50 households, six households per team; Sample 2 (2004) 88 households from one team; Sample 3 (2008) 80 households, ten households per team.

samples offer reasonably strong support for the proposition that child sex ratios in the village are abnormally high, and fluctuate at levels above 120. Levels this high used to be quite shocking, but are now no longer a surprise coming from China or India. It is quite evident that sex selection is part of the family decision-making process, at least for some families. The high sex ratio is not just a result of random variation, but part of a consistent pattern found across much of the north China plain (Attané and Guilmoto 2007; Cai and Lavely 2007).

How did Huang Tu end up with these imbalanced child sex ratios? Huang Tu villagers mentioned that in recent years, the population policy had become considerably more flexible than in the late 1980s and early 1990s when some villagers fled and had their houses boarded up and possessions confiscated because of out-of-quota pregnancies. The current flexibility includes the possibility of having a third child and paying a fine, which is considered worthwhile if ultrasound detects male sex during pregnancy. Remarks by villagers suggest that sex-selective abortion is fairly acceptable. Some villagers clearly recognized the pain and hardship women experience during abortions, but although it is illegal, they did not appear to consider it immoral. The 2008 survey showed an abortion rate of only 5 per cent out of 212 pregnancies, a rate which suggests effective use of other contraceptive methods. In another context I learned of two married women each with two daughters who had undergone abortions in the previous three years, and who subsequently had given birth to sons as their third child. The problem is clearly not that families do not want girls at all, but that most of them feel that they require a son (Johnson 2004; Zhang Qiang 2007).

Huang Tu family composition by sex of children shows that the vast majority of households (79 per cent) have at least one son and one daughter, but the demand for having at least one son stands out in the four-to-one ratio of son-only households to daughter-only households. Lack of a son appears to be a condition that Huang Tu families strive hard to avoid.

The average number of children (age 20 or under) per couple in Huang

Table 4.2   Huang Tu households: child sex composition, 2008

Family composition	Number	Per cent
Children of both sexes	63	79
Son-only households	13	16
Daughter-only households	3	4
Childless household[a]	1	1
Total	80	100
One-child households	4	5

Note: [a]This household consisted of a middle-aged bachelor.

Source: Author's 2008 survey.

Tu (2008) was 2.4. This figure is consistent with a scenario in which most families achieved their goal of at least one son after having two children, and those that still lacked a son went over the official quota of two children, until they had a son.

As Eklund details elsewhere in this volume, since the shocking census of 2000, the government has launched a Care for Girls Campaign, painting slogans about valuing girls on village walls, providing monetary subsidies at retirement to sonless or single-child families, banning and imposing fines for the misuse of ultrasound for sex determination, and confiscating ultrasound machines from law-breaking clinics. But the gap between national policy and local concerns is fairly wide. In Huang Tu, the family planning bulletin board on a wall facing the central square was splattered with mud, in what appeared to be deliberate defacement. No names were filled in. It is hard to say whether this reflected opposition or indifference.

SONG GOU CHILD SEX RATIOS AND FAMILY COMPOSITION

In contrast to Huang Tu, child sex ratios in Song Gou are marginally below the expected level of 106 males per hundred females. As shown in Table 4.3, from 1968 to 2008, the sex ratio of all 141 children born in Song Gou was 101.2. Asked about the use of ultrasound tests, villagers consistently denied using them although they knew of the technology. One woman admitted she had had one to check the health, not the sex, of the fetus. Song Gou women also had had nine abortions, one miscarriage and one case of (male) infant mortality.

Table 4.3   Song Gou child sex ratios over time

Year & sample	Number	Child sex ratio
Children born 1968–1988 (40 households)	83	102
Children born 1988–2008 (43 households)	58	100

Source: Author's surveys of all Song Gou households in 1988 and 2008.

Table 4.4   Song Gou family composition, 2008

Family composition	Number	Per cent[a]
Children of both sexes	19	44
Son-only households	14	32
Daughter-only households	10	23
Total	43	99
One-child households[b]	6	

Notes:
a   Per cent does not add up to 100 due to rounding.
b   One-child households, included in the son-only and daughter-only category, might still
    have a second child and end up with children of both sexes.

Source: Author's survey of all Song Gou households in 2008.

Table 4.4 shows that Song Gou also has a higher proportion of
households with single-sex offspring than Huang Tu. In a survey of all
households conducted in 2008, I found 14 son-only households, and ten
daughter-only households. Slightly over 50 per cent of the households had
single-sex offspring.

The pattern of reproduction in Song Gou suggests there is little insistence on having a son. The willingness to accept uxorilocal marriage as
an alternative to virilocality seems to make sonlessness less worrisome
to Song Gou families than it is to Huang Tu families. Song Gou families
also have fewer children on average (1.34) than those in Huang Tu. This is
consistent with the fact that Song Gou has not periodically allocated more
land to families that have gained members. Demographic studies in rural
China have found that the sex ratio climbs with strict family planning and
fewer children, as families try to make sure they have a son (Banister 2004;
Li, Shuzhou et al. 2007). Yet despite the fact that Song Gou has had fewer
births per couple, this study shows they have not intervened to ensure they
get a son.

Working against the equal valuing of daughters in Song Gou is the fact that there has never been an adjustment of land in this village. Daughters and sons born after the initial distribution of contracts both know they were not allocated land. However sons are the presumed heirs to village houses and land rights. Some wives marrying-in report that they still have land in their natal villages. If patrilineal inheritance continues over several generations, the individual entitlements of women to land in Song Gou could be forgotten. However this gender asymmetry may not have a great effect on the parental demand for a son, given that pressure on land is limited by low fertility, and uxorilocal marriage is permitted.

What underlies these observed differences in village culture? Having no dominant surname group in Song Gou may mean that lineage membership, ultimately assured through sons, is of less importance.[19] Other factors may be the long-standing participation of women in farming in many parts of Yunnan, whether in rice farming, tobacco farming, or vegetable production. Each of these requires a great deal of manual labour in the fields, and women are an important part of the labour force. Also, the history of uxorilocal marriage in this region, in which less populated areas may have recruited males through marriage, and in which ethnic minorities may have more flexible ideas about descent, could have diluted patrilineal traditions.

CONCLUSION AND PROSPECTS

These cases contain some lessons about development and the process of state-directed change. Customs and institutions are generally more complex and embedded than development planners recognize. In these two villages we saw that major policy changes were imposed for 'medium' durations. By 'medium' I mean decades, not one or two years and not centuries. The imposition of a state family planning or planned birth programme for more than three decades has produced a significant effect by lowering fertility even in rural areas. Some may argue that this process was underway without state controls. Still, there is no question that state controls, abortions, sterilizations and contraception were often fiercely resisted by rural populations (and sometimes secretly welcomed by women), but also implanted notions of controlled fertility. Would fertility practices have changed so rapidly without state policy? Unlikely. But the policy did not consider gender, and after two decades and a soaring sex ratio, it is obvious the planners missed something big: the persisting discrimination against girls in many parts of China, particularly in rural areas. It would not be the first time that leaders convinced themselves of their own propaganda that the sexes were now equal. China's glaring demographic imbalance shows how wrong they were.

Changing land policies have affected rural China for six decades – the first three through collectivization of land and farming, and the last three through the 'household responsibility system' and privatization of farm management. In the case of these land reforms, too, there was a failure to consider the effectiveness and resilience of underlying gendered institutions. The patrilineal corporation was bruised but not broken by collectivization. It lost its direct control over private and corporate property (clan lands) but made accommodations with the local Communist Party. The latter often empowered poorer families without changing the underlying structure of entrenched patrilineal control of land by corporate groups (collectives) which reproduced themselves along the familiar lines of patrilineal affiliation.

For this reason, three decades of allocating land to women and girls as collective members have had little effect on women's ability to exercise rights to property in housing or land. Women's rights are still truncated by marriage outside their natal village, and mediated by marriage into a different village, where the agents of mediation are the Village Committees which remain, to a significant degree, patrilineal agents. In neither the Song Gou nor Huang Tu Village Committees do women have positions with power over land allocation. Women's leadership roles are limited to Women's Director or Family Planning officer. The committees are composed of men from the dominant surname groups. In Huang Tu the position of Women's Director is part-time and paid less than the full-time positions held only by male committee members.

In patrilineal affiliation and virilocal residence, Huang Tu and Song Gou, like most Chinese villages, are broadly similar. In both, land management rests with a Village Committee which serves village members whose lives are structured by patrilineal affiliation. While many villages today do not have clearly defined dominant patrilineages, often they are effectively governed by clansmen, or sets of 'brothers' (a term encompassing patrilateral cousins) who share the same surname and exercise power through traditional patrilineal alliances.

These villages have adopted different land policies, ranging from no change in land allocations to adjusting them to accommodate population changes.[20] In Huang Tu, land adjustments were made every five years for the two decades prior to 2000, with each adjustment giving in-marrying women a sense that they contributed to the household's stock of land. In contrast, Song Gou distributed land only once, equally to both sexes at the time. For the next two decades, incoming wives did not acquire any sense of personally acquiring a plot of land or expanding the household land entitlement. Outgoing daughters who had been allocated land retained a lingering sense that they 'had land' at their natal home, given to them as a birthright, but those who spoke about it mentioned that they let their brother use it.

What about the sons and daughters born since the original land distribution? In both Song Gou and Huang Tu, the daughters expect to marry out and leave the village; they will not inherit land or houses from their parents unless uxorilocal marriages are arranged, typically if they have no brothers. The sons have a birthright to be heirs to family real estate. Their parents openly plan for them to bring in a wife. In recent years, new considerations have come into play. Daughters as well as sons now migrate to cities, earn money, rent apartments or invest in housing in urban centres where lineage is not relevant to property rights.

I began this chapter by arguing that variable sex ratios cannot be explained by a patrilineal constant. This exercise in comparing two village situations suggests that patriliny varies in its intensity and rigidity, and that this variability has a large effect on sex ratios. The examples above show that despite broadly similar institutions of patriliny and virilocality, the two villages differ in important ways in the intensity and rigidity of patrilineality. Song Gou has rituals and a temple that celebrate both sexes as protectors and givers of benefits. There is no single dominant lineage with a simple majority, and uxorilocal marriages are tolerated. Song Gou has been comparatively more successful in reducing fertility and its child sex ratio is close to normal. It is not obvious why this is so, but the policy of not adjusting land and weaker pressure to have a son may be factors. The contrast between two villages presented here is consistent with findings reported by Jin et al. (2007) for three counties in Shaanxi and Hubei. They found that the county in central Shaanxi with core elements of 'traditional Yellow River Culture' had large dominant family clans, strict virilocal marriage, rare uxorilocal marriage, and very high birth sex ratios. The other two counties, one in a less populated mountainous area of southern Shaanxi and the other in a plains region of southern Hubei with a high proportion of immigrant settlers, both traditionally had high rates of uxorilocal marriage and fewer dominant clans. These two counties, like Song Gou Village, had birth sex ratios close to normal, as well as low fertility.

Another factor affecting Song Gou's flexibility regarding uxorilocal marriage, its relatively low fertility and its relatively low sex ratios might be the village's longer history of female participation in farming. Generally in Yunnan, where rice was the major grain crop, women laboured in transplanting, weeding and harvesting. Although Song Gou was a wheat-farming village because it lacked water for irrigation, its commercial production of tobacco and vegetables has required significantly more manual labour input from women than wheat. The exchange of labour among women, including natal kin, has been common. By contrast, Huang Tu's land allocation and agricultural systems until recently encouraged high fertility. Families had little incentive to limit childbearing if each additional baby brought more land at the next land adjustment. Moreover, Huang Tu did not have a deep tradition of female participation in farming or labour exchange among women, and thus there was less need to maintain ties to married daughters. In the early 20th century, Huang Tu women were heavily occupied with domestic textile production for family and market.

Development planners are often able to change short-term or even medium-term institutions, but there may be other longer-term institutions that reproduce gender discrimination and resist policy changes and public education campaigns. As Sargeson and Song also argue elsewhere in this volume, the patrilineal corporations that persist under the nomenclature of Village Committees in much of rural China reproduce fundamental disadvantages for girls and women, granting them only secondary village citizenship rights when it comes to property in land and housing. Land and houses go first to sons. In Song Gou, they do sometimes go to daughters. In Huang Tu, patrilineal corporations are stronger and an outside son-in-law is more likely to be driven out (Bossen 2007a). Daughter-only families have much less likelihood of keeping property in the family for their descendents because they typically must depend on a single incoming son-in-law, usually a man without local kin, to help their daughter defend property rights.

China's rapid economic development over the past three decades has produced many positive changes for women in the realm of increased education levels, employment and housing choices, particularly in the rapidly growing urban centres that attract migrants. As women struggle to gain a more equal footing, development planners concerned with reducing China's disturbing sex imbalance should consider that rural areas still offer limited forms of social security to women. Without male descendants, rural women's claims to land and house are questionable. Prohibitions and penalties for sex-selective abortions, the provision of small pensions and publicity that girls and boys are equally important as descendents may not be sufficient to convince rural parents that they do not need a son.

This chapter has looked in detail at two villages, an infinitesimally small window on China's immense diversity. Can any development policy conclusions be drawn? By looking at 'hot' and 'cold' spots where sex ratios are particularly high and low, policy makers can identify elements of local customs and practices which contribute to such outcomes. Factors that prevent women from becoming equal property-owning citizens, particularly in rural areas, are prime candidates for consideration. One conclusion to draw from these two villages is that the relative strength of local patrilineal institutions and the resistance to treating village daughters as heirs appears to have more influence on the sex ratio and female deficit than variations in land adjustment policies. Child sex ratios in Huang Tu were high even though the birth of daughters and in-coming wives entitled families to additional land until 2000.

The development of real estate markets and migration to towns and cities across China may reduce the insecurities of parents who have daughters and no son. Looking beyond the village, women of the younger generations are purchasing housing in cities where property rights are less easily influenced by patrilineal groups, making it more likely that as widows or divorcees, they could retain some assets. For example, one Huang Tu woman, an unmarried university graduate with a good job in a foreign corporation, purchased a house in Shanghai, while a well-educated young man from Song Gou together with his wife purchased a house in Chengdu. Up to 2000, migration from Huang Tu was mainly temporary male migration. Now, many more young people of both sexes are migrating to distant provinces to work. Long distance migration from Song Gou is less common, but many grown children are finding jobs in the towns and cities of Yunnan. As Leslie Chang (2008) suggests, migration allows them to postpone marriage until they save enough to build a house in the village or secure a job and housing in the city. Experiences of urban employment and individual income earning opportunities away from home are changing young women's attitudes and perhaps their bargaining power. The point is illustrated by a segment in Chang's *Factory Girls*, in which a young migrant woman working in Guangdong was pressured by her parents to send more money, after she had given them almost 5000 yuan in two years:

> In Qianqian's village, parents traditionally built a house for a grown son to live in after his marriage . . . her parents were already worrying about the expense [for her 14-year-old brother].

> 'All the other people in the village have built their houses,' her father had said to her. 'How come mine hasn't been built yet?'

> 'I was going to ask you the same question,' Qianqian retorted. (Chang 2008: 109)

Yet while urban migration offers alternatives to young migrant women, the path to improving property rights for rural women remains long and difficult. As Liaw observed:

in the aftermath of legal reforms designed to secure land tenure for farmers, women in rural China lost rights to land at marriage, divorce, and widowhood. Despite a central legal framework that facially [sic] protects women's property interests, ambiguity in the property and marriage laws have allowed village leaders to reassert traditional social norms and deny constitutional equal rights guarantees for women. (Liaw 2008: 237)

Identifying variations in the intensity and rigidity of patriliny as they affect property rights has potential for enhancing our understanding of regional variations in China's sex imbalance. Governments at national and local levels must seriously address the denial of equal property rights to rural women, if policies aiming to reduce China's alarming female deficit are to be effective.

NOTES

1. This research was funded by a research grant from SSHRC, the Social Science and Humanities Research Council of Canada (2006). I thank Nathan Bossen, Jean Hung, Tamara Jacka, Sally Sargeson, Cheng Shaozhen, Yang Hui, Zhang Liren and the villagers. I am responsible for any errors.
2. Greenhalgh and Li (1995) used this expression to describe the bending of the original gender-neutral policy in response to fierce pressures from peasants who feared they'd be left without a son.
3. Various regions have been reported to grant extra land to men, considered to be 'labour force' while women, children, and elders were granted only 'subsistence' land.
4. By 'real property' I refer to property that is non-moveable: primarily land and houses in rural China.
5. Sargeson and Song (this volume) usefully emphasize the concept of 'village citizenship rights'.
6. Lineage strength can be measured by the concentration or diversity of surnames in a particular community. However, local lineage concentration cannot be measured by taking all the individual surnames of registered individuals or the surnames of the heads of household. Chinese women keep their own surname after marriage, and sometimes widows are listed as heads of households even though the inheriting children will have their father's surname. Lineage concentration can be measured by examining the surnames taken by the children of each household.
7. In some areas, however, land can be contracted by and exchanged among individuals and companies (see for example Sargeson 2004).
8. Although widows and daughters may have individual ownership of houses, this is more likely in peri-urban and urban areas. I have not encountered women regarded as sole owners in villages. Widows may be considered 'heads' of households, but they share the rights to a house with their sons.
9. In general, women seem to become more secure as owners as they age, but because older women generally have adult sons who share or protect their rights, it is difficult to determine whether these women's house rights would be secure if they were divorced or widowed without adult sons.
10. To protect privacy, pseudonyms are used in this chapter when referring to villages and individuals.
11. In 2008, a member of each household was interviewed: 19 men and 24 women in total.
12. In the one non-farming household, husband and wife work in transport, each driving

a separate vehicle. In one other household, the husband has a government job in town, but continues to help his wife who still farms in the village.

13. Discrepancies exist because marriage date and year of *hukou* transfer can differ, with *hukou* transfer sometimes occurring years later.

14. I adopt Johnson's formulation of parental reasoning from her book title (Johnson 2004).

15. Daughters receive dowries and gifts from their families at marriage. Depending on the family's resources, dowries can be quite costly, but they consist of moveable goods that can be usurped. They generally do not provide a house or a means to generate income that daughters can use to support parents.

16. More than 20 per cent of households contracted additional land. One explanation for the imbalance between those reporting contracting compared to those renting out land might be residual sensitivity about landlordism so that renting out is called 'giving'. Another explanation might be that some Song Gou villagers rent land from neighbouring villages.

17. 1 *mu* = 0.0667 hectares.

18. Youths aged over 15, both boys and girls, may migrate out to work or marry, even though they are underage (Chang 2008).

19. Lineage pressure to have sons is informal, and cannot be measured directly, but it is wrong to believe that the pressure comes only from within the family. Rural women without a son report disparaging remarks by other villagers, not just mothers-in-law. Loss of face at rituals and bullying by other families with more lineage 'man-power' are aspects of this.

20. This does not mean that Village Committees alone have the power to decide redistribution policy. Land management decisions may be set by county or town governments, but even subordinate 'small groups' or 'teams' may successfully resist a Village Committee's decision to redistribute land. Song Gou villagers did not refuse to readjust land; they accepted higher level policy. One of Huang Tu's 15 teams resisted readjustment.

5. 'Good citizens prefer daughters': gender, rurality and the Care for Girls Campaign[1]

Lisa Eklund

INTRODUCTION

In the 2000s a growing imbalance in the sex ratio at birth (SRB)[2] was identified by the Chinese government as a development issue, affecting harmonious and sustainable development, and ultimately the peace and stability of the country (SFPC 2002: 1). Imbalanced SRB is believed to cause an increase in violence against women, including sexual exploitation and the trafficking of women and girls, as well as the likelihood that tens of millions of men will be unable to find a marriage partner (CGC 2006a). In order to address the issue, the Chinese government launched the Care for Girls Campaign (hereafter referred to as the Campaign), which has as its objectives to improve the value of the girl child, promote gender equality, and normalize the SRB by the year 2020 (CGC 2006b). The Campaign was piloted in 11 counties in 2003 and in 13 counties in 2004, and has since been scaled up to a nation-wide campaign (Li, Shuzhuo 2007; Wei and Gao 2007). It consists of five core components: (1) awareness-raising and advocacy campaigns to promote 'new marriage and childbearing customs'; (2) a strengthening of reproductive health services and management; (3) beneficial socio-economic policies for one-child or two-daughter families; (4) strengthened management of sex determination and sex-selective abortions; and (5) improvements in statistical and reporting systems (CGC 2006a).

Although data show that the SRB has declined in the pilot counties of the Campaign from 133.8 in 2000 to 119.6 in 2005 (Li, Shuzhuo 2007), there has as yet been little systematic assessment of the impact of the Campaign on notions of son preference and the value of girls.[3] The few analyses of the design and implementation of the Campaign published to date have either portrayed it in favourable terms, pointing to the multi-sectoral character of the Campaign and the leading role of the government as 'champions' of gender equality (Tan, Liangying 2008), or have criticized it for not being gender sensitive (Li, Shuzhuo 2007; Liu, Sisi 2004; Lin Mei 2006). This chapter seeks to look beyond whether or not the Campaign is gender sensitive, and aims, first of all, to analyse the particular ways in which certain gender norms and understandings have shaped the Campaign's objectives and design, and its evolution as a political process and set of institutions. It further seeks to examine the relationship between the gendering of the Campaign and the gender norms and practices which prevail in rural China. It is hoped that by exploring this relationship, the chapter will contribute to a new understanding of the links between gender, development interventions and social change.

The chapter pays special attention to two of the Campaign's components, namely awareness-raising and preferential policies for families with daughters (Component 1 and 3 above). It will also discuss the Campaign in relation to the state's population policy, as an institution potentially reinforcing son preference. As well as primary and secondary literature, it draws on interviews with academics and government officials, and data from ethnographic fieldwork conducted in four villages in rural Anhui in 2007.[4] The chapter adopts an analytical framework wherein the 'state narrative' on son preference, as enacted through the Campaign, is compared with rural women's and men's representations of son preference. The concept of 'state narrative' is employed to signify that there is an official policy line, formulated and promoted by the party-state, which serves the purpose of (a) generating a unified and multi-sectoral response to a particular problem and (b) ensuring that the way policies and programmes are designed and implemented to address this particular problem does not contradict the overarching goals and strategies of the Chinese Communist Party (CCP).

Before discussing the main findings of the study, some more background on the state narrative on son preference will be provided, as such information is important for understanding both the design and implementation of the Campaign.

FORMULATING A 'STATE NARRATIVE' ON SON PREFERENCE

Son preference is nothing new in China. But, although illegal, its manifestations, of neglect, abandonment and killing of baby daughters, and foetus sex-selection, were not subject to active state intervention until very recently.

The state's imposition of strict population policies since the late 1970s has reduced the likelihood of couples having at least one son. A common response, in particular in rural areas, has been to defy the population policies, to continue childbearing until a son is born, or else to both reduce the number of births and secure a male offspring by undertaking the sex-selective abortion of female foetuses. The latter strategy is the main reason there is SRB imbalance in China today (Chu 2001). There have, hence, been two main incentives for the government to address son preference – to curb SRB imbalance and to keep birth rates down.

The National Population and Family Planning Commission (NPFPC),[5] the government organization responsible for implementing the population policy, became the leading body responsible for organizing, coordinating and monitoring the work of addressing SRB imbalance and son preference, together with a large number of other government organizations, non-governmental organizations (NGOs) and mass organizations (SFPC 2002). Drawing upon research results and experiences of a pilot project undertaken with support from the Ford Foundation in 1998, in Chaohu City, Anhui Province, the Chinese government began to develop its own approach to addressing son preference (Li, Shuzhuo et al. 2007). There has since been an increasing number of publications issued by the Chinese government, which contribute to formulating the state narrative on which the Campaign is designed (see for example CGC 2006a, 2006b).[6]

The state narrative on son preference attributes it to three main factors, namely, economic factors, cultural factors and factors pertaining to gender inequality (CGC 2006b). Economic factors refer to villagers' need to give birth to a son in order to secure male manual labour and security for old age. This need is related to the dominance of virilocal marriage arrangements, whereby daughters leave their native homes to move in with their husband's families, while sons stay with their parents after marriage. Cultural factors refer to traditional concepts such as 'the more sons the merrier' (*duozi duofu*), 'men are superior, women are inferior' (*nan zun, nü bei*), and the importance attached to 'the [patrilineal] transmission of the family line' (*chuanzong jiedai*). Gender inequality refers to different types of gender inequality and discrimination in society, such as the violation of women's land-use and property rights, women's lower educational attainment and discrimination against women in the labour market (CGC 2006b).

The state narrative emphasizes culture as a major factor explaining son preference. According to operational guidelines, compiled by the National Expert Group of the Care for Girls Campaign, son preference is rooted in 'feudalism',[7] which has had a history of more than 2000 years in China, and which still is typical for rural areas. The guidelines further state that, despite more than 50 years of Communist rule, including many changes in the social and economic landscape, as well as in the legal framework, feudal notions still prevail in China today (CGC 2006b). The view of son preference as 'feudal' or 'backward' is also supported in some academic work (for example, Wei and Gao 2007).

RAISING AWARENESS

Visiting rural China or street committees in urban China, one is likely to come across posters and slogans aimed at drawing attention to the value of the girl child. These slogans and posters are part of the awareness-raising activities which are one essential component of the Campaign.

The awareness-raising component of the Campaign largely overlaps with the Campaign to promote a 'new culture of marriage and childbearing entering into a thousand families' (*hunyu xinfeng jin wanjia*) which was

*Figure 5.1   A common sight in rural China where slogans related to
              family planning are written on the walls of people's houses.
              This slogan reads 'Nature will decide the sex of the newborn'.
              (Photo by Lisa Eklund.)*

launched in 1998 by the NPFPC (Li, Shuzhuo et al. 2007), and which is based on 'scientific principles, civilized behaviour, and progressive marriage and fertility behaviour, such as late marriage and childbearing [and notions of] fewer and better births, gender equality, giving birth to a boy and a girl is equally good, women are also inheritors, and husbands have responsibilities for family planning' (CGC 2006a: 41). As is evident from this quotation, adopting fertility behaviour free from son preference is associated in both these Campaigns with attributes that represent 'modernity', such as scientific principles, and civilized and progressive behaviour.

In order to promote the notion that 'giving birth to a boy and a girl is equally good', the Campaign has developed a range of slogans with different objectives (CGC 2006a). One set of slogans is based on the principle of equity between the sexes, emphasizing the equal capacities of males and females, such as 'Men and women build a harmonious society together' (*nannü gongjian hexie shehui*) and 'Nature will decide the sex of the newborn' (*shengnan shengnü shunqi ziran*). A second set of slogans focuses on girls only, aiming at promoting a positive role for daughters as beneficial to their families. Examples of slogans that fall under this category are: 'Daughters also constitute the next generation' (*nü'er ye shi houdairen*), 'Daughters can establish a household' (*nü'er neng lihu*), and 'Daughters can provide old age support' (*nü'er neng yanglao*). A third set of slogans directly urges people to value girls in general terms, such as 'Care for girls' (*guan'ai nühai*), and 'Protect girl children' (*baohu nütong*).

Contradictory Messages

The language used in the slogans and accompanying illustrations are two ways in which the gender norms and practices underpinning the Campaign are operationalized. In some cases, the slogans are worded in such a way as to convey multiple, conflicting messages about son preference. For example, the slogan 'Daughters also constitute the next generation' (*nü'er ye shi houdairen*), which, superficially at least, targets son preference as a problem, nevertheless signals that sons are the norm, through the use of the word 'also'. In other words, sons are the 'natural' ones to constitute the next generation, but daughters can also pass on the family line in case there is no son to do it. This slogan was subsequently changed and the 'also' was dropped in 2006–2007, suggesting that there is increasing awareness of the significance of gender-sensitive programming in the NPFPC (expert interview 2007).

Some slogans do not promote gender stereotypes in themselves, but the visual images that accompany them do. One example is a poster with the slogan 'To care for girls is to show concern for the future of the people' *(guan'ai nühai jiu shi guanzhu minzu de weilai)*. Nothing about the poster indicates that having girls is as good as having boys in terms of the social and economic status that they will acquire as adults or the labour power, income or other benefits that they will provide their parents. Rather, the poster emphasizes the stereotypical 'female' traits of being pretty and pleasing people. Another message conveyed by the slogan is that girls reproduce the people. These representations of girls and women stand in sharp contrast to the Maoist era, when women's productive roles were more often highlighted, and gender sameness and equality were emphasized (Evans 2005; Zhang, Jeanne H. 2003).

Figure 5.2   *Campaign poster at a township Family Planning clinic saying 'To care for today's girls is to show concern for the future of the people'. Although slogans are intended to increase the value of the girl child, they sometimes convey contradictory messages, based on gendered assumptions. (Photo by Lisa Eklund.)*

During my fieldwork in rural Anhui I observed that typical 'female' traits of daughters, such as being loving and caring and emotionally closer to parents in old age, are also promoted by local government officials as part of Campaign language aimed at enhancing the value of daughters in the eyes of their parents. However, such messages risk further reinforcing gender stereotypes and underlining the point that sons and daughters have different qualities. By explicitly stressing the advantage of daughters in terms of their pleasing traits and the emotional support they provide, they imply that sons are valued for something else; in many cases they are associated with providing economic security.

Clashes between Poster Messages and Rural Realities

The effectiveness of Campaign slogans is sometimes further hampered by the socio-economic context in which many rural women and men lead their everyday lives. For example, as the analysis of the baseline survey of the 24 pilot projects of the Campaign points out, in the absence of a social security system, the slogan, 'Daughters can provide old age support', means little as, in accordance with virilocal marriage patterns, daughters commonly move out of their natal families when they get married. Therefore, it is difficult for ordinary citizens to be persuaded by such slogans (Chen, Shengli 2006).

My fieldwork generated similar findings. This was particularly obvious with regard to the slogan 'Daughters can establish a household', which requires uxorilocal marriages, whereby a man becomes a son-in-law in his wife's native home. Among some of the informants interviewed in this study, there was much resistance to this type of marriage, both from families with experience of uxorilocal marriage and families who were facing the possibility of such a marriage (that is, only-daughters families), and from fellow villagers. Li, a man in his mid-forties with two teenage daughters explained that he did not want either of his two daughters to stay with him and his wife after they got married as he could not stand the thought of having a son-in-law under his roof (informant interview 2007). Wang, a 30-year-old man, who lived in his wife's natal family, described how fellow villagers would talk behind his back, tease him and make disparaging remarks, such as 'Are you on your way home to your mother-in-law, Little Wang?' when walking through the village (informant interview 2007). The examples provided illustrate that factors reinforcing son preference are multi-faceted and deeply embedded in local cultures, which are contingent on clear gendered social and economic arrangements. Consequently, the attitudes of both families with only daughters, potential husbands-to-be and fellow villagers contribute to the fact that

'Daughters can establish a household' is a slogan not easily translated into actual behaviour.

Capitalizing on Popular Fear – the 'Marriage Squeeze' Phenomenon

The state narrative on son preference uses the language of 'marriage squeeze' in order to mobilize citizens to end prenatal sex-selection. When asked about son preference, the villagers interviewed for this study often mentioned the problem of 'marriage squeeze'. Some of them explained that they did not want to have a son, since in the future men, especially those who are poor and uneducated, will have difficulty finding a wife. Being sonless is in some instances viewed as less humiliating than having a son who is a 'bare branch' (that is, unmarried).[8]

Another purpose of the state's focus on the 'marriage squeeze' seems to be to enhance the collective value of daughters, as, once they grow up, these women will be low in supply and high in demand as wives. During my fieldwork, I came across one family whose daughter had married recently. The family had received a cash transfer, effectively a bride price, from the husband's family of 40 000 yuan. The family had been very poor until then, but thanks to the money were able to build a house which was comparable to those newly constructed by migrant families. Both fellow villagers and cadres in charge of the Campaign interpreted this case as a sign that the value of young women had improved due to the shortage of girls.

However, as the examples above illustrate, the marriage squeeze issue is often phrased in a manner assuming virilocal marriage patterns. Scant attention is paid to challenging virilocal marriage customs wherein the man 'takes' (*qü*) a wife and the woman 'gives' herself in marriage (*jia*).

Feminists have been particularly vocal in their criticisms of the emphasis by media and government officials on the 'bare branches' phenomenon, which problematizes the shortage of women of marriageable ages from a man's perspective, while failing to acknowledge human rights violations of women and girls (Bu 2004; Wei and Gao 2007). However, there is little sign that this criticism has had a trickle-down effect on the grassroots level of implementation of the Campaign. In the four villages included in this study, there was little evidence that action was being taken to challenge virilocal marriage customs. Staying silent on the subject thus underpins one of the social institutions which feeds son preference.

Stigmatizing Son Preference

One of the consequences of the Campaign is that son preference has become politically incorrect. For individuals or couples to say that they want to have a (grand)son rather than a (grand)daughter is therefore associated with a certain level of stigma. Xie, a man in his early sixties, and who was a relatively well-off farmer thanks to migrant families subletting their land to him and his oldest son, denied that there was even such a notion as son preference in his village, both at present and in the past. At the same time, when asked how many children he had, Xie mentioned his sons only, and omitted listing his daughters as they were already married and hence 'belonged' to another family. Other informants in the four villages claimed that they did not mind the sex of their child or grandchild, and yet others announced that they in fact had 'daughter preference' (*nühai pianhao*).

Daughter preference was a concept often mentioned by local government officials as a sign that the Campaign had had an impact on people's gender values. Daughter preference was considered positive and 'modern', and seen as something in line with scientific principles and civilized, progressive behaviour. Paradoxically, daughter preference was not considered problematic from the point of view of addressing gender stereotypes or of addressing the Campaign objective of promoting gender equality. Rather, local officials implicitly encouraged daughter preference and portrayed families with daughter preference as 'good citizens'.[9]

The informants consulted in this study commonly discussed son and daughter preference in terms of slogans, and formulated problems in a way that resembled the state narrative, such as in terms of the 'marriage squeeze' mentioned above, and the notion that daughters are more loving and caring and provide better comfort in one's old age. Also, when asked about their personal views on son preference, many informants repeated the slogans of the Campaign (such as 'Boys and girls are the same'), but were unable to substantiate their opinions. This suggests that, although they had learned Campaign messages well enough to be able to recite them, the messages had not had any deeper impact on their attitudes.

Other studies of the Campaign have questioned whether the slogans can help bring about fundamental changes in norms and values related to son preference. In one of the pilot project sites of the Campaign, located in Hunan Province, a survey showed that whereas 81 per cent of the population surveyed knew of the Campaign, only about 50 per cent were familiar with its content and key slogans. The survey also found that the vast majority still possessed notions of son preference (Zeng Jianguo et al. 2006).

Fighting the 'Old,' the 'Rural' and the 'Traditional'

While conducting fieldwork it became clear that another dimension of the Campaign's awareness-raising activities is the assumption that son preference is intrinsically a 'rural' phenomenon. When discussing son preference with cadres from the local family planning bureau and rural women and men, the rurality of son preference was something that often came up. Typically, informants would avoid providing concrete reasons for son preference and make sweeping statements such as 'It's the countryside, you know! The city doesn't have it' or 'Old people have it, the younger generation doesn't mind'. When probing further, the importance of male labour in agriculture was another oft-stated reason for son preference. Hence, understandings of rurality incorporated the assumption that rural people are tied to a 'traditional' agricultural way of life, and often associated rurality with the past, and with norms and attitudes upheld by the elderly.

This representation of son preference was similar to the language of the state narrative, which credits son preference to 'feudal', traditional and rural norms and behaviour. For example, the Campaign guidelines state:

> [China] has experienced over 2000 years of a feudal society, which has gradually formed a traditional reproductive culture based on the importance of men and the insignificance of women (*zhongnan qingnü*) . . . According to old and traditional ideas the prosperity of a family depends on the man, a son will marry a wife who will add a son, and only sons and grandsons can provide old age support . . . This has upheld and strengthened the reproductive culture of men being important and women negligible in the traditional agricultural-based society. (CGC 2006b: 6)

Along the same lines of thinking was the portrayal by local government officials in charge of implementing the Campaign of mothers-in-law as carriers and transmitters of son preference. Although it would be misleading to argue that mothers-in-law do not hold values of son preference, assuming that son preference is something imposed on a woman by her mother-in-law is too simplistic. Although it is hard to separate individual choice and preference from that of a person's immediate surroundings and family members, among the villagers interviewed, in some cases the woman herself was the main person expressing the wish to have a son. This was illustrated in the quotation below, in which Yi, a woman in her early sixties described how she had given birth to four daughters before she bore a son, and her mother-in-law's reaction to this:

> She [my mother-in-law] was not at all disappointed. I gave birth to four daughters and I thought to myself that I had had too many daughters . . . The countryside is like that, you know . . . I wanted to kill her [my daughter] off . . .

wanted to kill her off, I didn't want her. But my mother-in-law brought me to reason. My mother-in-law said a daughter is also a piece of you that has been born, she said that she [my daughter] was also my own child, and that when she is grown up she will also be part of the family tree . . . (informant interview 2007)

Nevertheless, in two of the villages included in this study, where local government agencies were actively involved in the Campaign, in-laws, and in particular mothers-in-law were targeted with counselling sessions to 're-educate' them and address their presumed preference for sons. Similar activities have been documented by Wei and Gao, who refer to activities targeting mothers-in-law and daughters-in-law, with the purpose of establishing 'model cases' of mothers and daughters-in-law (Wei and Gao 2007). It can be seen, then, that activities conducted as part of the Campaign carry with them important assumptions about not only gender, but also rurality and generation, which do not always correspond with rural practices.

There are also some discrepancies between assumptions about gender divisions of agricultural labour as embedded in the state narrative on son preference, and actual work patterns prevailing in rural China today. The state narrative emphasizes the importance of male manual labour in agriculture as a contributing factor to son preference, and this is one reason why son preference is depicted as 'traditionally rural'. However, over the last three decades, China's rural economy has diversified and industrialized at a very rapid rate, and a large proportion of men have moved out of agriculture (Bossen 2007a). This, in combination with the mechanization of agriculture, land shortage and the lower status attached to farm work, has led to a 'demasculinization of agriculture', meaning that male manual labour in agriculture has become increasingly dispensable. Hence, the 'traditional' gender division of labour, which accords primacy to the role of male manual labour in agriculture, has been undergoing transformation, undermining the argument that son preference in rural China is based on the need for male labour in agriculture (Eklund 2009).

SOCIO-ECONOMIC INCENTIVES FOR SOCIAL CHANGE

Material Benefits

The state narrative on son preference acknowledges that certain socio-economic circumstances reinforce son preference. In order to alter those circumstances, the Campaign includes a range of policies and programmes aimed at improving the living conditions of girls and their families (CGC 2006a; Li, Shuzhuo et al. 2007). The range and scope of the programmes implemented differ between geographical areas, depending on the commitment of local governments to allocate resources to the Campaign and whether or not local budgets can accommodate financial benefits to concerned families (Zeng Jianguo et al. 2006).

Li and colleagues have grouped the programmes into two categories. The first category provides financial benefits to couples who adhere to the population policy, typically those who have only one child or two daughters (Li, Shuzhuo et al. 2007). The most common benefit is an old age pension for persons registered as rural residents of 600 yuan per person per year, or 50 yuan per person per month (CGC 2006a). In some instances local governments contribute to this basic pension to allow for adaptation to local costs of living. In two of the villages included in this study, the local government added 10 yuan to the basic monthly pension for couples who had one daughter. The second type of programme aims at helping poor families with only daughters to reduce problems related to housing, schooling and employment in order to support the development of girls (Li, Shuzhuo et al. 2007). There are many such programmes in existence, including job training programmes, cooperative medical services, poverty alleviation schemes, and the preferential allocation of housing and land (CCP 2007; Zheng, Zhenzhen 2007). As an example, in my research sites, daughters without brothers and with no or a maximum of one sister were given extra credits when applying to senior secondary school, in order to improve their chances of pursuing an education. Only-daughter families were also given preferential access to credit and training opportunities.

There are also provisions within the population policy regulations in some provinces which, although not officially part of the Campaign, are formulated implicitly to help realize the objectives of the Campaign. For example, in Anhui, the local population policy regulation gives preferential treatment to couples who marry uxorilocally, entitling them to two children, regardless of whether the first-born is a boy or a girl (APFPC 2002). However, if a family has two daughters, only one daughter can benefit from this rule. This effectively means that daughters-only families have to decide and come to an agreement on which one of the daughters will take on the role of a 'son'.

Even though programmes providing material benefits are welcomed by rural residents, there are several problems with the way they are designed as well as implemented, from the point of view of combating son preference. For example, the amount associated with the monthly pension is relatively small, even by rural standards (Wei 2006). In fact, it is well below the poverty line and does not replace the reliance on children for old age support. Among the informants in my study, none of the older persons were able to get by on their pensions alone, but received remittances from their migrating children or engaged in income-generating activities.

In addition, preferential policies for daughters-only families convey mixed messages and risk reinforcing the gender inequalities upon which son preference is based. On the one hand, such policies contradict the message that 'Women and men are equal', as families with sons are left without benefits (Lin 2006). On the other hand, some of the policies, which are aimed at boosting the value accorded to daughters, may instead undermine that value. For example, the pension scheme for families with one child or two daughters indicates that a family needs two daughters to be able to provide what one son can do alone.

Lin Mei, a researcher at the Central Communist Party School, argues that such policies are based on an underlying assumption that daughters will marry out of their natal families, leaving their parents without anyone to provide old age care, or alternatively they will stay with their parents but still be unable to provide old age care. Hence, the government support to those families is based on the idea that not having a son creates vulnerability (Lin Mei 2006). This may sanction the notion that sons are essential and thereby underpin son preference.

The same dual message is conveyed by the population policy rule which allows uxorilocal families to have two children regardless of sex. Although this rule serves to challenge virilocal marriage patterns, it only applies to women who have no brothers. Again, this preferential treatment, aimed at easing son preference, is formulated in a manner that allows for daughters to take the traditional role of sons only if there is no son, confirming that sons are the norm.

Other ethnographic work has documented that rural residents believe it is unfair that families with two daughters receive financial benefits, while families who first had a daughter and then a son get no financial support (Wei and Gao 2007; Zeng Jianguo et al. 2006). As a matter of fact, it is deeply contradictory that, although both types of families adhere to the population policy, only families with two daughters qualify for financial support. This suggests that the support is more a compensation for not having a son than a reward for reducing the number of births, as will be discussed below. This way of implementing preferential policies effectively means that families who accept the Campaign slogan, 'Giving birth to a boy or a girl is the will of nature' (*shengnan shengnü shunqi ziran*), are discriminated against.

Finally, the fact that a substantial part of the financial benefits is granted to poor rural families with daughters only builds on the assumption that son preference, poverty, rurality and backwardness are linked. However, granting financial benefits to poor families with girls only is not necessarily going to alter gender relations within these families or in the local community. Moreover, providing financial benefits to daughters-only families as a means to enhance the value of daughters has been questioned, as many people doubt the preferential policies will last (Wei and Gao 2007).

Championing 'Daughters-Only Households'

Another strategy to promote small families and prevent daughter-only families from continuing childbearing until a son is born is to promote the labels 'only-child household' and 'daughters-only household' *(dansheng zinühu* and *chunnühu)* as markers of status. In the villages included in this study, daughters-only households were issued a certificate and awarded five yuan a month as a 'daughters-only allowance', provided the parents practised long-term contraception, such as IUD or sterilization. When interviewing villagers, I noticed that even though the financial contribution was mostly symbolic, the fostering of the label initiated pride in the sense that the families were doing 'common good' for the well-being of the nation. Similar to the notion of 'daughter preference' as something 'progressive', many of the daughter-only families that I interviewed were proud to have made the decision to have only daughters. This was particularly evident among families who had decided to have just one daughter, even though they had the right to have a second child according to the local population policy regulations. Those families typically stated that 'boys and girls are the same', which is one of the slogans of the Campaign, and that daughters are more caring and loving.

However, it was unclear whether or not the decision to have only daughters and the positive feelings associated with this were present before the children were born: given the lack of choice under the population policy, the positive attitude evinced by those with daughters only may have been simply a matter of rationalization. Other research has confirmed that having one child or two daughters is not necessarily an active choice or an indicator that the families have been convinced that the value of a daughter is as high as a son, as communicated by the slogans of the Campaign (Lin Mei 2006).

Although the intention with the 'daughters-only household' label in the villages studied is to reward the families who adhere to the population policy regulations, there is a risk that the creation of the social category 'daughters-only household' signals that families who stop childbearing while having only daughters have made a 'sacrifice' and suffer 'hardship' (Murphy 2003), and therefore need care and financial compensation for their lack of a son. Hence, there is a fine line between being 'rewarded' for making a contribution to the country (having fewer children) and being 'compensated' for making a personal sacrifice (having no son). This ambiguity is compounded by the fact that not all families who adhere to the population policy regulation qualify for a certificate and a monthly allowance. As mentioned above, families who first have a daughter and then a son are not included in the programme.

THE POPULATION POLICY AS AN IMPEDIMENT TO THE CARE FOR GIRLS CAMPAIGN

When reading documents about the Campaign and when discussing its objectives and activities with local cadres, it becomes clear that the impact of the population policy is largely absent from the state narrative on son preference. Although it has been documented that the one-child policy has had a 'daughter empowerment' effect in urban China (Fong 2004), as will be discussed below, there are contradictory elements in the population policy, as well as in the way it is implemented, particularly in rural China. This sends messages that work against the objectives of the Campaign.

The 1.5-Child Policy

When the population policy was first implemented, there were few exceptions to the one-child-per-couple rule. However, the discrepancy between the policy and the preferred number and sex composition of children among the general population was very large, particularly in rural areas. Consequently, the implementation of the policy met a great deal of resistance and, as evident by a brief spike in the birth rate in the early 1980s (Greenhalgh and Winckler 2005: 18), local cadres in charge of implementing the population policy did not manage to implement the policy as strictly as they had planned. Following this phase was a period of mass sterilizations and abortions, combined with a revision of the policy to make it more feasible to implement. Beginning in 1984, many areas introduced an amendment to the policy stating that rural families with only one girl could have a second child (Zeng, Yi 2007). This amendment effectively supported the notion that one girl was not sufficient for a rural family, whereas two girls or one boy was good enough, ascribing half the value of boys to girls. In most provincial regulations which operationalize the Population and Family Planning Law of 2002, the same stipulation is present. For example, in the Anhui Provincial Family Planning Regulations of 2002, families who meet certain criteria can have two children. Those criteria include that families must be registered as rural, and have one daughter or a son with a disability (APFPC 2002). Here, a daughter is not only ascribed half the value of a son, she is also equated with a disabled child. In other words, the '1.5-child policy' sanctions the notion of son preference, potentially not only 'giving in' to the pressure to bear a son, but also reinforcing the belief that bearing an able son is essential for the survival of rural families.

Sanctioning Late-Term Abortions

Given the population policy and the fact that some couples prefer to have sons, undertaking foetal sex determination and sex-selective abortions in order to have a son are common practices. These practices are referred to as the 'two illegalities', and efforts to combat them are one component of the Campaign (Li, Shuzhuo 2007).

To understand the availability of sex-selective abortion it is important to examine the goals and values of those working in reproductive health (RH) services. In this context, one must remember that many RH service providers have been trained within a system in which RH services are delivered in order to meet administratively set demographic targets (Sai 1997). In this system, service providers have been mandated to perform abortions in order to keep birth rates down, and to ensure high contraceptive prevalence rates. This mandate has been extended to include the performance of second trimester abortions. In other words, health staff have performed abortions in the interest of the state for decades, and little consideration has been given to the fact that the abortions have been performed in the second trimester. Although a client-centred approach, which is based on the needs and rights of the client, quality of care and informed choice (Costello et al. 2001), has been promoted in China since the International Conference on Population and Development in Cairo in 1994, there is still a legacy of the administrative approach remaining.

Accounts from family planning cadres at grassroots levels reveal that couples who want a son sometimes evoke the population policy and regulations to seek late-term abortions (UNFPA 2005). Although lifted in some provinces, many provinces still have birth spacing requirements of three to four years between births, in cases in which a second child is allowed. Both couples and family planning cadres and medical staff have sometimes taken advantage of this spacing requirement. The birth of an unwanted child before the spacing requirement is met is a lose–lose situation for both couples and family planning cadres in the sense that couples will have to pay social compensation fees and family planning cadres will fail to meet the requirements of reducing 'out-of-plan' births. Under such circumstances, medical staff have sometimes turned a blind eye to the real reason for late-term abortions so as to contribute to keeping the birth rates low. Hence, there has been an unspoken understanding on the part of medical staff that couples need a son, and therefore late-term sex-selective abortions for non-medical purposes have been made available, signalling that the urge for sons is sanctioned by the health and family planning authorities.[10] However, in 2003, a regulation was jointly issued by the NPFPC, the Ministry of Health and the State Food and Drug Administration, stating that a woman, whose pregnancy is compatible with local population policy regulations regarding the number of children allowed, and who has had an unauthorized abortion[11] after 14 weeks, loses the right to have another child (NPFPC et al. 2003).[12] This may reduce the demand for sex-selective abortions, as the sex of the foetus can most reliably be determined through ultrasound from 16 weeks gestation onwards (Harrington et al. 1996). However, women who are pregnant with an out-of-plan child can have the pregnancy terminated up to week 27 of gestation, which is the latest time for an abortion according to the Standard Service Delivery Protocol on Family Planning (SSDP n.d.).

CONCLUSIONS

This chapter has analysed the particular ways in which certain gender norms and understandings have shaped the Care for Girls Campaign's objectives and design. It has shown how the Campaign has evolved as a political process, responding to the population policy and the demographic imbalance in favour of new-born boys. It has also examined the relationship between the gendering of the Campaign and the gender norms and practices which prevail in rural China.

The chapter concludes that there is a complex set of relationships between the gendering of the Campaign, as manifested both in its awareness-raising component and in its constituent socio-economic policies, and rural gender norms and institutions. First of all, in the formulation and illustration of messages that aim at raising awareness about the value of girls, the Campaign capitalizes on prevailing gender norms, including the understanding that women are loving and caring, and closer to their parents emotionally. It seems that using gender stereotypes is not considered problematic and that such stereotypes may even fit into an ideal of modernity because they divert from the norms of gender sameness and equality that prevailed during the Mao-era. With regard to social change, the chapter suggests that capitalizing on gender stereotypes may attract attention and sympathy in the short term. However, in the long run, it may contribute to the reinforcement of popular gender stereotypes which may, in turn, contribute to the maintenance of son preference.

Secondly, the Campaign's preferential socio-economic policies targeting one-child and only-daughters families are partially based on the assumption that having daughters creates vulnerability. These policies risk further contributing to gender inequalities, as they convey the message that daughters are not as valuable as sons, and that families with only daughters are in need of financial support.

Thirdly, the state narrative on son preference which underpins the Campaign partly formulates its arguments in relation to rural gender institutions, but does not challenge them. A key example of this is the lack of a systematic approach within the Campaign to addressing virilocal marriage patterns as a factor contributing to son preference.

Fourthly, both the state narrative and popular conceptions of son preference tend to frame and explain it in stereotypical terms, such that rurality, the old, and the past are understood as forming a single institution which underpins son preference.

Finally, this chapter has shown that missing from the state narrative is an acknowledgment of the role of population policy in both underpinning the notion of son preference and providing conducive circumstances for undertaking sex-selective abortions. Until this consequence of population policy is addressed, the Campaign may not be successful in reaching its objectives.

In conclusion, I argue that the Campaign pays too little attention to different rural institutions and to women's and men's agency and experiences of development and transformation of these institutions. There are many lessons to be learnt from the people with regard to fostering positive social change that can ease son preference. If it cannot heed and respond to these lessons, there is a risk that the Campaign will cement a rigid perception of son preference and that this will prevent a deeper understanding of how changing social and economic institutions may contribute to altering son preference, with or without direct state intervention.

NOTES

1. I am grateful to the Swedish School of Advanced Asia-Pacific Studies (SSAAPS) and the Swedish International Development Cooperation Agency (Sida) for financially supporting my PhD project, of which this study is one part. I am also grateful to Cecilia Milwertz at the Nordic Institute of Asian Studies in Copenhagen for comments on an earlier draft of this chapter.
2. Sex ratio at birth refers to the number of boys born per 100 girls and normally ranges

    between 103 and 107. According to official figures, in 2005, the average sex ratio at birth across China was 120.5 (UNFPA 2007).

3. However, for a small-scale study on this topic, see Zeng Jianguo et al. (2006).

4. The fieldwork was carried out in four villages, two of which were located in northern Anhui and two of which were located in a semi-urban area in eastern Anhui. It lasted for 22 days spread out over three periods between May and July 2007. The main methods used for producing data were household interviews, individual in-depth interviews and participant observations of village women and men belonging to 48 separate households. The names of the informants referred to in the text are fictive.

5. The NPFPC was preceded by the State Family Planning Commission (SFPC), which was the government agency responsible for implementing the population policy until 2003.

6. Some of the documents are not available to the public, such as the 'Action Plan for Extensively Unfolding the Care for Girls Action and Comprehensively Addressing the Issue of Abnormally High SRB', issued by the State Council.

7. It should be noted that, in the Chinese official and popular discourse referred to here, 'feudalism' does not have the same connotations as it does in historical scholarship, in which it refers to a type of governance. In China, 'feudal' is a pejorative term. According to official discourse, contemporary Chinese governance is not feudal, but there are elements of feudalism remaining in Chinese society.

8. It should be noted that 'bare branch' in historical terms has been used to denote a criminal man. Using this value-laden word fosters fear of being categorized as a bare branch.

9. Daughter preference has also been documented in one village in rural Jiangxi, where uxorilocal marriages have been promoted actively, and 52 out of 138 households are uxorilocal households. In this village, no skewed SRB was observed. Rather, daughters were ascribed equal value in terms of being able to provide old age support and taking on the responsibilities associated with inheriting family assets and land-use rights. Adding the fact that daughters were considered to be more loving and caring, daughter preference was observed (Lin Mei 2006).

10. It should be noted that research has found that sex selective abortions predominantly take place in health facilities that fall under the Ministry of Health and not the NPFPC (Chen Shengli 2006).

11. The term 'unauthorized abortion' refers to an abortion which takes place without medical grounds.

12. The same provision can be found at provincial level (see e.g. APC 2004).

6. Challenging the gendered dimensions of schooling: the state, NGOs and transnational alliances*

Heidi Ross

INTRODUCTION: THE 'WICKED' CONTEXTS OF GIRLS' SCHOOLING

> Schooling may be a subversive or a conservative activity, but it is certainly a circumscribed one . . . The faith is that despite some of the more debilitating teachings of culture itself, something can be done in school that will alter the lenses through which one sees the world; which is to say, that nontrivial schooling can provide a point of view from which what is can be seen clearly. (Postman 1996: ix–x)

This chapter presents a modest attempt to reveal the 'what is' of gender discrimination in China by exploring how it is (re)produced, maintained, and sometimes countered primarily through schooling.[1] The context for analysis is a 'Spring Bud' partnership begun in 2000 between an international non-governmental organization (INGO) and the Shaanxi Province Women's Federation (SWF). This Spring Bud project, which has funded the primary and secondary education of 1000 out-of-school girls, sheds light on what Sutton (1998: 382) has called the ABCs of girls' education: access to schooling; benefits of schooling; and constraints to full participation in schooling. The project has aimed for educational equity rather than equality. If equality is the same education, equity is the right education. This definition contrasts sharply with the Chinese state's deficit model of girls' education, in which achieving gender parity in participation in schooling has been seen as key to poverty alleviation.

The project helps us answer two questions critical to understanding the gendered project of Chinese schooling. What discourses of female education inform school policies and practices? How are these discourses shaped by top-down forces of state policies and agencies, bottom-up forces of communities and women's groups, external forces of INGOs and donor agencies, and middle forces, bridging civil society and state, of domestic non-government and semi-non-government organizations, and government-organized non-government organizations (GONGOs), particularly the All China Women's Federation (henceforth, Women's Federation)?

Gender socialization and discrimination neither begin nor end at the school gate. Stromquist has characterized gender issues as 'wicked problems', 'complex, interrelated, and less amenable to technical or scientific solutions since they depend primarily on value preferences' (Stromquist 2004: 5). Formal education is but one of several institutions (and policy arenas) that make up the fluctuating, wicked environment that genders human beings. The family (marriage, property and population policies), the economy (employment and market policies), and culture (values and preferences regarding appropriate roles and aspirations for sons and daughters, fathers and mothers) are sites of gender construction that influence a female's ability to receive and use formal education.

Reforms associated with market socialism have transformed these institutions, simultaneously enhancing girls' and women's opportunities and reconfiguring barriers to their full participation in society (Mak 1996; Movius 2004: 116). During the Maoist years 'women' barely registered in public discourse, because the achievement of socialism and the achievement of male and female equality were thought to share the same trajectory. This assumption proved false. While school participation rates in China have basically equalized over the last decade, persistent gaps in earnings and political representation favouring men in both revolutionary and reform periods challenge 'the state-as-equalizer model just as it challenges the market-as-equalizer model' (Bian et al. 2000: 131).

Since the late 1970s, when the Chinese Communist Party (CCP) and state approved the end of collective farming, allowed private ownership, implemented strict population control policies, broke the iron rice bowl of employment and urban social safety nets, and gradually opened China's market, media and culture to global influence, 'what counts as work, what counts as household, and what constitutes properly gendered behavior' (Entwisle and Henderson 2000: 11) have been transformed. Women's expanding educational and occupational opportunities and liberating explorations of identity, femininity and sexuality in high and popular culture have been accompanied by the feminization of agriculture, discrimination in the job market, disproportionately high layoffs of 'surplus' women, and a skewed male/female birth ratio. In this contradictory context, schools are necessary but far from sufficient to secure for girls and women productive and equitable positions in their communities (Stromquist 2003).

A comprehensive international review of state policies on women between 1975 and 1998 indicated that the most important predictors of strong and effective state action on behalf of females were '(in addition to contact with transnational networks) the proportion of women in ministerial positions, the degree of democracy in the country, and the extent to which women had similar access to men to secondary education' (Stromquist 2003: 196). In relation to China, only the last of these has changed. Given continuing low levels of participatory democracy and low numbers of women at top levels of government, progress in providing females access to education has been the state's primary means for making good on its commitment to gender equity. The truth about the ABCs of Chinese schooling is that girls and women have made greater strides there than in employment or in political participation.

The case study in this chapter illustrates how gender relations and discrimination are intimately tied to China's integration into the global economy. Educational challenges facing girls and women are simultaneously national and international, and their exploration requires coming to terms with the 'dialectic of the global and the local' (Arnove and Torres 2003). Theorists have used this insight to create the neologism 'glocalization', sometimes explained as globalization through localization. Anthropologist Anderson-Levitt (2004: 251) describes this process as global models inhibiting and inhabiting local practices. The 'global' is not an autonomous space, but rather a 'terminal point' for educational signs or targets like the 'girl child'. Detached from any specific context, these signs and targets circulate through the global educational community, ready for appropriation. Popkewitz has envisioned this process with the metaphor of 'indigenous foreigners' (John Dewey or Bill Gates, for example), who when locally appropriated 'take on the characteristics of that context before they move on to other contexts and become the target of further interpretations and reinterpretations' (Hultqvist and Dahlberg 2001: 251). The girl child as mother of development has for the last decade and a half been one of the world's most recognized 'indigenous foreigners' (Kristof and WuDunn 2010).

CHINA'S DISCOURSE OF DEVELOPMENTALISM AND THE INTERNATIONAL CONSENSUS ON GIRLS' EDUCATION

In 1990 leaders from 180 countries convened a world Education for All (EFA) conference and set three strategic objectives – to universalize primary education, eliminate illiteracy, and end educational inequality between men and women – for the end of the decade. China became a high-profile player in female education as one of the Summit of Nine, with the other most populated countries with high illiteracy rates: Brazil, Bangladesh, India, Egypt, Indonesia, Mexico, Nigeria and Pakistan. Girls and women accounted for two-thirds of the world's out-of-school children and adult illiterates, figures that closely matched the Chinese experience in 1990. Female education was declared the single most important investment a country could make in enhancing household income, improving family health and nutrition, reducing infant mortality, improving the skills and knowledge of agricultural workers (the majority of whom are women), democratizing decision making at household, community and national levels, and in alleviating poverty. In short, female education became the magic bullet of development (see Seeberg and Ross 2007).

Despite an almost fetishistic celebration of girls' education throughout the 1990s, EFA goals went unmet worldwide, as both the number of children in school and the number of children without access to school climbed (Goldstein 2004). Recognizing the failure of many nation states to act decisively on behalf of widening educational access and ensuring literacy, new EFA targets were set in 2000. The United Nations reaffirmed EFA commitments by approving eight Millennium Development Goals to be achieved by 2015. Millennium Development Goal 3, gender parity in primary and secondary education, was considered crucial to the success of the other seven goals. Consequently, its target date for achievement was pushed up to 2005, and a flurry of international reports heralded the importance of girls' education to global development, sustainability, and well-being (UNESCO 2004; UNICEF 2003; World Bank Gender Development Group 2003).

By 2000 China ranked high on 'gender scorecards', which generally include girls' net enrollment and survival rates over five years in primary school, girls' secondary net enrollment ratio, and a country's gender development index (Unterhalter et al. 2004). Of 31 Asian countries, China ranked number four (after Japan, Korea and Singapore). China's legislative and policy contexts also supported gender parity. The Constitution stipulated that women should enjoy equal rights with men in political, educational and social domains. The Compulsory Education Law asserted that every child at the age of six, irrespective of gender, ethnicity and race, should have the right to nine years of schooling. The 'Program for the Development of Women' and the 'Program for the Development of Children' called for equal access to education, employment and leadership opportunities and to improvements in health, social protection and quality of life.

The challenges faced during the last two decades of educational expansion provide a useful context for this chapter's case study. At the beginning of the EFA movement in 1990, Chinese schools were grappling with the consequences of state policies to decentralize school funding, which began as compulsory schooling and was expanded through junior secondary school. The collision of these two policies precipitated retrenchment of village schools and declining enrollment rates. In response, the government launched a massive campaign to support education for poor children between 1995 and 2000 (Hannum et al. 2010). At the end of the campaign the national percentage of school age girls able to enter primary school had increased from 96.31 per cent to nearly 99.1 per cent (climbing to 99.58 per cent in 2008); and the percentage of primary school age girls attending five years of schooling had increased from 82.2 per cent to over 94.5 per cent (reaching 99 per cent in 2008) (Ministry of Education 2003).

Even as a 2003 report on China's EFA policies published a sobering picture of low educational expenditure, inaccurate reporting of enrollment rates, failure to eliminate obstacles to schooling faced by China's poorest children, and use of legal guarantees as 'the end rather than merely a means for human rights protection' (Tomasevski 2003), the State Council was hosting its first conference on rural education since 1949. Building on momentum to expand educational access, the state re-committed itself to universalizing education among China's most marginalized children. In 2006 a revised Compulsory Education Law spelled out the 'right' of school age children to receive free education. The Law was accompanied by significant reform of the financing system for basic education making compulsory schooling virtually free for all children. In addition, strategies and regulations for the training and provision of highly qualified teachers, the construction of boarding schools to facilitate access in remote areas, and the implementation of a new national curriculum have all been put into place.

Results have been largely encouraging. Female enrollment has increased at every level of formal schooling, up to and including the first years of college. In 2008 the proportion of female students in undergraduate institutions exceeded that of males at 52.96 per cent (in contrast to 19.8 per cent in 1949 and 24.1 per cent in 1978), and at the masters and doctoral levels reached 48.16 per cent and 34.70 per cent respectively. Of course, these aggregated numbers conceal persistent lower access among minority girls (and boys) in rural areas. As China's most recent EFA report reminds us, if even 1 per cent of Chinese children are out of school that means that over one million girls and boys are not receiving their 'right' to education (Jing, Zhao and Wenbin Hu 2007).

In this context of transformation and remaining obstacles, Chinese EFA policies continue to problematically hinge on two utilitarian narratives that define girls (and women) as 'important mediators in the modernization process' (Stromquist 2003: 177). First, state policy rests on the premise that education provides the master key to poverty alleviation and to development (see Seeberg and Ross 2007). Second, China's embrace of the global consensus on girls' education has been constructed through the logic of developmentalism. Educated girls become valued as mothers of development, and the means for reducing poverty, containing population growth, engendering public health, and strengthening the nation. In the discourse of developmentalism girls are assumed to be both recipients and agents of development, not its victims. However, this version of agency is built on a narrowly utilitarian assessment of female lives, lives rarely considered as ends in themselves. Developmentalism thus reflects a 'gender trap within the market solution' of neo-liberal development policies (Young 1989).

Two additional gender traps, the 'naturalization of gender' and 'strong China nationalism', constrain girls' education. The naturalization of gender is a central motif in China's post-socialist story (Rofel 1999: 116–131). This story reads that the Maoist state repressed natural distinctions between males and females through egalitarian discipline and labour. In the era of opening and reform, women reclaim their sexuality and family, and men their virility and the state. Schools and the public further the discourse of natural difference just as they previously furthered the discourse of egalitarian sacrifice and productive labour. In the post-Mao era the naturalization of the gender paradigm for human relationships and abilities 'holds out hope and excitement; it celebrates national strength and private pleasures; it appears to move beyond the regulatory politics of Maoist socialism; it seems to carve out a space separate from the state' (Rofel 1998: 255). Accepting this paradigm, however, reinforces gender stereotyping in families, schools and the workplace (see Ross and Lin 2001).

Linking expanded opportunities for females to the cause of strong China nationalism has provided a strategic cover of respectability for activists working on behalf of gender equality. Yet it also weakens the possibility for transnational alliances on women's rights. Many transnational feminist non-governmental organizations (NGOs) conceptualize full citizenship not in terms of specific cultures or nations but in terms of women's (and men's) common humanity. Any exclusion of Chinese women from the dialogue on women's rights as human rights means a loss to women around the world.

ARENAS OF DISCOURSE AND ACTION ON BEHALF OF GIRLS' EDUCATION: THE STATE, TRANSNATIONAL ALLIANCES AND THE WOMEN'S MOVEMENT

China's agenda for educating females is created in three arenas: the state's education bureaucracy, which sets school policy and funding paths; domestic and international NGOs, including women's groups, which use, accommodate and resist state policies to provide education for females; and international aid and cooperation agencies that help the state and society educate females. While overlapping relationships among these arenas are in flux, the state is still paramount, mobilizing the non-state sector to finance and regulate education (Mok 2003: 208). The state also directly influences the key GONGO representing Chinese women, the Women's Federation.

The Indispensable State

One of the common explanations for rising educational disparities that impact negatively on China's vulnerable populations is the decentralization of educational funding and provision begun in the 1980s (Lin, Jing and Heidi Ross 1998; Mok 2003). Since 1978, the state's reorganization of education has been primarily to support economic policies associated with market socialism. As funding was gradually decentralized to lower levels of government, provincial and local governments were allowed to retain part or most of their revenue and decide how to spend it. Taxation reform codified legitimate authorities of taxation and helped stabilize incomes of central and sub-central levels of the government (Cheng 1998). Educational policies promoting decentralization expanded to include: (1) the reduction of the central state's regulation, provision and subsidies of education services; (2) the devolution of responsibility and power to localities; (3) the diversification of resources (i.e. the encouragement of multiple channels of funding, including cost recovery measures like tuition); and (4) enhanced flexibility and autonomy in governance of education institutions.

That the state continues to play a strong guiding role in a decentralized educational market will surprise few readers who have followed the processes and conditions of decentralization worldwide. Decentralization defined as the redistribution of power and responsibility does not necessarily mean that states do less (Bray 2003; Mok 2003). It does mean that their role as 'education service providers' changes 'from carrying out most of the work of education itself to determining where work will be done, by whom and how' (Mok 2003: 213). Indeed, the Chinese state's legitimacy increasingly depends on whether it successfully organizes the education system.

In general, the state has garnered public support for its ability to guide educational expectations and futures with a deft, pragmatic hand. However, stresses in the system and the public's faith in it are apparent, particularly around issues of the increasing costs of schooling; unequal educational opportunities for minority, rural, working class and migrant children; and scandals involving enrollment bribes, illegal school fees and land grabs by private universities and local university complexes.

Scholars often argue that:

> there exists much more political and even financial space for governments to condition the way globalization is brought into education than is usually admitted . . . That states generally choose not to be responsive to more equitable versions of knowledge production is at least partly the result of ideological preference rather than helplessness in the face of new competitive pressures and new, globalized thinking. (Carnoy 1999: 83)

China presents a case in point. Devolution of authority in educational governance has increased educational flexibility. But it has also periodically allowed the state to pass the buck on social justice issues.

The international literature on girls' education provides abundant evidence that many of the most important changes affecting gender relations have been generated not by the state but by women themselves, often in the form of actions and programmes organized through NGOs at local levels before they became issues incorporated in national policies (Cortina and Stromquist 2000). Ethnographic accounts of contemporary Chinese society detail how three decades of reform have eroded the state's monopoly on 'framing the conditions of social existence' (Mueggler 2001: 4–5). One intriguing argument is that while the state's partial withdrawal from individual and community life worlds has precipitated a confusing, corruption-inviting lack of moral authority at the local level, paradoxically 'widespread changes in Chinese society have formed a moral space at large, making possible a new grounding for social interaction and individual experience' (Liu 2000: 182). Extending anthropologist Liu's argument about community life to schooling, the 'lack of a moral economy in communal life in conjunction with the emergence of a moral space at large' (Liu 2000: 183), has provided a crucial condition for the development of China's educational NGOs.

The Middle Ground of NGOs

The rise of NGOs in China has produced a large body of divergent commentary regarding their ambiguous relationship with the state. When they first appeared in China in the 1980s, NGOs were seen as one more example of decentralization – a way to release the state from social welfare burdens. Some Chinese social scientists remain sceptical of the extent to which China has a civil society (Yan 2003). In contrast, others document the state's encouragement of NGOs, because they serve areas the state cannot reach without unleashing potentially uncontrollable social forces. In his analysis of how China developed markets for educational institutions and various international development assistance organizations, Zweig explains how resisting but opportunistic bureaucrats came to support transnational exchanges critical to civil societies in a global age (Zweig 2002). Rofel (1999) has argued that when the Maoist state was rejected, policies of state feminism were also questioned. The logical consequence was that supporters of women's rights looked elsewhere, spurring the development of the non-state public sphere (Ma 2002).

There is now a tangible NGO and non-profit foundation community in China, receiving hundreds of millions of dollars each year in project funding directly from or channelled through hundreds of groups. With the exception of environmental NGOs, the most visible education-related NGOs, such as Project Hope and the Spring Bud programme, are involved in poverty reduction (Du, Jie 2004: 172–192). These NGOs and non-profit social organizations reflect a diverse set of assumptions about the purposes of development and many are aligned with state policies of global economic integration and strengthening.

While Chinese NGOs seem to retain as their guiding principle, 'Do not criticize government policy' and emphasize constructive and mutually dependent relations between society and state, their memberships are also asking questions about political purposes and consequences (Young 2003). In the 1990s, prominent activists in the women's movement favoured keeping their eyes on China's structural inequalities and called the possibility of an effective grassroots women's movement 'absurd' (Chen 1994). This assessment has since been refuted on the ground. In at least four ways, NGOs in China create supportive conditions for thinking and acting on behalf of girls and women. They facilitate women's right of association in a political culture where such a right had not been practised for decades (Ma 2002). They also increase women's consciousness of citizenship and community participation, and they nurture female leadership and significant learning about lobbying and mobilization. Finally, their actions widen the state's definition of acceptable *renquan*, which can mean basic human rights or grassroots people power.

In the project discussed in this chapter, NGO action takes place in a semi-autonomous, middle ground for change that serves to mediate among international support, community advocacy and state interests.

Community-based action flows in the Spring Bud programme through a network of homeroom teachers and principals (who serve as parents' representatives), local and provincial SWF representatives and members of an INGO. SWF representatives have played a pivotal role in mediating potential conflicts among various government units, school officers and the INGO. This is no small task given the scope of the project, which has involved 1000 girls and their families; scores of schools; county and city educational officers; county, city, provincial and national Women's Federation representatives; and INGO donors. In championing the significance of the project while ensuring its accountability, the SWF has had to act like both a grassroots organization and a state agency. From a comparative perspective, the SWF's attempt to 'walk on two legs', one the state's and one civil society's, complicates the international finding that 'there are very few cases of alliances between women's groups and the state education sector' (Cortina and Stromquist 2000: 82).

Women's Activism and Women's Studies

Women's Studies emerged contemporaneously with NGOs, likewise propelled by economic reforms of the post-Mao era (Min 1999). Li Xiaojiang and Liang Jun (1998: 598–600) summarize the beginning of the contemporary Chinese women's movement in three periods. A 'theoretical exploration' period between 1980 and 1985 brought professionals in the Women's Federation and in academe together to explore women's problems associated with economic and social transformation. In 1982 the name 'women's studies' was introduced to conceptualize these activities. In 1983 the Women's Federation announced its 'four-selfs' slogan. Twenty-eight years later a version of that slogan – 'self-respect, self-support, self-confidence and self-strengthening' – remains the dominant paradigm for female education.

In 1985, the Society of Women's Studies was founded and the first women's studies symposium was convened in Zhengzhou. The same year Li Xiaojiang, often described as one of the mothers of Chinese women's studies, taught courses at the Henan Provincial Institute for Women Cadres. Her proposals for a women's studies curriculum were published and widely circulated.

The years 1986 to 1988 witnessed the establishment of NGOs dedicated to female equality, the continued growth of women's studies at Chinese universities and increased collaboration between the Women's Federation and scholars in those programmes. As access to social services deteriorated in rural China, the Women's Federation became more proactive in seeking aid for girls and women. However, the Women's Federation's identity as a GONGO constrained its direction, funding and purposes.

From 1990 to 1993, the economic and social dislocations of market socialism experienced by women had become headline news. In 1990 the State Council established the Women and Children Work Committee and passed the Law on the Protection of the Rights and Interests of Women. Faced with growing evidence that market socialism advantaged some women and disadvantaged others, the Women's Federation sponsored research on the social status of females that disaggregated the category of women and recognized the particular concerns of ethnic minority groups. In 1993 an influential exchange conference, 'Engendering China: Women, Culture, and the State', brought together Chinese and US women's studies faculty at Harvard University, Wellesley College and the Massachusetts Institute of Technology. The same year at a seminar in Tianjin, scholars introduced the concept of *shehui xingbie* (gender or social sex) to articulate how males and females are socially constructed.

During the 1990s gender studies programmes mushroomed in tertiary educational institutions. Women's studies institutes were also created at the provincial level, including Heilongjiang Women's Studies Institute (set up in 1986), Jiangsu Women's Studies Institute (1990) and Sichuan Women's Studies Institute (1994). These provincial-level institutions served as consultation agencies for local governments on gender and women-related issues and therefore had at least some influence in the policy-making process. In order to bring together these institutional strands, the Women's Studies Institute of China set up the China Women's Studies Association as an extensive network of institutions and organizations devoted to women and gender studies (Yang Yujing 2009). In 1995, the year of the UN's Fourth World Congress on Women, China Women's University was established in Beijing, which was the first and only women's university in China awarding bachelor degrees including those on gender studies. By 2001, more than 40 universities and colleges and 10 social science academies had set up gender studies or women's studies programmes (Chen Fang 2008).

These programmes and institutions, coupled with the research and collaboration generated at numerous international conferences on women and gender studies hosted by China, have played a positive role in shaping and influencing many national policies towards women's education, healthcare and employment opportunities (Du, Jie 2004). Such influence indicates that by 1995, China's women's movement was no longer directed just by the state or the CCP but also by diverse groups concerned with the 'mutual promotion and encouragement of social development and women's progress' (Li, Xiaojiang and Liang Jun 1998: 596). During this period, the partial de-politicization of the Women's Federation allowed it more autonomy in its 'bridging role' between the CCP and NGOs and other groups, 'voicing the interests of women upwards to the Party elite, while also transmitting CCP policy downwards to women' (Howell 2003: 192–193). A decade of 'separatism', when Chinese scholars remained relatively isolated from the international women's movement and intentionally distant from state policy on women, had ended.

Scholarship on Chinese women's relationships with the state since the 1980s has shifted from strong critique (Stacey 1983; Wolf 1985) to more positive interpretations of limited agency across region and political level (Diamant 2000) to analyses that contrast the state's proactive efforts on behalf of women from the 1950s to the 1970s with reversals during the reform decades (Davis and Harrell 1993). Two decades ago Young described Chinese women as the vehicle through which the state deploys and constrains its population. As the previous analysis of the state, NGOs and women's organizations has illustrated, new social spaces have emerged to expand transnational collaboration and women's social imaginations (Lu 2008).

THE SHAANXI SPRING BUD PROJECT: EDUCATIONAL REFORM THROUGH TRANSNATIONAL ALLIANCE[2]

Project Context and Purpose

Mapping the contours of girls' opportunities is an exercise in sorting through contradictions. The girls who have participated in the Shaanxi Spring Bud programme stand on the downside of what sociologist Sun Liping calls China's 'cleavage', what *The New York Times* calls China's 'great divide', and what Whyte (2010) more recently calls 'one country, two societies'. In spite of dramatic overall improvements in China's standard of living during the decade the project has existed, rural income is only about one-third of urban income, rural child mortality is double that in urban areas, and maternal death is five to ten times higher in rural areas than in urban areas. In 1985 the disposable income of urban citizens was on average 1.89 times higher than that of the rural population. By 2003 the disparity had reached 3 to 1 and it climbed to 3.33 to 1 by 2008 (Fu 2010). Disparities have been aggravated by a 'tidal wave' of migration of people from the countryside to the city (Yardley 2004). At least 140 million people have left China's countryside and that number may swell to 300 million. The difficulties rural communities face in accommodating the mammoth social, economic and cultural dislocations associated with this shift have a direct and powerful impact on the abilities of those communities to provide schooling for their children (Guldin 2001; Link et al. 2001).

To reverse such trends, equity has been high on the government's policy agenda, indicated by the state's willingness to pay for improved rural social services, including education. A recent bright spot in enhancing educational equity is the Two Exemptions and One Subsidy (TEOS) policy. Along with the establishment in 2005 of the Rural Compulsory Education Assured Funding Mechanism, which has rationalized and re-centralized to the central and provincial levels universal support for rural and urban compulsory schooling, TEOS ensures that primary and junior secondary school students are exempt from textbook costs and miscellaneous school fees, including tuition, and that rural students receive subsidies to defray some of the expenses of attending boarding school (common in rural areas to consolidate educational resources). With TEOS as a linchpin, the state made central to its efforts to 'build a new socialist countryside' genuinely free basic education (Lou and Ross 2008). These policies have been successful. In 2008 China's net enrollment rate for pupils in junior secondary school (grades seven to nine), reached 98 per cent, up from 88.6 per cent in 2000 and 69.7 per cent in 1991. Attention to expanding access to senior secondary schooling, China's chief bottleneck in achieving equal educational opportunity, also shows a positive trend for net enrollment rates, which have risen from 42.8 per cent in 2000 to 74.0 per cent in 2008.

Nevertheless, rural schools continue to struggle with funding shortfalls, debt, inferior infrastructure and poor teaching. Pressure on junior secondary school students to become migrant workers explains drop-out rates that in some areas reach 30 per cent or higher (Lou and Ross 2008). Nearly 70 million children of migrant parents have been 'left behind' in homes with one or no parents, leaving rural schools overwhelmed with custodial responsibilities. In 2008 as many as 20 million migrant children under 18 years of age were living in cities and working as labourers, many without access to schooling.

Admission to senior secondary school is difficult for rural students who have proportionately fewer secondary school options than their urban counterparts. Many rural students who are successful in university preparatory secondary schools cannot take full advantage of the dramatic expansion of tertiary education, where gross enrollment rates were 23 per cent in 2008 compared to 3 per cent in the early 1990s. High tertiary tuition fees on top of heavy secondary school costs (which are not covered by TEOS policies) create a financial burden beyond the means of poor rural families. Likewise, mid-western and western provinces have fewer quotas for the entrance of their students into prestigious institutions of tertiary education.

Intersecting gender discrimination with constrained opportunities provides a challenging context for achieving educational equity. Fifty million women have left the Chinese countryside to work in cities. While this shift is often positively correlated with increased female wage-earning capacity, educational attainment and status within the family, it also separates vulnerable young women from the protections they receive from their natal families. Whereas 39 per cent of China's paid workforce is female, 50 to 60 per cent of those laid off during the years up to 2005 were women. Attempts by the Women's Federation to help unemployed women find jobs as housekeepers and nannies place more women in unregulated working conditions.

Finally, women's (and men's) futures are profoundly influenced by China's skewed sex ratio, which averages above 120 males born for every 100 females. Some scholars are so alarmed by this destabilizing trend that they suggest it could 'tip the scales toward war' (Hudson and den Boer 2004; Kristof and WuDunn 2010; Lee, Felicia A. 2004). Concerns about the trafficking and kidnapping of females have penetrated to the villages of Shaanxi where Spring Bud parents and leaders worry about the safety of girls walking to school. Dubbing China's 'missing girls' phenomenon 'gendercide' may sensationalize a profoundly complex social issue, but the Chinese government took the problem seriously enough to launch a Care for Girls Campaign – a national movement aimed at 'changing the traditional preference for boys to girls, safeguarding girls' legitimate rights and interests and striving to enhance their status in the family' – and to begin paying rural parents US$144 per year as a bonus for having one child, two girls, or a disabled child, when they reach 60 years of age (see Eklund, this volume, for further discussion).

No easy solutions for narrowing the divide between China's haves and have-nots will be found within schools. Nevertheless, education is the first place anxious leaders turn to for an answer and this Spring Bud story is partially about the constrained power of education to bridge divides.

The Spring Bud project, initiated in 2000 by a US-based INGO,[3] takes its name from a nation-wide strategy to provide educational access to girls. In 1989 China's Fourth Population Survey revealed that 4.8 million children between seven and 14 years old were not attending school and girls comprised 83 per cent of these children. More than half of these girls, estimated at 2.61 million, resided in western China. To help such girls finish the nine years of compulsory education, the Chinese Children and Teenager Foundation, administered by the Women's Federation, launched a national Spring Bud project to be implemented by all provincial and local children and teenagers' and women's foundations.

Described as the largest INGO Spring Bud initiative, the Shaanxi

Spring Bud Project is also considered one of the most successful. The 1000 girls who have participated in the project are overwhelmingly Han Chinese and from impoverished, and in most cases remote, mountain villages in south-eastern Shaanxi Province.[4] Per capita income of the villages ranged from under US$100 to US$125 in 2000. The girls' lives had been beset by material and social hardships, including devastation of land and home by flooding, the deaths of parents and severe illness. Each of the 1000 girls was out of school when selected by the SWF (using low household income to measure greatest need) to receive INGO funds to attend fourth grade in the autumn of 2001. A handful of these girls are singletons; most have one or two siblings. On average, parents' education reached the elementary level (father: 4–6 years; mother: 1–3 years). Seventy per cent of parents hoped their daughters could attend university and perceived schooling primarily as a vehicle for escaping rural poverty. For girls, schooling seemed the only hope for fulfilling personal, natal family and INGO donor obligations to matriculate to college and/or earn a living.

Taking Identity Work Seriously

> I was born into a poor farming family. I have several sisters, and parents aged and weakened by years of hard work. Three years ago we had a most unfortunate surprise. Father's liver had hardened to an advanced stage. This added substantially to the family's burden. Mother bravely hid her constant tears, but we knew things needed to change. Older sister quit school to earn money to help pay for father's treatments. To lessen the financial strains on the family, I too left school to help out at home. The instant I stepped out of the schoolyard for what I thought was forever, tears streamed down my face. (A Spring Bud girl)

The state's developmentalist approach to girls' education and to poverty alleviation implies that children spend their time in schools responding only to dominant lessons. The problem with this sort of modernization theory is that it imagines becoming modern as uni-directional, something that happens to individuals only from the outside. In contrast, the assumption that 'educated persons' have agency (Levinson et al. 1996), influences this analysis of how collective ideas about what is modern and what is 'traditional', 'local', 'rural', or 'cultural' emerge in how girls imagine themselves and their futures.

Multiple and sometimes contradictory processes of globalization dig deep into Spring Bud girls' identities and recognitions of social place and status. The transnational support they receive to go to school makes this inevitable. Images projected by the mass media and the 'urbanization' of township life also teach girls lessons about the space they occupy in the status hierarchy of China. Girls who watch village friends go to school when they cannot, experience the humiliation and sadness of rural inequalities (which are now larger than inequalities within urban areas).

Interviews with Spring Bud girls highlight the contradictory consequences of schooling for rural children and depict with utter clarity how much 'economic reforms have introduced global space as a source for social imagination' (Ong and Nonini 1997: 102). Schools get formulated in rural spaces 'as a civilizing practice that implies and confers proximity to the modern' (Jeffery 2001: 25). Rural education operates through a discourse of lack, a discourse of compensatory education designed to take girls who hear themselves called low quality (*suzhi di*) (Murphy 2004), backward (*luohou*), poor (*pinqiong*), unenlightened (*yumei*) and ignorant (*wuzhi*), and make them modern. Rural girls are confronted with an ideal of success and of quality that is defined through market and modernity. If their parents were not driven by those discourses, then whose fault is it? Poverty becomes their parents' marker, their 'culture'. Just like that, poverty is explained away by culture, the state is absolved from its obligation to provide compulsory education, and the school is empowered to further the state's development programme by making sure rural girls are remediated to live up to 21st-century standards of quality.

Just as modernization is used to dilute ethnicity in minority schools in China, it stakes out ignorance in rural schools. Most programmes in China created to widen educational access for (usually rural, female and minority) children of 'poor and backward regions' are firmly rooted in progressive, nationalistic and universalistic definitions of modernity that by design or default denigrate local cultural practices and knowledge (Hansen 1999). They are run on the premise that schools can and should align local communities with urban/global forces and that this interface is a relatively unproblematic cultivation of human capital.

One of the most successful elements of this Spring Bud programme has been its attention to careful selection of homeroom teachers (many of whom were raised in local communities) who recognize that modern schools produce both knowledge and ignorance. Teachers help girls evaluate and counter the exclusionary, urban-centric categories (of what is progressive and what is backward, for example) that are the inevitable outcomes of market socialism. Put a different way, what anchors the moral politics of the Spring Bud programme is taking identity work seriously as a way of empowering girls.

> It was a hot summer day three years ago, unusually hot. Suddenly dark clouds rolled in, thunder struck and lightning streaked. Rain poured, driven by strong winds. In an instant one could not distinguish where the sky ended and the earth began. Water was everywhere. In that engulfing darkness, our home swayed as if it was ready to crumble. At father's command, we ran out to seek safe refuge.

But then father remembered that the ginger mother and I crisscrossed mountains and valleys to dig up for so many days was still in the house. That ginger was to pay for the fees of my next school term. The moment father went back into the house, it collapsed. The gush of rain washed away our home. It carried away father. (A Spring Bud girl)

Spring Bud students commonly introduce their school experiences with stories about the precariousness of life. In contrast to interviews with students attending privileged schools, which are characterized by entitlement and optimism, as well as weariness at the pressures of schooling, Spring Bud girls are painfully earnest, yearning for recognition, articulate about the costs of market socialism (particularly to their mothers), and truly grateful they attend a school that actually cares about them. They are also aware of the opportunity costs of schooling, which they describe as adding to the intense demands rural life makes on their parents. School fees mean sacrificing family welfare and parental health. They (and their parents) perceive 'success in school' as an overwhelmingly positive yet contradictory resource, one that will produce skills, desires and associations that will both complicate and enhance their future identities, family relationships and career opportunities. International scholarship on girls' education indicates that parents 'calculate' both the costs and the benefits of their daughters' schooling from their own points of view rather than from the point of view of their daughter (Colclough 1996). One of the findings from the Spring Bud programme is that fathers and mothers perceive their daughters' schooling not only as a sound investment for the family's future but also as part of their obligation to support their daughters to complete compulsory education. Parents who could not do so expressed great anxiety.

Local officials in the two municipalities participating in the project, and now parents of girls in the Spring Bud project, have a favourite saying: '*zhi yu mian qiong*' (cure foolishness to alleviate poverty) – reaffirming the state's narrative that education is the key to alleviating poverty. In fact, education and poverty are interrelated in much more complex and compounding ways. Gender as well as economic and cultural factors all influence household educational decisions along with the quality of local schools. One of the salient examples is that the quality of the local vocational school really influenced decisions of parents and students on whether to continue schooling.

Research on rural schooling in China indicates that parents want education for both boys and girls, but they believe it is more useful for boys, who presumably will support families and elderly parents (Hannum 2003). Some studies conclude that son preference persists in the face of sweeping economic and social change and that urbanization, female education and employment only slowly change incentives for sending girls to school (see Li, Danke and Mun C. Tsang 2003). Still other researchers agree that patriarchy (son preference, for example) still matters, but that it is being more quickly weakened by economic development (Michelson and Parish 2000).

Interviews with Spring Bud parents suggest that 'traditional' attitudes (such as son preference) no longer erect severe barriers to girls' education, and placing too much weight on 'culture' obscures equally or more important material obstacles that girls and their families contend with. Parents hold relatively egalitarian attitudes towards their daughters and sons, although their educational and employment aspirations for sons are higher. However, participation over eight years in the Spring Bud project has raised parents' expectations for their daughters – and raised the aspirations of girls well beyond what their families would be able to support without INGO funding. Finally, the Spring Bud project has created a local community ethos of the importance of girls' education, prompting local leaders to seek more outside funding to support out-of-school childrens' 'return to the school gate'.

> [We] girls established a 'Love Bank' to further the spirit of The 1990 Institute. We pool together what we can save of our pocket money and make loans to those amongst us who need it most . . . Unfortunately, all around us, there are still many students who cannot afford schooling. I have thought about this a great deal, and I have made a vow. When I grow up I will work very hard and help those who have lost the opportunity to learn because of their poverty, so that like us they will swim carefree in the ocean of knowledge. My friends, let us, shoulder-to-shoulder, hand-in-hand, build a 'Great Wall of Love' and spread the spirit of The 1990 Institute. (A Spring Bud girl)

The national Spring Bud logo is inscribed with a diagonal line representing the power of hands, symbolic of social mobilization. While helping hands from afar are not always welcomed in a postcolonial world, one of the transformational consequences of the Spring Bud project is the extensive network of social capital it has extended to participating girls and their families. Girls (and their teachers) are seen and see themselves as part of a larger enterprise of training China's future female leaders. In this sense, the influence of schooling on girls' lives lies in what schooling signifies locally, not just in its literal content.

> I knew that this special opportunity was a rare gift . . . Whenever I regressed I seemed to hear the American grandaunt and aunties saying, 'Child, don't slack off, go back to work!' Every time I earn less than perfect marks I see the American grandaunt and aunties appear before me, looking at me with gentle but firm eyes . . . Rest assured that with your help, under the guidance

of my teachers, I will study hard, make progress, and grow up to be a valuable member of our society. Finally I would like to say, 'Love and family can be found all over this country.' 'Love and family can be found all over the world'. (A Spring Bud girl)

How the Spring Bud girls frame themselves as passionately hard-working, honour-bound students recalls Mary Jo Benton Lee's (2001) interviews with minority students in south-west China. Successful minority students feel compelled to work hard to succeed in school out of obligation to and gratitude for the sacrifices of parents and hometown supporters. With the currency of their college degrees, students then confer honour and service upon family, village and ethnicity. A cycle of high expectations, success, obligation, achievement and empowerment creates social capital.

> Teachers, neighbors and parents of successful minority students expect them to go on to college – and tell them so repeatedly. Finally, those minority students, who are repeatedly defined as achievers by significant others, begin to see themselves the same way and to share these same expectations. (Lee, Mary Jo Benton 2001: 19)

RURAL GIRLS' ASPIRATIONS AND MOBILITY PATHS: SCHOOLS' POSSIBILITIES AND LIMITATIONS

This chapter was revised in 2010, just after 124 Spring Bud participants received notification that their college entrance examination scores would likely give them entrance to second-tier colleges. Five anxious girls might yet succeed in gaining entrance into an elite university. Nearing year 10 of a 13-year project, we have begun to draw conclusions about how complex schooling's impact is on girls' aspirations, life chances and family well-being; and they are simultaneously uplifting and cautionary. Our summary of the most salient themes resonates with much international scholarship on the critical importance of secondary schooling for girls who face multiple sources of social exclusion (e.g. being poor and rural in China) (Lewis and Lockheed 2006; Rahini 2006). This literature generally advocates consistent strategies for countering exclusion and raising educational attainment, ranging from implementing stronger, more coherent and enforceable policies to improving educational quality, for which China gets high marks, and increasing the relevance of schools for girls, for which China might receive a generous 'C'.

Spring Bud girls graduated from elementary school in 2004 and the vast majority entered and graduated from compulsory junior secondary school in 2007.[5] Two hundred girls with excellent marks studied in four 'key' junior secondary schools,[6] and the remaining 800 studied in regular junior secondary schools. Upon graduation from junior secondary school, Spring Bud girls have followed three distinct mobility paths: to academic senior secondary schools; to vocational schools; and to work. Specifically, 274 girls passed a highly competitive senior secondary school entrance examination and matriculated into university preparatory secondary schools. The fact that over 27 per cent of Spring Bud participants took this crucial step towards university education was a mark of success. Their entrance rate exceeded by 10 per cent (rich and poor) their peers in the region. However, the distance between this 'success' and Spring Bud participants' educational aspirations for further education when they were in eighth grade is poignantly large. Then 67 per cent hoped to attend secondary school. And while only 7 per cent of the girls expected to leave school after ninth grade, 550 girls (55 per cent) did so, the vast majority joining China's migrant labour force. Migrant work is considered by girls on this path to be a somewhat temporary, dead-end condition, although in the process of sending remittances home, they are changing local understandings of the social roles of girls and their ability to provide immediate and old-age support to their natal families.

The remaining junior secondary school graduates opted to study in vocational schools, 74 entering vocational secondary schools (specializing in nursing, forestry, pre-school teaching, tea production, accounting, computer graphics and medical technology) and 79 in short-term programmes offering training in hair styling and cooking. Given their cost, questionable quality and pay-off in terms of stable employment, vocational schools represent a second choice option for most students and their parents. In contrast, migrant work provides a pay cheque for worker and family (most Spring Bud girls save a certain portion of their earnings for themselves and share the rest, to help construct a brother's new home, for example), but rarely provides skill training that will further a young worker's future beyond the construction site, factory, or restaurant. Vocational and technical schools have been advocated by the government as an alternative path for rural teenagers in the process of 'transforming a country with a large population into a country with sound human resources' (State Council of the People's Republic of China 2005). However, most parents and girls, who see around them a tightly constricted job market, remain convinced that the only way for a girl to have a better life is by following the academic path.[7]

The distance between aspiration and reality noted above can ironically be explained by the INGO's success in raising Spring Bud girls' expectations, aspirations and financial resources for continuing education. The project began as a crisis intervention action in a region of China reeling from economic and cultural disruption. Impoverished girls were out of school and needed, in the words of the INGO leader, 'a safe environment for learning', and further, 'The homeroom teachers were important, because they represented kind and caring adults'. Over time, the INGO focused on supporting talented rural girls to enter post-compulsory schooling and eventually bring back to their home regions expertise, experiences, social networks and leadership skills.[8] By definition, these expectations, which provided girls with a complex mix of high aspirations, encouragement and anxiety, conflicted with the highly competitive structure and chief mission of secondary schools, as well as the gendered expectations of their teachers, principals and families.

Participation in the Spring Bud project did increase girls' confidence, educational aspirations and expectations and general school satisfaction. As mentioned above, the girls have benefited from their proximity to the INGO's global network, a form of 'social capital' that has probably done more than any school activity to model for them leadership in the service of individual and social advancement. Research shows again and again that strong social support is an effective, even necessary means for empowering disadvantaged groups (Ross and Lin 2006). The Spring Bud project has succeeded for many of its participants in fostering comparatively strong levels of self-esteem and confidence, as well as high educational and career expectations, characteristics often associated with the potential for leadership (Ross and Wang 2008). For example, Spring Bud girls *and* non-Spring Bud girls in the same homeroom classrooms reported significantly higher educational expectations than female students in the same school who were not in Spring Bud classes. By interacting with Spring Bud donors, volunteers, and specially selected homeroom teachers who encouraged girls to achieve in school, even non-Spring Bud girls (who were also rural and generally poor students who had to fund their own schooling) came to hold similarly high expectations and aspirations, and had the self-confidence to say, 'if I work hard, I can also be successful'.

Unfortunately, schools are sometimes mis-educative, limiting students' 'capabilities to achieve . . . the kind of life that they have reason to value' (Aikman and Unterhalter 2005: 246). This is the case with Chinese secondary schools, particularly materially stretched rural ones. Recent reform that challenges their examination orientation is called essential-qualities-oriented (EQO) education (UNESCO 2000). The EQO model is designed to encourage students to take the initiative, engage in independent inquiry – verging towards the Spring Bud project's expectations for young female leaders. However, over half of the junior high schools attended by Spring Bud girls had classrooms that did not meet national safety and resource standards. In addition, schools transferred pressures to assist students 'escape the countryside' onto teachers. Teachers' bonuses were tied tightly to the number of their students who matriculated to the next level of schooling. The principal of a key school where 50 Spring Bud students studied told us that his teachers 'must ensure' that at least 19 girls would be accepted into key senior secondary schools. This reality forced teachers to train students for an encyclopedic control of information and Spring Bud girls were in monitored classes more than 10 hours each day for this purpose. It is hardly surprising that they (and their teachers) were risk-averse, chained as they were to the causal link between examination success and educational credentials.[9]

In addition, an enervating mix of gender and class-based discrimination created an environment that subtly questioned Spring Bud girls' new-found identities as 'modern girls with a future'. Spring Bud junior secondary school principals, all of whom were male, unanimously agreed in one of our surveys that, 'Boys and girls are different in terms of intelligence'. While teachers' views were more diverse, they still reflected an explicit biological determinism. Girls' survey and interview responses confirmed that teachers acted on such attitudes in the classroom.

> Teachers, especially science teachers, look down on girl students. You can see their attitudes in class. If we answer questions slowly, he will say that girls are not as smart as boys. Teachers say that girls are slow at thinking. I like science, because I want to prove my ability. (A Spring Bud girl)

The Spring Bud girls were also caught between two images that mirror a contradiction found in much of the literature on girls, education and development. On the one hand, policy discourse (which is repeated at the school level), teachers' expectations and wealthier classmates' slights labelled them somehow as poor children of circumstance in need of 'charity and uplift'. On the other hand, their teachers, the SWF, and to an extent the INGO, asked them to take to heart the struggles they had overcome and the help that they had received and 'serve confidently', 'give freely of themselves', and 'live life with gratitude'. Many girls took away from their experiences a contradictory set of lessons that kept them grounded somewhere between grateful recipients of aid and active subjects for whom risk-taking is neither modelled nor desired.

Of course, poverty and its indirect effects also matter. Although financial obstacles to schooling for many Spring Bud families have significantly declined over the last decade as a result of government policy and improving local economies, even with INGO scholarships and the introduction of China's TEOS policies when they were junior secondary school students, some students struggled to keep up with the fees associated with boarding schools. High levels of out-migration by working parents, parental sickness or death, number of siblings, and perceptions of low quality schooling, *particularly* when coupled with a girl's poor academic performance (which in the minds of parents and teachers predicted likely future failure to enter and perform well in expensive secondary schools), all lowered girls' expectations to seek higher levels of education. Nevertheless, financial support provided by the INGO and the government was not the essential factor in girls' decisions to continue their schooling. The most important factor, after taking into account the girls' performance in school, was whether further schooling would be relevant, attainable and deliver a stable, preferably state, job.

CONCLUSION: DEVELOPMENTALISM VS. PEOPLE-CENTRED DEVELOPMENT

The real question for girls in China today is not whether to attend school but to attend for what purpose, on whose terms, and at what cost. The project described above engaged participants constantly in such questions and in doing so offered students, teachers and local leaders significant opportunities to reflect upon and debate the gendered nature of schooling, and expectations and aspirations for girls.

In contrast, the state has measured progress on female education almost solely by school access and participation ratios. In 1999 I was assured by a policy maker that educators in many regions of China had 'no need to worry about gender issues', as gender gaps in enrollment and attainment had disappeared. Bolstered by the global consensus on girls' education, the discourse of developmentalism continues to be difficult to dislodge.

Nevertheless, China's 'reform and opening' era has been characterized as a struggle to balance the needs of two civilizations, one spiritual and one material. Education has been conceptualized as part of spiritual civilization, an underpinning of a new social ethos that could ameliorate the negative social consequences of the strong national get-rich-is-glorious forces of market socialism. Much has been made recently in the Chinese and international press of the pains China's leadership has taken to represent the Chinese government as more caring. Progress is to be measured not in terms of growth but in terms of 'people-centered development' (*yi ren wei ben*).

The UNESCO 2008 EFA China Country Case Study defines 'the key dimensions of disparity and barriers to education in China' as 'poverty, gender, social exclusion, people with disabilities and children in exceptionally difficult circumstances' (Zhao, Jing and Wenbin Hu 2007).

Interestingly, and reflecting the distance between the state and development agencies around the issue of girls and women in Chinese society, gender is not mentioned in China's most recent educational reform document, the '2020 Blueprint' (China, Ministry of Education 2010), which will set the educational agenda for the next decade. Yet, the Blueprint has made 'overcoming disparity' one of the main goals of educational development, singling out migrant children as the 'most pressing problem' and defining educational disparities 'between the prosperous coastal east and the underdeveloped west; between rural and urban areas; and between different ethnic groups' (Cheng 2010).

A significant lesson from global educational initiatives is that to succeed 'an educational agenda must be accompanied by a political agenda' (Stromquist 2003: 196–197). The *Blueprint 2020* document lays out an unusually transparent and ambitious political agenda with equity as one of the most salient themes. The *Blueprint*'s publication presents a timely opportunity for Chinese educators to rethink developmentalism and its negative impact on providing girls (and boys) with 'nontrivial' schooling.

NOTES

*   Adapted from Heidi Ross (2006), 'Challenging the gendered dimensions of schooling: the state, NGOs and transnational alliances', in Gerard A. Postiglione (ed.), *Education and Social Change in China: Inequality in a Market Economy*, Armank: NY: M.E. Sharpe, pp. 25–52. Used by permission of M.E. Sharpe, Inc.

1.   The author wishes to thank Ms Yimin Wang and Ms Lei Wang, Indiana University, for their able assistance and generosity in suggesting revisions to this chapter, which was originally published in 2006, just as state policy pressed forward on 'education for all' commitments, particularly in the countryside, one consequence being a diminishing gender gap at all levels of schooling.

2.   China has two national EFA-related projects. The first programme, Project Hope, was launched in 1989 by the Chinese Communist Youth League to solicit donations for primarily rural children too poor to attend school. By its tenth anniversary, Project Hope had assisted over two million poor students to return to school. The Spring Bud Plan, sponsored by the China Children and Teenagers' Fund (CCTF), was established in 1981 as the nation's first national-level welfare fund organized through a non-profit organization. In 1992 CCTF formally established the Spring Bud Plan under the guidance of the Women's Federation to assist impoverished girls to return to school. By the end of 2003, US$65 million had been raised and 1 350 000 drop-out girls had been sponsored to go back to school.

3.   Drawing on school achievement data, teacher assessments, interviews, student essays, and surveys of all participants, the research project is a longitudinal study to understand whether, how, and in what ways participating in the project improves girls' lives and futures (and by extension the lives and futures of their family members and communities).

4.   One of the participating municipalities has 2.4 million residents spread across seven counties and 2800 villages. Each county supports an average of seven senior secondary schools and 28 junior secondary schools. About 30 per cent of the municipality's

ninth-grade graduates can enter secondary school, 10 per cent lower than the provincial average. The second municipality is home to 1000 of the 25 000 primary-school aged girls out of school in Shaanxi Province.

5. Since 2000, only 10 girls have dropped out of the project. With the exception of one 'over age' student, these girls moved away from the project area with one or both parents seeking work. The INGO's 13-year project is committed to funding all qualified girls through college.

6. In China, key schools and ordinary schools are all public schools. However, key schools have more experienced teachers, better facilities and more financial resources.

7. Parents believed that boys might find high enough paying 'blue collar' work, for example as heavy machinery operators, drivers, welders, carpenters, painters, or mechanics – jobs they considered unsuitable for their daughters.

8. For more details on the developing goals of this INGO project, as well as contradictions surrounding the aim to cultivate 'leadership' skills in young women, see Ross and Wang (2008).

9. I want to thank Jingjing Lou, Assistant Professor, Beloit College, and Lei Wang, Indiana University, for sharing these insights from their fieldwork related to the Spring Bud Project.

PART III

The global, the local and the project

7. Developing Yunnan's rural and ethnic minority women: a development practitioner's self-reflections

Zhao Jie

INTRODUCTION

For more than a decade, I have been engaged in Gender and Development (GAD) research and intervention, specializing in the area of rural women in Yunnan.[1] Frankly speaking, in all these years I have never paused to consider the question of why we GAD practitioners pay special attention to rural women in Yunnan. I have not questioned the received wisdom that rural women are illiterate or semi-literate, impoverished, have inadequate healthcare and lack basic rights. In this chapter, I take the opportunity to reflect on and question orthodox views and, indeed, my own beliefs about the development of rural women in Yunnan. I begin with a simple question: how is this subject, 'rural women in Yunnan', constructed and deployed in development research and practice? Why are rural women characterized as illiterate, and as suffering poverty, inadequate healthcare and the absence of basic rights? Are these accurate descriptors, or just constructed labels that allow us to arrive at simplistic affirmations or refutations because we actually are unable to explain the situation clearly? Or, is the construction 'rural women in Yunnan' itself actually a manifestation of gendered political processes of development?

It has become a commonplace that in recent years China has experienced rapid, overall development. Yet despite that development, the gap between rich and poor continues to grow, and the gap between the economic and social status of urban and rural women becomes ever wider. These contrary trends also are part of the reason for my inquiry, and for self-examination. What effect has the idea of 'rural women in Yunnan' and GAD methods exerted on my research direction and development interventions? What are the interconnections between rural women,

communities and nation; what are the interconnections between existing rural development systems and policies, and those global and local
experts who are engaged in GAD? What is the relationship between
project activities focused on 'rural women in Yunnan', and globalization
and 'modernization'? This chapter provides a Yunnan GAD practitioner's
self-reflections on, and reconstruction of, the problematic subject of her
research and practice. It begins by clarifying my understanding of the constructed subject, 'rural women in Yunnan', then turns to examine different
aspects of GAD projects, and introduce some of the ways my colleagues
and I have sought new, organizationally sustainable ways to adjust GAD
ideas to Chinese realities.

YUNNAN'S DEVELOPMENT AND 'RURAL (AND ETHNIC MINORITY) WOMEN': WHO IS CONSTRUCTING THE IMAGES?

Yunnan is a unique province. Mountains account for 94 per cent of its
total terrain, and its area is bounded by more than 4000 km of national
borders. The province is home to the greatest number of ethnic minority
peoples in China. Over the past 20 years, Yunnan has become synony-
mous with 'marginal, impoverished minority areas', 'endangered ecosys-
tems needing protection', 'lagging educational standards', 'inadequate
public health systems', 'HIV/AIDS', 'illicit drug use', and 'economic
underdevelopment'. In short, any developmental issue in need of close
attention is associated with Yunnan.

Yet, at the same time, Yunnan has a positive image as an 'animal and
plant kingdom' and home to many minority peoples, a place which has
conserved the original ecology, music, dance and cultural customs of the
'ancient kingdom', and as an important hub in the political economy of
the Mekong sub-region. Under the standards of so-called 'modernization', Yunnan is categorized as 'economically underdeveloped', but with
original ecological 'natural advantages'. These contradictory images of
Yunnan are projected onto the development practitioner's map.

According to the evolutionary logic of development theory, the area
in which Yunnan's development is most 'lacking' relates to rural women.
Research reports reveal that in the course of China's systemic transition
and rapid social, economic and policy reform, traditional gender relations have re-emerged in the form of 'women's issues' (Zhao Qun 2004).
Examples include the 'feminization' of agriculture, women's reproductive
health issues, a lack of political participation among women, the problem
of female school 'drop-outs', and the abduction and trafficking of women

and children. Of course, these kinds of 'women's issues' are described in the context of international GAD discussions as frequent occurrences in underdeveloped countries generally. In China, however, there is concern that they will affect various aspects of the modernization process. These concerns typically are coupled with a mainstream, instrumentalist commentary on whether or not the advancement of women is an important criterion for measuring social progress. In this way, Yunnan's rural and ethnic minority women have become the index of, and the focus for 'development', a proverbial bargaining chip, a signifier that infuses our colonial discourse of gender-related development, and a tag connoting Yunnan's progress towards 'development'.

Although ideas of gender equality and justice increasingly have influenced the scope and focus of development activities aimed at remedying Yunnan rural women's 'underdevelopment', the contradictions between 'backwardness' and 'natural advantage', 'women's issues' and 'national interest', continue to manifest in our work. Yunnan's 'economic underdevelopment' and potential 'natural advantages' have attracted the attention of a wide array of global development organizations and relevant Chinese agencies and organizations. International organizations involved in paying attention to 'women's issues' in rural Yunnan include global organizations such as the United Nations Development Fund for Women (UNIFEM) and other UN bodies, and the World Bank; regional bodies including the Asia Foundation, the Asian Development Bank, and the European Union; developed countries' embassies and associated development organs, such as the UK Embassy and the British Department for International Development (DFID); and international non-governmental organizations (NGOs), such as Médecin sans Frontiéres (MSF), World Vision International (WVI), the Ford Foundation (FF), Oxfam, and the Partnership for Community Development (PCD). These organizations have run projects in Yunnan with the help of authorized local partners, including government departments, research institutions, government-organized NGOs or GONGOs[2] and grassroots NGOs. Some overseas organizations such as Britain's Save the Children and Oxfam Hong Kong have set up offices in Yunnan. Thus, GAD projects in Yunnan are the result of concurrent globalization and localization processes.

Almost all organizations engaged in development projects in Yunnan are, to some degree, involved with disadvantaged women and call for gender sensitivity in their development interventions. This phenomenon can be attributed to the orthodoxy of GAD and gender mainstreaming. Just as the inclusion of the term GAD came to indicate conformity with international standards of development practice, so is attaching resources (knowledge, skills and funds) to the operationalization of gender-sensitive approaches now established local development practice. Superficially, there is consensus among development practitioners about the need for GAD and for the participation of poor women, in particular, in development projects, even though in practice there are deep rifts between the GAD plans and strategies of different organizations. The consensus is reinforced by mainstream intellectuals, whose data and case studies constantly are rehearsed, replicated and recycled, thus producing in the final freeze-frame the undifferentiated form of rural women's and ethnic minority women's problems, which are characterized by poverty, backwardness and the preservation of difference. In short, at international, national and sub-national levels, through organizations, stakeholders, GAD policies, strategies and project activities, we development practitioners continuously give assistance to and strengthen the construction of Yunnan's rural women and ethnic minority women as those who are 'underdeveloped' and in need.

Inevitably, then, in a wide array of Yunnan development projects, including those targeting poverty alleviation, migration, environmental protection, and community governance, targets for integrated development and social change are, to varying degrees, locked to an iteratively constructed static image of 'underdeveloped' rural and ethnic minority women. This construction occludes the multi-layered interactions between women and their environment, between family and social relations and local culture, and the interplay between national and global forces. As a consequence of this construction, people's thinking, conceptual associations and involvement are all narrowly framed. Why is it that rural women born in the 1970s and 1980s still are viewed as a semi-literate, and backward, disadvantaged group? Perhaps it is, as reports often claim, a result of rural communities' maintenance of old customs and traditions. Though there may be some truth in this explanation, it lays the blame too heavily on the ancestors who play no part in development, much less 'modernization'. The argument has its utility, however, not least of which is that it allows people to forget mainstream, expert and authoritative people's own gender bias and interests, and so avoids reflecting on the systemic political, economic and social factors that are currently producing rural and ethnic minority women's poverty and backwardness, and, from that perspective, exploring flexible and effective responses.

Aid donors, scholarly experts, all levels of government agencies and non-government organizations, both at home and abroad, are concerned about and want to help meet the needs of 'underdeveloped' 'rural women in Yunnan'. This is certainly a good thing. However, because of our different identities and perspectives, our conviction in our own superior knowledge (evidenced by our production of endless, objective reports), our central location, the roles we play and our intense desire to control change, not to mention our professional and personal interests, all of which admittedly enable us to promote GAD, we become disoriented and have difficulty realizing the ultimate point of our endeavours – to enable women to articulate, represent and protect their own diverse interests, to construct their own subjective identity and citizenship rights.

YUNNAN GAD PROJECTS: RURAL WOMEN'S ISSUES ARE NOT JUST RURAL 'WOMEN'S ISSUES'

During the 1980s and early 1990s, much of the emphasis on women's participation in traditional agriculture, forestry and livestock farming focused on providing women with income-earning opportunities and better living conditions. In that regard, development goals and strategies clearly resembled the Women in Development (WID) approach. For example, in the 1980s the United Nations Development Programme (UNDP) began working in Wenshang, Yunnan, on projects aimed at providing loans to rural women to help them develop agro-forestry projects. The World Food Programme (WFP) experimented with participatory methods to empower women, giving them opportunities to participate in project activities, processes and evaluations.

Following the 1995 Fourth World Women's Conference in Beijing, more and more organizations came to Yunnan to promote projects aiming to develop some aspect or capacity of 'rural women'. The gender issues encompassed by these projects were seemingly endless, and ranged from the old WID focus on the education of rural girls and their improved access to secondary and tertiary education, poverty reduction and women's microcredit, and rural women's migration and employment, to projects claiming a GAD approach to promoting gender-equal reproductive health education and AIDS prevention; gender equality in political participation; gender-sensitive agriculture and forestry; the prevention of human trafficking of women and children; gender in the development of minority cultures; improving and safeguarding women's legal rights; and gender in natural resource management and biological diversity conservation, and the archiving and promotion of women's traditional medical and pharmaceutical knowledges.

From the late 1990s, Yunnan GAD projects returned to a focus on agriculture, forestry and livestock farming, but from the perspective of gender discourse sought to reposition and give voice to women in their diverse, particular gender relationships and environments, and explore structural improvements in small-scale, integrated management. Compared with the initial understanding and development interventions which had solely related to women's development, or the more critical variant, which sought to expose women's vulnerable status, these strategic interventions in agri-business and forestry development constituted a gender main-streaming approach.

The introduction above illustrates the breadth of GAD projects in Yunnan, and the integration through concurrent processes of globalization and localization, of GAD ideas and international, regional, national and grassroots organizations and actors. This integration is exemplified by projects seeking to prevent the trafficking of women and children, which have involved analysis of the significance of the gender system in contributing to the phenomenon of trafficking, and prevention strategies aimed at changing gender relations in the community. Interventions in this field have been implemented by the International Labour Organization (ILO), The United Nations Educational, Scientific, and Cultural Organization (UNESCO), The United Nations Children's Fund (UNICEF), Save the Children UK, DFID, World Vision, and other international organizations, in partnership with local agencies including bureaux of Civil Affairs and Public Security, Women's Federations, provincial and municipal research institutions, and community and other NGOs. Reports indicate that the combined research, intervention, advocacy, support, facility building and network mobilization activities of these organizations have been quite successful in combating trafficking (see Zhang Qiang 2004). Another project, 'Girls Forum', organizes and trains young women from remote rural areas who may be at risk from trafficking, and involves bridge-building by an alliance of provincial Women's Federations which engages girls in direct face-to-face dialogue with provincial decision makers. As a result, more government departments have taken positive action to remove barriers to young women's education and training and address their reproductive health needs (Zhao Jie and Li Yi 2007). Concurrently, the 'IEC' (information, education, communication) project centres on publicizing prevention measures and communicating issues arising from the trafficking of women and children. In rural and minority communities, ideas about trafficking and measures for prevention are combined with, and presented through local folksongs, dances and other customary activities.

THE SIMULTANEOUS DEVELOPMENT AND UNDERDEVELOPMENT OF RURAL WOMEN IN GAD PROJECTS

Each year, the Yunnan provincial government Bureau of Statistics compiles and publishes data showing improvements in rural women's economic status and employment; participation in government and social affairs; access to education and years of education; improved access to, and quality of, basic healthcare services; quality of life; and progress in the implementation of laws and regulations guaranteeing the rights and interests of women (Yunnan Funü Ertong Gongzuo Weiyuanhui 2003). Women's Federations at all levels similarly have a large number of real case studies and stories demonstrating that rural women now have a presence, and that among them are many capable farmers and entrepreneurs (Yunnan sheng Fulian 2008). 'Strong women' are everywhere in Yunnan. NGOs that have implemented projects in villages, such as Oxfam Hong Kong and the FF, have achieved many breakthroughs and innovations in rural women's development, and this is particularly apparent in their training of grassroots women's organizations. Local NGOs also have innovatively built on their foundation of local experience to promote minority cultures' respect for mother spirits, thereby encouraging ethnic minority women to participate as empowered agents in project activities (Jing Niyan 2007; Su Cuiwei 2005). This wealth of data on the positive outcomes of various development interventions shows, indisputably, that rural women in Yunnan have 'developed'.

Nevertheless, there is still a belief – supported by numerous reports – that rural and ethnic minority women in Yunnan remain 'underdeveloped', beset by 'women's issues', and in need of assistance from development practitioners. This is exemplified in internal research reports of the Women's Federation, which note, for example: 'regarding rural women's participation in politics, the problems of rural women's fluctuating rate of political participation continue, and their participation in general is declining throughout Yunnan; the participation of women is still rare during decision-making processes and in democratic management in village self-government' (Yang Jing 2007); and 'In certain prefectures of Yunnan, rural women's reproductive health issues, such as reproductive tract infections, are still serious' (Chuxiong zhou fulian 2009). In a speech given in 2005, the Secretary of the Lijiang Municipality Communist Party School noted: 'Women in mountainous areas still face poverty, and there is a lack of funding to encourage their political participation and social development. These areas need to be addressed to raise rural women's quality of life, in addition to strengthening grassroots women's organizations' (Li Chunri 2005). Such statements continue to influence government policies and our selection of development project targets and strategies.

Moreover, women with whom we have worked continue to report that, despite our interventions, they still face difficulties in realizing their own interests. For example, rural women who have participated in microcredit poverty-alleviation projects report that even when loans assisted them to increase their income, income expenditure was still determined by family decision making. If they first had to choose technology to run business projects, by degrees women exited project activities. Equally disturbing is that over the last 20 years, when women-centred reproductive health projects that excluded men were being implemented across Yunnan, the ratio of females to males in Yunnan's population of HIV infected persons increased from 1:40 to 1:1.52 (Zhao Jie 2009). And it is incontrovertible that women still comprise the majority of people with low levels of education in Yunnan (Guojia Tongji Ju 2007). In sum, clearly there are many shortcomings in our approaches to the development of rural women in Yunnan. How are we falling short?

There is a great deal of diversity among rural women in Yunnan. The major axes of difference include ethnicity, geography, kinship and marriage, class and family wealth, and mobility. Yet these differences tend to be overlooked in participatory projects, which are based on the assumption that participating female community leaders (*funü gugan*) will act as representatives of, and exemplars for, other rural women. GAD projects, goals, strategies and practices in rural China increasingly have centred on encouraging a select group of local female community leaders to participate in project activities, undertake relevant training, attend conferences, and act as spokespersons and advocates for women's economic and social rights and interests. These outstanding community leaders are expected to assist in changing the behaviours, capacities and public image of rural women, irrespective of the diversity of others' circumstances and interests. Yet the reason why most of these women are selected as community leaders and become active participants in development is that they are relatively experienced, well educated and courageous, or their households are already relatively well-off and have good political connections.[3] And it is these rural elite women who we charge with leading the development of less advantaged rural women. Indeed, many do conscientiously exemplify and promote the image of the traditional hard-working rural woman. But in fact, the great majority of rural women's interests cannot be realized by relying on elite exemplars to lead change, especially as they lack a supportive social environment. Moreover, there is no doubt that our utilization of and focus on models' performance obscures many fundamental facts about 'rural women' that should be brought to light.

In addition, the evolutionary logic that underpins our understanding of development gives rise to progressivist aspirations that are expressed in temporal comparative evaluations, between past, present and an imagined developed future. In this way, we see only progress towards milestones that we, the development experts, have pre-determined. Little comparison is contemporaneous, and directed at gender, or – among women – geography, or family wealth. Consequently, we have little insight into contemporary sources or expressions of in/equality or in/justice. Importantly, if GAD organizations and projects, much less the mainstream of government and society, continue to use temporal changes in 'rural women's issues' as indicators, and do not scrutinize measures currently taken to promote rural women's development, or examine policies, institutions and organizations tasked with undertaking gender-sensitive analysis, critique and reform, then any answer we produce relating to the development of rural women in Yunnan, whether positive or negative, will be severely limited.

In constructing our problem we also need to acknowledge and address structural inequalities, rather than just focus on 'rural women's issues'. For example, what are the relationships between the human trafficking of women and children and our current strategies of market-led modernization? How are gendered socio-cultural phenomena relating to violence and abusive power expressed in, and reinforced by, structural gender discrimination? Is the emphasis we place on rural women's reproductive health and our neglect of other diseases affecting them evidence of the incorporation of gender relations into the state's modernization strategies; a sign that we still manage women's uteruses in pursuit of the national interest? In a country undergoing transition, does our promotion of health projects based on market models of public health provision simply serve to justify the nation's disinvestment in social welfare and healthcare and the diversion of resources into the construction of 'modernization'? These things have directly impacted on the health of the rural population and their quality of life, and ill health remains a major cause of rural impoverishment. Is the emphasis we have placed on improving rural women's income (irrespective of the wealth differences among them) by promoting their education, training and mobility, not just a new angle on how to direct rural household investment into 'human capital accumulation' and transform women into flexible wage labour? Also, our emphasis on the development of women's agribusiness overlooks the fact that even if these women desperately want to make money, in increasingly open markets they cannot control and may be unable to deal with external factors, such as changes in the prices of commodities and inputs such as seeds, fertilizers and irrigation water.[4] Yet these external market factors are among the most important reasons why farming women fall back into poverty.

It is not hard to imagine that some of those least able to see through these development and modernization plans are those who are still in poverty, those who are 'backward' and who preserve their so-called difference: rural and ethnic minority women, still considered to be rendered 'stupid' by low literacy, still struggling to acquire and learn to use modern production technologies to increase yields and profits, and who, in the course of development and swayed by commercial advertising, unknowingly damage the environment and discard their cultural and spiritual heritage and the knowledges that once were critical in sustaining production and daily life. Thus, 'rural women' become implicated in the reproduction of their own 'underdevelopment'. As Shiva (2000) has shown, this kind of lesson has been learned in other developing countries, and China now is heading for the same cul-de-sac.

In the field of GAD, practitioners appropriate a variety of negotiating resources and positions, but rarely acknowledge their vested interests in, or the problematic consequences of, those appropriations. For example, domestic and international development organizations, their staff and experts all emphasize the 'protection' of rural and ethnic minority women's culture, interests and rights. In this manner, our rhetoric demonstrates respect for the cultural authenticity and diversity of the bargaining chips which serve as the basis for our international and domestic negotiations of, and interventions in, development. But in emphasizing the 'neediness' of Yunnan's impoverished, backward rural women we overstate some aspects of their circumstances while ignoring equally important factors such as social structural inequalities. In this way, we development scholars and practitioners may unwittingly be involved in colonizing a social construction of gender relations which reinforces stereotypical images of disadvantaged women in developing countries. It is standard practice for GAD practitioners and scholars to assert that, as rural women are unable to represent their own interests, they perform this role on their behalf. But, in fact, if the many Chinese laws granting women equal rights in all spheres of life were truly understood, implemented and respected, we actually could not represent these women. Our representation of rural women must give some of those same women cause to wonder to what extent, and in what respects, they must rely on development practitioners and women's rights activists and, indeed, it poses a real question for us all.

How do communities and countries struggling to survive in the course of modernization, and constrained by political, economic and cultural circumstances, construct 'rural women'? Do we tend to position them first and foremost as women, or as rural, or as members of a minority group, or as members of the nation-state? Might we position them as another interest group? If we are not clear about how we position rural women conceptually and in our discursive constructions and activities, it will be impossible to resolve real gender issues. In fact, to date, one of the consequences of our purported representation of 'rural women's interests' is not that of assisting them to develop, but rather, of using that freeze-framed construct, 'rural women', to further our own production of development knowledges, positions and practices. Though we participate in the relay race of globalization and modernization, we are oblivious as to which section of the race we are running or even whose team we actually are on. By endlessly recycling statistics and case studies regarding 'rural women', locking them in as target populations needful of our assistance to participate in markets and governance, and representing their interests, we have constructed binary categories of knowledge and positioning. How can we assist Yunnan villagers, and especially rural and ethnic minority women, to express and represent their own interests?

IMPROVING GAD APPROACHES IN YUNNAN

In the process of implementing GAD ideas in any developing country, we have to face the harsh realities of complex and changing structural inequalities, the sublimation of women's interests to the national interest, the pursuit of market power and globalization, and the impacts of environmental change. In the specific context of a socialist country such as China, the framework of our gender advocacy and activities cannot be based solely on either WID or GAD approaches. It must also comply with state and society's institutions and organizational models. Hence, in attending to gender issues, we Chinese development practitioners must also consider the use of approved concepts, models, measures and methods to promote structural and systemic changes in gender relations. This requires us to pay more attention to rural women and their families, and men and women of all ages in their communities. With local government agencies, we must adhere to state principles guiding national and global interactions and, in word and deed, uphold equality and mutual respect. In the interests of all parties, we must design development strategies which are consistent with, and capitalize on, the goals, methods and reach of the Communist Party and government, have the support of civil society, and uphold socialist ideals of gender equality and justice. Yunnan rural women's development has to be anchored in the unique circumstances associated with China's globalization and modernization as a socialist country.

Under these circumstances, who is best equipped to represent the interests of rural women? It is generally agreed that rural women are best placed to realize their own rights and represent and pursue their interests through their selection of rural women representatives to grassroots organizations. But the reality is, GAD development projects are initiated by organizations, and are subject to the influence of domestic and international development experts. And, with few exceptions, the scholarly and mass organizations[5] in which women participate, not to mention rural women's own grassroots organizations such as the village Women's Committee,[6] are rarely either independent or sustainable. They lack the efficacy and influence that civil society organizations have in other societies. Their existence is not unimportant, but, because they are the sole forces women can deploy in their collective interests, they require a more supportive environment.

The Communist Party and government should bear the greatest responsibility for safeguarding and enforcing the rights of women to represent their own interests. In addition to the Women's Federation and women's grassroots organizations, other civil society organizations should endorse and take some responsibility for improving gender equality and justice. GAD practitioners are all responsible for promoting gender equality as a basic national policy and as a project goal.

How can we transform this interlinked, multi-level system and division of responsibilities to enable it to operate to produce a sustainable, comprehensive strategy to assist women to realize their own interests in gender equality and justice, and a series of indicators showing whether (and which) women actually are developing towards their goals, rather than continuing to focus on our static construction of needy 'rural women'? At the Gender and Participation Research Centre (GPRC) of the Yunnan Academy of Social Sciences, it is our opinion that in rural areas of Yunnan, two organizations can and should represent the interests of rural and ethnic minority women. One is the emergent village self-government organization – the Village Committee – the other is the Minority Folk Association, organized by minority elites. These are important organizational resources that could help realize the interests of rural and minority women. Below, I discuss two projects in which I and my GPRC colleagues collaborated, which illustrate how the Party, government, and mass and civil society organizations can be encouraged to take responsibility for helping rural women to articulate, pursue and realize their own development interests. The projects also shed light on how the particular characteristics of China's socialist state organizational and institutional structures – characteristics that sometimes have been viewed as constraints on GAD activities – might be used to embed GAD activities and research in everyday governance. These cases represent a critical departure from previous GAD goals, plans and methods which, by only targeting rural and ethnic minority women, failed to build on and take advantage of existing distributions of responsibility, resources and support for gender equality and justice, and thereby perpetuated organizational and institutional weaknesses.

Working with Party Schools to Enhance the Gender Awareness of Village Committee Members

The villagers' self-governing committee is a new type of democratic political organization in rural China. In recent years, the election of village leaders has become a matter of concern for government at all levels, but the skills of those elected, and their ability to effect change once they have assumed office, have received less attention. Yet, once elections are over and the new Committee members assume office, they must quickly show their expertise in deciding how to recognize and deal with the range of gender issues facing rural areas. In theory, the Village Committee should represent, and bring about changes in the interests of rural women. However, it is clear that currently, Village Committee members, both male and female, do not possess the knowledge, attitudes, skills and conditions to perform those tasks. In particular, they lack awareness of gender in/equality, and the capacity and leadership skills and experience necessary to promote gender equality and justice. For this reason, grassroots democratic elections and Village Committee mechanisms have thus far failed to integrate gender equality and justice into village policies and management practices.

Having identified this problem, with the support of the World Bank, we put into practice a training project titled 'Enhancing village leaders' gender awareness and leadership capacity'. The project was relatively successful. However, such projects can only train a handful of village leaders and are not sustainable over the medium term. What could be done about the multitude of Village Committee members? We began to consider the county and township Party Schools, which constitute unique channels for training grassroots level cadres in politics, administration and governance. The Party Schools are a long-standing institution in the Chinese Communist Party state system, possessing educational facilities and training teachers. In order to implement the New Socialist Countryside policy, the government has directed that tens of thousands of village leaders should receive training in Party Schools.

We therefore, with the support of the FF, set ourselves the challenge of increasing the knowledge of Party School leaders and teachers about laws and policies relating to gender equality, training them in gender awareness and issues relating to gender equality and methods of gender analysis, and assisting them to incorporate these subjects into their curriculum for village leaders. By utilizing existing Party and government training resources at a grassroots level, we aimed to enhance village leaders' gender sensitivity and leadership skills, and thereby improve their capacity to represent rural women's interests. Our project was conducted at county and township levels over a two-year period between July 2007 and June

2009. Its pre-set target groups included both leaders and teachers in Party Schools and village officials. In the preparatory phase, GAD related materials and training courses were developed. We established relationships and technical support to assist Party Schools to obtain approval for the training programme from the provincial government. In the second phase, we trained Party School teachers. Phase three centred on the provision of assistance to Party School teachers in developing relevant curriculum content and methodology for use in their training of village leaders. In the final phase, we worked with Party School teachers to evaluate lesson plans and their experience of, and outcomes in, systematic gender awareness training of village leaders.

In the Party School classrooms, village leaders were trained not only in matters typically regarded as 'women's issues', such as domestic violence, women's right to contract land, and family planning and reproductive health, but also in village management techniques, so that village leaders were better equipped to handle all aspects of village affairs. Village leaders were invited to compare and connect their implementation of basic national gender equality policies with mainstream official discourse on the 'three rural issues' (i.e problems relating to agriculture, the countryside and the rural population) and comprehensive harmonious rural development. Moreover, in keeping with the orthodox discursive framing of, and pedagogic approaches to, the transmission of knowledge in China, gender analysis and participatory methods were introduced to village leaders as 'scientific development' concepts based on objective research and new knowledge. In short, rather than proceeding from our own pre-determined list of the needs of Yunnan's 'underdeveloped' rural women, this project aimed to create sustainable training methods that could be embedded organically in the daily operations and training activities of Party Schools. By scaling up the gender awareness training of male and female village leaders, the project worked to provide villages with leadership that is sensitive to gender relations, and knowledgeable about gender equality and justice institutions and methods, and thereby give Yunnan's rural women channels through which to represent and realize their different interests.

Supporting Ethnic Minority Women's Subjective Needs in Minority Associations

In the context of development, Yunnan's ethnic minorities and minority women have been subjected to the combined phenomena of feminization and 'othering' (Liu Xiaochun 2007; Schein 1997; Zhu 2005). Some Chinese scholars argue that, to some extent, these phenomena have been exacerbated because some people have been dazzled and diverted by the influx of GAD theories and foreign-funded projects in Yunnan. For example, Du Juan, of the Yunnan Academy of Social Sciences, suggests that some Western feminist theoretical perspectives may not be appropriate for Yunnan's present situation (Du Juan 2005). For, the reality is that in some ethnic minority cultures, genders are not defined and practised as binary oppositions. Rather, there is much overlap in the connotations of gender and sexuality, and, because of this, there is also greater potential for mutual understanding and harmony between the genders. Another point to note is that among GAD public intellectuals and practitioners in Yunnan are several minority women who possess situated knowledge of gender relations in ethnic minority cultures, gender analysis skills and the ability to publicize and advocate on behalf of their minority cultures and callings. These include Gu Wenfeng of the Miao, Su Cuiwei of the Lahu and He Zhonghua of the Naxi, all researchers at the Yunnan Academy of Social Sciences. Instead of relying on 'imported' GAD experts, ethnic minority women should be at the fore in identifying the values and goals, and acquiring the resources that will allow women to pursue their own plans for sustainable development.

The Chinese government has granted a limited measure of 'democratic autonomy' to ethnic minority groups, and organized and provided support for representative associations and institutes for each of the 26 ethnic minority populations in Yunnan. Some of the Minority Folk Association leaders are concurrently Communist Party and government leaders, and hence exert influence among both the Han majority and ethnic minority publics. Thus, the Yunnan Minority Folk Associations constitute a potential platform for collaborative dialogue with the state, and the representation and resourcing of minority women.

Our new approach is to encourage and assist ethnic minority women intellectuals to join the leadership ranks of their associations and, from that position, apply gender-equal principles, gender-just governance and gender-participatory concepts in the development and catalytic growth of the nation's civil minority associations. This represents a sustainable strategy to enhance women's capacity to identify and respond to latent risks posed by processes of globalization and modernization, and give play to the active agency of ethnic minority peoples (including, of course, women) to represent, defend and realize their diverse interests. In three provinces with large ethnic minority populations, Yunnan, Guizhou and Guangxi, we formed partnerships with five ethnic Minority Institutes (Miao, Lahu, Bulang, Shui and Zhuang) to implement the 'Southwest five Minority Associations experiment in designing gender enhancement'. The project, which ran for two years between July 2006 and June 2007, was coordinated by the Yunnan Minorities Research Association, with the

GPRC providing advice and training. Project activities centred on training Institute and Association leaders in gender analysis, gender-integrated development planning, good governance, finance, team building and participatory working methods. Through these means, the project sought to produce a group of gender-sensitive leaders in non-governmental organizations representing ethnic minorities, and, inter alia, provide them with skills and strategies for planning the gender-equitable organizational development of their Institutes over the coming five years. Four of the Institutes formally established internal councils for women in the workplace.

Participants' feedback suggests that the projects are succeeding. For example, in an interview conducted in 2008, two of the participants who had been elected Vice-Presidents of their associations, Gu Wenfeng and Su Cuiwei, reported that the project:

> really is based on the study of gender analysis, participatory concepts and methods, which enables us to find our own approach to development, enhances our capability, makes us sensitive to the importance of promoting the development missions of minority ethnicities, and enables us to rely on our own organizations and pay more attention to the sustainable development of our own ethnic groups. (Gu Wenfeng 2008: 50)

Both said they had acquired a new, and stronger, sense of identity, not only as individuals but also as members of their communities and ethnic groups. Such statements also are indicative of the emergent expression of ethnic minority women's interests. Follow-up research also found that all associations involved in the project had established strategic plans that continued to promote participatory gender analysis in ethnic minority areas, focusing on gender roles, the status of women and changes in gender-unequal relations, local understandings of gender equality and justice, and communities' tracking of their own progress towards realizing their objectives with regard to gender-equal development.

CONCLUSION

Promoting the development of women is by no means a substitute for, or solely an instrument in, the promotion of social equality and justice. If GAD is limited to efforts to raise women's status, it will face thorny problems; if it is only concerned with women, it will simply show that 'good deeds' cannot transform structural inequalities. The term GAD actually refers only to a strategy and methods, rather than to the ultimate goal of achieving social, including gender, equality and justice. In China at present, although gender equality is guaranteed in national law and policy, in terms of both scope and depth, the work being done to promote gender equality remains marginal. The reason for this is that mainstream institutions and organizations genuinely do not understand the import of gender inequality, and do not agree that unequal gender relations adversely affect people's development, including people within their own institutions and organizations, and their efficiencies and achievements. In addition, personnel and organizations within the current state-society system certainly are not clear about how they might conduct their work in ways that help to implement the nation's legislation and policies on gender equality.

To transform this situation, we first need to recognize the risk that, under the influence of the colonial discourse of WID or GAD, we might overlook and fail to capitalize on China's socialist resources. In China, the institutionalization of gender equality and gender mainstreaming should be synchronized, and comprehensively implemented in day-to-day development work. The two projects described above illustrate how we can adjust GAD strategies and utilize an existing system of Party, government and civil society organizations to improve gender equitable representation, leadership and management in a vast number and diverse range of grassroots rural communities. The reason adjustment of GAD strategies is necessary is that in a socialist country such as China (and, perhaps, not only in China), primary responsibility and the resources necessary for advancing gender equality rest with the state. Hence, we need to focus attention on, train and support state agencies to address gender inequality from within, as well as in their policies, procedures, training projects, and operational interactions with all sections of society. In other words, we must co-opt and transform existing state and societal organizations into a machinery producing gender-equal, impartial, participatory and representative developments. Gender mainstreaming is implicit in this goal, but it also encapsulates a feasible, sustainable strategy that responds to the realities of China's political, economic and cultural context and allows us to work as, and with organizations and members of the socialist system.

Only with the destruction of the present system of patriarchy, under which women are controlled by concepts such as 'concern' and 'protection', can we truly establish equality in the rights and interests of women. The current emphasis given by China's government to the 'protection of women', especially rural women, is of positive significance. Nevertheless, that paternalistic 'protection' clearly continues to place strong constraints on women. In addition, from the platform of development, many individuals and organizations with differing positions perpetuate gender power relations by manipulating the freeze-framed image of vulnerable, needy 'rural women in Yunnan' to pursue their own needs and propagate their own knowledges. The current development and 'underdevelopment' of rural women is not a simple, unmediated objectivity, but rather results from various political, economic and cultural constructions, and is the operation of a type of 'collective patriarchy' (Bai and Du 2009).

When thinking about who rural women are, we should also ask ourselves, who are we Chinese feminist intellectuals: what is our position, and how will we carry out our mission? What is our responsibility? In the context of globalizing GAD, those of us local GAD practitioners who are regarded as influential and who, to a large extent, indeed do influence other 'experts', must avoid becoming colonizers, central tools or controlling conspirators. We need to reflect on what actually can be introduced in China's rural areas, and what room we have to produce lasting impacts on what is there. How can we preserve diversity and enhance others' agency, while still taking the initiative? And how can we use the rich organizational resources of a socialist country like China to establish a sustainable system that enables women to articulate, represent and protect their interests and, most importantly, that upholds our core, interrelated values – the promotion of social and gender equity and justice? It is by seeking answers to these questions that we must proceed with the reconstruction of GAD in China.

NOTES

1. Development practitioners and scholars in China began to adopt the rhetoric of GAD, in favour of that of WID (Women in Development), after the UN Fourth World Conference on Women held in Beijing in 1995. In theory, GAD strategies and projects address gender inequalities and the institutions and relations of power which underpin them, rather than merely giving aid to women or adding them to existing institutions, as in WID strategies. In practice, both in China and elsewhere, many so-called GAD projects are similar to WID projects in targeting women, and in not mounting any significant challenge to existing gendered institutions. Yunnan GAD practitioners mostly are trained and employed in academies of social sciences and universities and colleges, and are engaged in women's studies and gender studies research and teaching. As a result of our work and interests, we petition international organizations and the Chinese government for sponsorship to implement development projects relating to the development of women in rural areas. Others, employed by foreign NGOs, work with gender experts or advisers involved with projects or organize to form grassroots NGOs to undertake more targeted research, interventions and activism. GAD practitioners are presently the most powerful force for gender and development in Yunnan.
2. Gender-related GONGOs rely on and work with mass organizations, such as the Women's Federation. Strictly speaking, the latter is not part of the government or Communist Party. However, its leadership, core policies, and funding are determined by the government and Party. The Women's Federation is also itself sometimes referred to as a GONGO.
3. Such women often have family members in Party or government departments at the township or county level.

4. Seeds were traditionally self-cultivated, but now because of the reliance on hybrid and genetically modified seeds, farmers must purchase seed stock. This has increased farmers' production costs.
5. See note 2 above for an explanation of the position of mass organizations.
6. The village Women's Committee is the lowest representative body of the Women's Federation. According to Article 22 of the Constitution of the All China Women's Federation (2003), it should consist of a head, deputy head, and an unspecified number of committee members. In practice, most villages have a village Women's Committee head, but few have a functioning committee.

8. Engendering the local: globalization, development and the 'empowerment' of Chinese rural women

Sharon R. Wesoky

The objective of the Platform for Action, which is in full conformity with the purposes and principles of the Charter of the United Nations and international law, is the empowerment of all women. (United Nations 1995)

INTRODUCTION

The 'empowerment' of women is a central theme in contemporary global feminism and development discourse, as is evident in its centrality in the Platform for Action resulting from the 1995 United Nations Fourth World Conference on Women in Beijing and the UN's Millennium Development Goals, adopted in 2000.[1] Empowerment has moved from being a rhetorical flourish to becoming a concrete goal in the projects of many women's organizations in both the developed and developing worlds.

At the same time, feminist activists and scholars often highlight the negative effects on women of the neoliberal-led forces of globalization, especially women in the developing world (see e.g. Hawkesworth 2004). Yet, as Valentine Moghadam notes, there is 'at least one positive aspect of globalization – the proliferation of women's movements at the local level, the emergence of transnational feminist networks working at the global level, and the adoption of international conventions' regarding the status of women (Moghadam 2005: 19). This caveat signals the need for interrogation of the more specific relationships between women's empowerment and globalization. How does women's empowerment work when the discourses and resources of globalized feminism encounter local-level power structures?

In this chapter, I examine the potential for globalizing feminism to shape local-level, gendered power relationships in rural China. I begin with a discussion of globalization and the local, with special attention to the centrality of empowerment in contemporary global discourses of gender and development. I then look at one channel of globalization in China, the emergence of a largely internationally funded sector of women's non-governmental organizations (NGOs), telling the stories of two women whose fates have been altered through one such NGO, the Beijing-based Cultural Development Centre for Rural Women. These stories provide an illustration of how globalization contains the potential to challenge local power relationships, as well as a way of considering the implications and meanings of local ideas of women's empowerment in a rural Chinese context.

GLOBALIZATION AND LOCAL EMPOWERMENT

Much scholarly attention to the relationship between global and local has centred on the economic or cultural effects of globalization. Yet globalization also has effects on local power relationships, including those shaped by gender norms. One lens through which to assess such effects is that of empowerment, a rhetoric that has been central to development projects in recent years. In this section, I will briefly trace some of the theoretical approaches to the question of globalization and local power, and then consider the effects of globalization in relation to ideas of women's empowerment through organization in rural China.

Some theorists have observed that ultimately the global can only be understood through its local manifestations. For instance, O'Byrne adopts a largely Habermasian approach to examining the ways that 'Hitherto abstract concerns with rights, emancipation, self-discovery, and so on have been transformed into political action in a direct, unmediated, pragmatic way', particularly through social movements that construct the 'global lifeworld' at a localized level (2005: 84). Similarly, Sassen examines the varied ways that globalization affects the local in order to understand the relationship between globalization and 'actors typically represented as powerless, or victims, or uninvolved with global conditions' (Sassen 2005: 155).

The feminist discourse on empowerment is one which specifically connects to local-level power relations, for while feminists assert the need for a nuanced and context-specific notion of empowerment, they most commonly focus on the challenges that it presents to local, rather than global, gendered power relations. For instance, Datta and Kornberg maintain that 'empowerment occurs most definitely when women mobilize themselves and take leadership positions in work settings and in the community' (2002: 5). A United Nations Task Force on the Millennium Development Goal to 'Promote Gender Equality and Empower Women' defines empowerment in a somewhat more complex way, noting that 'The core of empowerment lies in the ability of a woman to control her own destiny'. This requires an expansion of what Sen refers to as her 'capabilities', understood as access to resources and opportunities and the ability to exercise agency (Sen 1993; UN Millennium Project 2005: 3). While the Task Force's attention spans the implications of women's empowerment in the private sphere and familial relations, the operationalization and measurement of empowerment primarily focuses on the public-sector goals of education, employment and political representation. This potentially obscures the more complex, ground-level manifestations of empowerment, in which a person may have position or stature in the public sphere but limited ability to 'control her own destiny', or, conversely, may have such control over her personal destiny without a public position. Consideration of the actual empowerment promoted by development programmes at the local level needs to take account of such multi-layered positionings and dynamic interactions between them.

Under China's post-Mao reforms, globalization has had complex, ambiguous impacts on rural gender relations. While socio-economic inequality generally has increased (see e.g. Wong 2004), some observers note that this has had particularly detrimental effects for women. Sargeson declares, 'It is indisputable that at the beginning of the 21st century, rural women were one of the poorest population categories in China' (2006: 579; see also Jacka 2006a: 590). At the same time, globalization creates opportunities for rural women. For instance, Lin Chun maintains that although globalization and marketization potentially diminish the 'hard-won achievements for women' made during the Maoist era, they also expand the potential to create a 'social realm' in which 'socially empowered voices and forces' could promote women's rights and interests (2001: 1285).

A core component of this 'social realm' is comprised of women's non-governmental organizations (NGOs), a large variety of which have emerged in China since the 1990s. Until that time, the women's movement was dominated by the quasi-state body, the All China Women's Federation (hereafter, Women's Federation). However, in the late 1980s and early 1990s, preparations for Beijing's hosting of the United Nation's Fourth World Conference on Women (FWCW) and the arrival of new international donor organizations in China (described by Zhao Jie in the preceding chapter of this book), opened spaces for non-governmental women's organizing in China.[2] It is important to stress the global origins and resourcing of these new women's organizations: many largely rely on international donors such as the Ford Foundation and the Global Fund for Women.[3] Clearly, then, globalization has provided significant resources for the formation of an emergent women's civil society in China.

Although scholarly attention has recently focused on forces shifting local power relations in reform-era China,[4] the effect of globally-funded NGO activism on gender power relations in rural areas remains under-theorized. What are the ground-level effects of NGO development projects aimed at empowering women? After briefly examining two of the projects initiated by the Cultural Development Centre for Rural Women, on women's political participation and suicide prevention, I turn to examine the stories of two rural women and illuminate how their access to globalized resources both empowered them and presented challenges to local power.

GLOBALIZATION, GENDER, AND NGO ORGANIZING IN CHINA: *NONGJIANÜ* AND THE TALES OF TWO RURAL WOMEN

The Beijing-based Cultural Development Centre for Rural Women (referred to hereafter as the Cultural Development Centre) is an offshoot of the magazine, *Rural Women* (*Nongjianü*). Founded by Xie Lihua in 1993, *Nongjianü*[5] was the first, and remains the only, magazine in China geared toward China's population of rural women, and was founded as part of the group of new women's organizations in the 1990s. *Nongjianü*, partially as a result of global influences and funding opportunities, expanded rapidly beyond being just a magazine to becoming a service and activist-oriented organization. In 2001, Xie also established the Cultural Development Centre to operate as an umbrella organization for these various projects.[6]

One important project of *Nongjianü* relates to suicide prevention, an issue to which it has been devoting attention since 1996. China has a number of unique and disturbing patterns in terms of suicidal behaviour. In contrast to the West, about 93 per cent of suicides in China occur among rural residents (Phillips et al. 2002), and China possibly is the only country in the world where more women commit suicide than men (Lee and Kleinman 2003). The advocacy of Dr Michael Phillips, a Canadian psychiatrist who for a long time worked at Beijing's Huilongguan Hospital, was crucial to raising awareness regarding China's unique patterns of suicidal behaviour. Thus, the 'naming' of this problem partly occurred as a result of global connections. *Nongjianü* started focusing on suicide with a column titled 'Why Did They Choose the Road of Suicide?' and later began a suicide prevention project centred on creating Women's Health Support Small Groups (*Funü jiankang zhichi xiaozu*) in villages. The project adopts a multi-faceted approach to suicide prevention, by promoting ideas about living 'a good life in a more general sense' (Wu Fei 2005: 17) and 'harmonious families and happy lives' (Nongjianü Wenhua Fazhan Zhongxin 2008), as well as gender consciousness.[7]

Another activity of importance both to *Nongjianü* and the Cultural Development Centre, has been the promotion of rural women's political participation and leadership. For several years, the Cultural Development Centre has been conducting training sessions for officials from rural areas, which include aspects relating to gender awareness. In 2006, it convened a National Conference for Women Village Heads, which was followed by the development of a network for rural women village heads that includes a new magazine, *Women Village Heads* (*Nücunguan*), and an interactive website. These projects facilitate women village heads' collaboration in their work as well as increased awareness of women's legal and political rights.

These projects are almost solely funded by international foundation support. The suicide prevention project has been supported by the Ford Foundation and the Global Fund for Women, while the Washington, DC-based International Republican Institute largely funded the political participation project.[8] Indeed, international funding arguably is a *raison d'etre* of some of the projects pursued by the Cultural Development Centre. As its founder, Xie Lihua, remarks, international donors 'are more willing to support new projects, such as suicide prevention and political participation, rather than supporting a magazine year after year' (Qian and Young 2006).

The *Nongjianü* website emphasizes that the Cultural Development Centre's projects are 'aimed at creating opportunities for self-empowerment and development together with rural women', and, it notes, 'In all our activities we seek to advocate awareness of gender and citizenship, and we aspire to maintain a dedication to openness, democracy and participation in all our work'.[9] Commensurate with the discussion above regarding the centrality of empowerment to United Nations programmes on gender and development, Xie Lihua recognizes the role played by her connections to global feminism in making 'self-empowerment' (*ziwo fuquan*) an aim of the organization's projects. In the magazine's early years, she considered the readers of *Nongjianü* as 'friends', but became more consciously aware of the term 'empowerment' in the mid-1990s, in encounters with the Ford Foundation's Mary Ann Burris and during her trip to Senegal, where she observed women self-organizing rather than relying on top-down organizational structures such as the Women's Federation (Xie 2009). Such notions of empowerment, I argue, distinguish the Chinese women's NGO sector from the Women's Federation.

The Tales of Two Rural Women

The experiences of two rural women and their encounters with the Cultural Development Centre's projects demonstrate how China's processes of globalization intersect with and transform local power relations. The narratives of these women's experiences come from various sources, including personal interviews, quasi-official documents, magazine articles, and blog postings.[10] Here, I trace the women's global connections and participation in development projects. Below, I will analyse their stories in more depth, in terms of the varied ways they demonstrate how globalization complicates local power dynamics.

The project on rural women's leadership perhaps most obviously empowers women in ways that lead to new negotiations of local power relations. This is illustrated by the example of Li Huaqin, who recently served as the first female head of Dongzhao Village, in Mancheng County, Hebei. For a rural woman, Li is relatively 'cultured' (*you wenhua*), a high school graduate who aspired to attend college but gave up on taking the university entrance examinations due to illness and poverty in her natal family. Li married into another village, and she and her husband were fairly quickly successful at various small business ventures, including selling agricultural chemicals on credit to villagers at a time when many elsewhere fell prey to those selling fake chemicals. This led to a view in the village that Li was an enterprising but honest businesswoman. Li then dared to take a contract to use land on a barren mountain, and through painstaking labour she turned the mountainside into terraced orchards that, ironically in light of her previous venture, she named 'the Phoenix Slope Organic Farm and Ecology Garden' (Xu Xu 2007).

In an article about her in the magazine *Women Village Heads*, Li explained that it was her business acumen that initially attracted the attention of the women's movement: 'After the experiment on the desolate mountain was so successful, the County Women's Federation really took me seriously and gave me an opportunity to attend training at the Beijing Cultural Development Centre school' (quoted in Xu Xu 2007: 12). The County Women's Federation, for its part, described how Li was so excited by the training that she was 'unable to sleep for several nights'. Li herself wrote of gaining a fresh consciousness from her exposure to the discourses promoted in the training curriculum. However Li encountered antagonism from the leadership of Dongzhao village: the village's Communist Party secretary would not give his approval for a water pump that she had been awarded by county officials in recognition of her achievements with the 'Ecology Garden' (Xu Xu 2007: 13). As a result of these experiences she decided that she wanted to become active in village governance.

Despite having no previous political experience, Li decided to stand directly for election as head of the Village Committee in Dongzhao. Starting in the 1980s and becoming fully institutionalized in the 1990s, China introduced a system of direct, competitive elections for membership on the committees that govern villages, the lowest administrative level of the political system. While not without problems, these elections are regarded by many villagers and outside observers as having increased the efficacy, legitimacy and democracy of village-level governance.[11] However, the democratization of village-level governance has had, at best, mixed results for rural women. Li stood for election as village head against three male opponents. In an interview, she recalled that:

> When I stood for election, people [i.e. the other candidates] were afraid of me because they could see that I can do things. In the three rounds of voting, they all used every kind of method to gain the voters' ballots, for example, giving money, inviting them out to eat, all kinds of tricks. I didn't do any of this. I just depended on my personal character and I finally was elected by a narrow margin.[12]

The Mancheng Women's Federation noted that because of her intelligence and her economic successes, Li Huaqin had a 'good base in the village public' and villagers who wanted to improve the village 'placed their trust in her'. Consequently, Li was elected the first female head in the history of her village in April 2006. However, old village power-holders, including its long-serving Party secretary, 'really understood Huaqin's upright, honest, and conscientious character, and so were not willing to let her be elected and put up many obstacles for her, but the people's vision was clear and Huaqin was finally still elected' (Mancheng Women's Federation n.d.). When she won, Li took the official village seal, and 'she tied it to her pocket, and took it wherever she went' (Xu Xu 2007: 14), as a visible symbol of her new authority in the village.

Nevertheless, as I shall show, the challenges that Li's election posed both at home and within her village exemplify the ways that even rural women who occupy positions of authority still have to negotiate for power. Her husband, while claiming to be supportive, was critical of her neglect of 'domestic duties' as she focused on her position as village head. And she encountered continued obstacles from other men in the village, particularly in her desire to fix the long-neglected village road.[13]

The second story is that of Xu Fengqin, an activist on suicide prevention. Xu Fengqin is a 60-year old woman, a member of the Manchu minority ethnicity, who hails from Hebei Province's Qinglong Manchu Autonomous County. She is a Party member who served as the head of the Qinglong Women's Federation from 1989 to 1998 and then in the county Commerce Bureau, from which she fully retired in 2004. Before her full retirement, from 2001 to 2003 she served as the vice-principal of the suburban Beijing campus of the Practical Skills Training School for Rural Women, which had been founded by *Nongjianü* in 1998. In 2003, she returned home to rejoin her family and establish her own NGO, the Qinglong Rural Women's Health Promotion Association (*Qinglong Nongjianü Jiankang Cujinhui*), which follows the model utilized by the Cultural Development Centre in preventing rural women's suicide. Since many suicides emerge out of family conflicts, Xu's project centres on forming support groups in which women can discuss their feelings, and organizing cultural activities (Fan, Maureen 2007; Xu Fengqin 2007). This project was largely funded by the Global Fund for Women, in response to applications submitted through the Cultural Development Centre. Initially, support groups were formed in two villages, Donghao and 36 Rollers.

In December of 2007, the Qinglong suicide project was visited by a journalist from the *China Philanthropy Times*, who wrote an article reporting on the high rate of suicide in Qinglong County, where 1014 cases had occurred over three years, among which were 476 fatalities. Seventy-one per cent of these fatalities were women (Xu Fengqin and Xu Rong 2004: 18; Zhao Guanjun 2006). The article went on to discuss the suicide prevention projects initiated by the Beijing and Qinglong rural women's organizations. After the publication of the *Philanthropy Times* article, it was re-published on governmental websites elsewhere in Hebei Province.[14]

But whereas public prominence brought Li Huaqin official support, in the context of scheduling a visit to Qinglong, Xie Lihua told me that it had earned Xu Fengqing local officials' disapproval:

> Yesterday I already spoke with Xu Fengqin, and of course she will welcome you. Recently the *China Philanthropy Times* reported on our suicide project, mainly writing about the Qinglong example. Their county government has been giving her trouble (*mafan*), but she is very persistent and will make even more people understand her work, but also there are some people who oppose her doing this project. Therefore, if you go in April it will be better, because some time should pass . . . You can read my blog on sina.com[15]

As Xu later told me, she had been called by government officials and basically informed, 'you're in trouble!'

GLOBALIZATION, WOMEN'S EMPOWERMENT, AND LOCAL POWER

For Xu Fengqin and Li Huaqin, empowerment is a polysemous concept. It means an acknowledgement that rural women, empowered in part through globally connected non-governmental activism, are obligated to exercise their 'power' in other-directed local activities in which they might then confront resistance. But it also means a recognition of the various ways that power relations perpetuate gender inequalities at the local level.

For Li, empowerment involved gaining a political position that would allow her to assist her fellow villagers in economic development and cultural enrichment. Her empowerment therefore is motivated by a sense of reciprocal obligation: 'I am not serving for myself. Why did the villagers want to elect me? It is because they believe in me, they hope I will be able to bring them a better life' (quoted in Xu Xu 2007: 14). But she also notes that she herself is obligated to the Cultural Development Centre for her empowerment: 'the change from engaging in business to politics is entirely the result of the Cultural Development Centre training'.[16] In other words, Li's empowerment ultimately has not just derived from her business success and electoral popularity amongst villagers. Xu Fengqin also regards economic development to be only one aspect of women's wider empowerment, stressing that her organization acts to promote women's legal and political awareness, as well as to provide them with opportunities to become economically self-sufficient.[17]

In this respect, both Li and Xu connect economic development with a superficially utilitarian, but nonetheless politically loaded meaning of empowerment that echoes Xie Lihua's notion of empowerment. Xie describes empowerment as utilizing the great 'untapped potential' of rural women in order that this 'marginalized group becomes a force promoting the development of civil society' (Xie 2009). Yet the empowerment projects funded by Xie's organization encompass a range of pragmatic interventions, including not only economic development but also the promotion of women's political leadership, 'harmonious families and happy lives', and mutual support to prevent suicide. To understand the relationship between globally derived and distinctly local ideas of women's empowerment in rural China, I will now examine shifts in local power dynamics, local-global communications and media, agenda setting, and discursive power.

Local Power Dynamics

Local power relations in rural China remain gender unequal, despite the state's nearly 60-year commitment to the promotion of gender equality (see e.g. Howell 2002). Patriarchal institutions such as virilocal marriage and gendered divisions of labour are central to the perpetuation of power inequalities in public life, as in the household (Jacka 1997, 2006a). There is substantial evidence that women's political status has stagnated or even declined in the post-Mao reform period (Edwards 2007), with several village-level studies showing that 'grassroots democratic processes, together with rapid marketization in rural China, have hindered women's political participation' (Zhang, Weiguo 2006: 2; see also Ding Juan 2006). Women are especially under-represented in politics at the lowest, village, level. As Howell writes, 'only 1% of village committee chairs are women and 16% of village committee members are women' (2006: 607). Men significantly outnumber women as village Party members (Zhang, Weiguo 2006: 17).

Both Li Huaqin and Xu Fengqin have offered challenges to local power dynamics. Li's challenge is quite obvious. Merely by standing for and winning election as village head, she has sought to overturn male dominance in the local political power structure. Li was encouraged to enter politics not only by her local Women's Federation but also by the township Communist Party Committee. Her husband was concerned that the political situation in the village was 'too disordered' (*tai luan*) and that her honesty and desire to improve the quality of government in the village, especially by being more responsive to the wishes of ordinary people, would add to the difficulties she would face as head of the village. Nevertheless, because the villagers praised her as an 'honest and capable person', she was elected (Xu Xu 2007: 13–14). Yet, as her husband had predicted, she did indeed face obstacles from the Party secretary who had served in the village for over a decade. Reflecting a general problem associated with parallel structures of power in China's political system, Li noted that her biggest difficulty was 'disagreement between the two committees [Party and Village Committees] – our village's Party Branch secretary does not always support my work'.[18] Li's election, not surprisingly, also challenged power relations in her family. Her husband, while generally supportive, was unhappy with her attention to village matters rather than to domestic labour; one night he locked her out of the house when she was late back from a meeting and she had to plead with him about her desire to not disappoint the villagers (Xu Xu 2007: 14).

Xu Fengqin's challenges to local power dynamics differ from those of Li Huaqin's, because they hinge on both the idiosyncratic and conflicting interests of different levels of Party and statist organizations. Whereas the Mancheng County Women's Federation encouraged Li to receive training in political participation at the Beijing Cultural Development Centre for Rural Women, the chief obstacles to Xu's suicide project emerged from the very same Qinglong County Women's Federation which she once headed. The Qinglong County Women's Federation was 'dissatisfied' (*buman*) with Xu's suicide project, and particularly with its public discussion in the *Philanthropy Times* article at the end of 2006.[19] On the other hand, the head of the Qinglong County government, Wang Liancheng, in an interview, expressed support for Xu Fengqin's work as 'having an irreplaceable function in constructing a harmonious society' (*hexie shehui*), and noted that NGOs can be 'very beneficial for government work'.[20] While not surprisingly looking at NGO work in terms of its utility in building the 'harmonious society' that is central to contemporary Chinese statist rhetoric, Wang also noted that, after its initial concerns, the county government affirmed the value of Xu's projects.

As I will discuss below, in relation to agenda-setting, the differences in who supported the empowerment of Li and Xu have much to do with the ways that they added new ideas to local political agendas. At the same time, however, globalization contributed to their emergence as new political players who threatened established power relations: Li, by herself becoming involved in village government; and Xu, by creating a new NGO that challenged the Women's Federation's traditional monopoly on organizing on the basis of gender.

Local–Global Communications and Media

Mittelman writes, 'the redefinition of political life in China is shot through with technological innovations and more mobile spaces, as on the Internet' (2006: 387). The cases of Li Huaqin and Xu Fengqin reveal the contribution of new forms of communications and media to processes of women's empowerment. Especially the Internet, but also the diverse forms of media used in China today, are closely connected to globalization and marketization, and, while still subject to restrictions, contribute to a widening of the space available to new political constituencies.

Most obvious in these shifts is the way that new media platforms connect people in rural China to more extensive social and political networks, providing alternative channels through which actors can circulate information and build support for their initiatives. This is evident in Xu Fengqin's case. At the same time as some local officials were causing her trouble over the publicity surrounding her suicide prevention projects, Xie Lihua was reporting on Xu's victimization in her blog on the popular website sina.com. Xie wrote that, while she coincidentally was attending a seminar in Beijing on suicide intervention, Xu Fengqin text messaged her with the news that Qinglong doctors who were supposed to attend the seminar had been called back by county officials due to their concerns over the *Philanthropy Times* article. Moreover, in the blog, Xie noted that, 'Xu Fengqin received great pressure and the county leaders looked for her to discuss this matter, because it seemed that she had done something to blacken the name of Qinglong County'. In Xie's view, although the Qinglong project was successful and the newspaper article 'reflects a situation that is fundamentally true', nevertheless 'in the exposure of the media, no leaders are willing to claim authority over a negative situation – compared to the lives of rural women, they value their "face" and their own official achievements more' (Xie 2006a).[21] Alternative venues such as blogs allow for the circulation of unauthorized (and, therefore, not sanitized and possibly more accurate) statistics and information, even if it is detrimental to local officials' 'face'.[22]

According to Sassen, 'the technologies, the institutions, and the imaginaries that mark the current global digital context inscribe local political practice with new meanings and new potentialities' (2005: 164). *Nongjianü* certainly makes advantageous use of the Internet to develop women's political practice. This is illustrated by the organization's creation of the network of rural women village heads and the website in which those women can exchange information and ideas.[23] Li Huaqin had received coverage in that magazine, as well as in *China Women's News* (*Zhongguo funü bao*) (see Tong 2006). And Xu Fengqin's troubles with the County Women's Federation sprang from the coverage of her project in various Chinese media sources. Even prior to the *Philanthropy Times* incident, her activities had been reported on in national outlets such as China Central Television and the investigative newspaper, *Southern Weekend* (*Nanfang zhoumo*) (Xu Fengqin and Xu Rong 2004: 18), as well as in some international venues (Fan, Maureen 2007) and several local county and provincial newspapers and websites (Xu Fengqin 2007: 11). Hence, diverse media forms do provide opportunities for new actors to establish the legitimacy of their work among broader audiences, even though this potential currently is limited by political censorship of China's media.[24]

Agenda-setting

Another way in which globalization has altered local power relations is through shifts in agenda-setting for policy and activism. New organizations and actors on the political scene led to new issues becoming salient, posing a challenge to more top-down means of agenda creation.

This is especially evident in the ways in which globalization spurred the formation of new women's NGOs, such as Xu Fengqin's Qinglong Rural Women's Health Promotion Association, which provide an alternative base for women's organizing to the previously dominant Women's

Federation. Xu Fengqin herself acknowledged the importance of having an organizational basis for work such as her suicide prevention projects, in part to diminish pressures from the government, and in part to provide 'the support of international organizations' that enables many 'popular organizations' (*minjian zuzhi*) to exist.[25] Yet these sources of protection and support potentially challenge the hegemony of the Women's Federation in setting agendas for women's organizing. While providing a sometimes-useful venue for women's political organization and representation, as a state-funded organization, the Women's Federation also tends to foster careerism, and adopts a conservative programme of activities. For instance, the Qinglong County Women's Federation stressed its work in choosing 'Outstanding Mothers' and 'Harmonious Families' as well as organizing 'Two Studies, Two Competitions' (*shuangxue, shuangbi*) activities to promote women's market participation.[26] NGO activists such as Xie Lihua therefore point out that in developing organizations like *Nongjianü*, 'We walked a road that depended on the Women's Federation but also was differentiated from the Women's Federation, and we created an entirely new model of conducting grassroots women's work' (Xie 2006b).[27] Elsewhere, Xie implicitly critiqued the Women's Federation's emphasis on the emancipatory potential of women's market participation:

> I feel that in the past we paid more attention to rural women's economic development, and even more attention to their families becoming rich. But in fact, in the countryside we did a survey, and found that whether rural women were happy or not happy, sometimes was connected with their economic situation, but did not have a major relationship with their wealth. It was even more closely related to their family's psychological health and their family's relationships, so therefore I felt that we should do psychological health work, in order to raise rural women's quality of life, to raise their total quality (quoted in Zhao Guanjun 2006).

Moreover, as Xie argues in her blog, NGOs propagate different ideas about women's empowerment: 'Everyone is accustomed to regard women's issues as Women's Federation issues', so China's women consequently 'lack their own initiative to positively and energetically participate' in their own liberation. In contrast, by creating an organization primarily centred on women's mutual support to prevent suicide, Xu Fengqin not only produced an alternative power structure to the Women's Federation, but also brought new ideas about empowerment strategies to the policy agenda. According to Xu Fengqin's own writings, such activities have also improved village life in ways that the Women's Federation has not, including providing cultural activities that grant new colour and meaning to village life (Xu Fengqin 2007: Xu Fengqin and Xu Rong 2004: 19).[28]

In addition, rural women's empowerment has made agenda-setting in villages more gender inclusive. Women who attain political office in villages more often than not are appointed head of the local village Women's Committee,[29] and their role on this committee is to enforce highly unpopular family planning policies (Edwards 2007: 382; Howell 2006: 608, 613; Zhang 2006: 16). Ultimately, this 'limits the range of "women's interests" represented' (Howell 2006: 613). Yet NGOs' creation of networks such as the Women's Health Support Small Groups assist rural women to shape agendas in their own villages, and to transcend the focus on family planning that has previously characterized women's political leadership positions. This in turn generates new foci for gender-based activism, and contributes to more inclusive approaches to village governance. Li Huaqin, for example, particularly sought the advice of previous power-holders in her village when she first took office as village head, and then sought to tackle 'the problems that the ordinary people were most concerned about' (Xu Xu 2007: 14). Fixing the village road emerged as the issue of greatest concern to villagers; this was something that, in the words of local Party member Wang Shuzhai, 'when men were in power, they did not do' (quoted in Xu Xu 2007: 15). Looking at issues beyond economic development, Li also spoke of her desire to improve the lives of women, the young and elderly villagers. As a result, she established a Women's Activity Centre, to encourage village women to engage in activities other than playing Mah-jong (Xie 2006b). Li's responsive leadership therefore represented a potential loss of 'face' for earlier male power-holders (Mancheng Women's Federation n.d.; Xu Xu 2007). Greater inclusion of women in structures of political power is commensurate not only with the democratization of village policy agendas, but also with global feminist 'insider' strategies to increase numbers of women in elected and appointed institutions of government (Hawkesworth 2006).

Discursive Power

Finally, and perhaps most significantly, women's empowerment has begun to shift some of the cultural norms and discourses that perpetuate gender power inequalities in China. To give an example, Howell critiques the smoking, drinking and banqueting culture of village politics, which impedes women's more equal political participation (2006: 616). In an interview, Li Huaqin agreed with Howell's argument about the obstructive effects of this political culture, noting that 'men get together to smoke and drink and eat, but women cannot smoke and drink'. Such behavioural norms inhibit the ability of women to construct the social capital and networks so crucial to political efficacy in any context. However, Li claims that her training experience at the Cultural Development Centre enabled her to 'dare to stand up to the old traditions' of male domination in local politics.[30]

Elitist discourses in China emphasize rural women's 'low quality', rather than sexist norms and institutions, as a reason for gender disparities in village political participation and representation (Howell 2006; Jacka 2006a; Zhang Weiguo 2006). Li Huaqin herself echoed the 'low quality' logic, claiming that it hampers female village heads in comparison to their male counterparts. At the same time, she attributed her own motivation to pursue political office to her origins and the discrimination she experienced as one of five daughters. This led to her having 'a kind of a psychology to want to triumph over men', and to 'make every effort to succeed' as a way of contesting assumptions about women's 'low quality'.[31] It is women like Li Huaqin who provide the most convincing public refutation of the 'low quality' discourse: Li has a higher educational level than her husband, and her successes in various business ventures contributed to the 'certain prestige' that allowed her to run for and win election as village head (Mancheng Women's Federation n.d.). Li Huaqin also found the courage to critique the discourses of 'low quality' through her participation in training run by the Cultural Development Centre, noting that this training 'really allowed me to deeply and beneficially open my viewpoint, and from that time I felt that we women could do the things that men do, that if men can serve as village head, so can women' (quoted in Xu Xu 2007: 12). Similarly, the mobilization of village women through Xu Fengqin's formation of Women's Health Support Small Groups also operates in counterpoint to notions of rural women's 'low quality'. Xu writes that villagers' spirits and sense of pride were lifted when county officials attended the launch of the project in 36 Rollers Village (Xu Fengqin 2007: 11). One of the project's Small Group leaders in Donghao village, Li Guimin, subsequently became head of the village's Rural Women's Resource Centre and was elected to the county-level People's Congress (Xie 2008).

Finally, as these women's stories illustrate, and as Yuqin Huang details elsewhere in this volume, Chinese cultural constructs of 'face' that turn on gender power inequalities, are complicated by women's empowerment. In this process, masculinist 'face' can be used in a reverse fashion. Observers of the work of both Xu Fengqin and Li Huaqin noted how they challenged the 'face' of local power-holders in their efforts to empower women and broaden the policy agenda in their localities. Edwards discusses how 'international shaming' is used as a tactic to improve women's political status in China (Edwards 2007: 384). International statistics and discourses on women's political participation combine with the Chinese state's own rhetorical commitment to gender equality to create a source of pressure for greater gender equality. Such pressures are one explanation for why the state allows women's NGOs to pursue their work on issues such as women's political participation. At the same time, such activism can also 'destabilize the accepted narratives' about the dynamics and effects of globalization (Sassen 2005: 155). For instance, the Qinglong suicide project, which drew attention to the alarming suicide statistics in Qinglong County, presents a counterweight to the largely triumphalist narrative of China's globalization and modernization emanating from the Chinese state, despite occasional critiques that do emerge from within the system.[32] The global-local circulation of counter-narratives can produce subtle but nonetheless significant shifts in discursive power relations.

CONCLUSIONS

The stories of the empowerment of Xu Fengqin and Li Huaqin are ongoing. In this respect, their empowerment is both process and outcome (Datta and Kornberg 2002: 1). In Spring 2009, Li Huaqin was defeated in her effort to be re-elected as her village head, despite the fact that during her tenure as head she did succeed in fixing her village's road and the Cultural Development Centre opened a Women's Activity Centre in her village.[33] However, she is now a member of her village's Communist Party Branch Committee. Xu Fengqin still lacks the support of her local Women's Federation, but she continues working with Rural Women's Health Support Small Groups and establishes new groups with financial support from the Global Fund for Women, channelled through the Cultural Development Centre's Beijing office.[34] Like their mentors, Xie Lihua, *Nongjianü* and the Cultural Development Centre, Li and Xu accommodate mainstream arguments connecting economic development and women's empowerment, while also promoting a wider conception of how power might be attained through participatory citizenship. Though their promotion of women's self-organization and political leadership resembles global approaches to advancing gender equality in the public policy arena, their promotion of activities aimed at preventing women's suicides is linked to improved familial relations as well as gender consciousness. Used in these ways, local ideas of empowerment and globally derived resources and discourses can create new sources of power for rural women. While economic development is one important component of empowerment, to truly succeed at changing power relations at local levels, a multi-faceted approach that includes attention to gendered family relations, village political structures, and Party and governmental institutions, is essential to women's realization of power.

NOTES

1. The third of eight Millennium Development Goals is 'Promote gender equality and empower women' ('About the MDGs: Basics' http://www.undp.org/mdg/basics.shtml).
2. This sector self-consciously identifies itself as 'non-governmental', despite some of the different meanings of that concept in China than in the West.
3. For discussions of women's organizing in contemporary China, see for example Du Jie (2004), Howell (2003), Hsiung et al. (2001) and Wesoky (2002).
4. See for example the edited volume by Perry and Goldman (2007).
5. The magazine was originally called *Nongjianü Baishitong*, or 'Rural Women Knowing All'.
6. For more on the specifically 'global' discursive and organizational aspects of *Nongjianü*, see Wesoky (2007).
7. Interview with Xu Rong and Xu Fengqin, 18 June 2009.
8. For information on the funding of the suicide prevention project, see Nongjianü Wenhua Fazhan Zhongxin (2003: 5; 2005b: 2; 2006: 21) and Xu Fengqin and Xu Rong (2004: 18). For the political participation project, see Nongjianü Wenhua Fazhan Zhongxin (2003: 5; 2004: 15; 2005a: 18).
9. See *Nongjianü*'s website at http://www.nongjianv.org/web/english/aboutus/index.html. While agreeing that the approach of NGOs, including *Nongjjianü*, is different from the All-China Women's Federation (ACWF) in their tendency to emphasize women's 'empowerment', Jacka (2006a) questions whether their approaches are ultimately so very different. Wesoky (2002: 190–192) provides an account of the translation of the idea of 'empowerment' into Chinese.
10. Aspects of both the stories have been published either in magazine articles or online, and so it is possible to discuss them without the need for pseudonyms. All translations from the Chinese are mine. Field research for this chapter was funded by a 2007 Fullbright Research Fellowship.
11. See for example, Li, Lianjiang (2003) and Jakobson (2004). Jakobson notes that the international sector, including foundations and other experts, have played an important role in implementing village-level elections in China.
12. Interview with Li Huaqin, 8 May 2007.
13. Jacka (2008) writes of a similar project for promoting women's political participation initiated by the Shaanxi-based NGO WestWomen, and observes that such projects may not have a transformative effect on gender relations. The difficulties experienced by the two women and narrated here would seem to offer some qualified support to that observation, but my discussion below will suggest that these women have also experienced forms of empowerment through their encounters with the 'global'.
14. Interview with Xu Fengqin, 16 April 2007.
15. Personal correspondence, December 2006.
16. Interview with Li Huaqin, 8 May 2007.
17. Personal correspondence, October 2009.
18. Interview with Li Huaqin, 8 May 2007.
19. Interview with Xu Fengqin, 16 April 2007.
20. Interview with Wang Liancheng, 17 April 2007.
21. Apparently, county government officials were initially concerned about Xu's project and the publicity surrounding it following the publication of the *Philanthropy Times* article, but county committee members 'met to affirm Xu's achievements' in the wake of the article's publication (interview with Wang Liancheng, 17 April 2007).
22. Yongnian Zheng (2008: 119) finds that because the Internet in China has enabled its users to 'access information and communicate with other people despite the often tight control on the part of the government . . . social members can no longer be atomized by the government but are able to form voluntary groups'.
23. See the website at http://www.nvcunguan.org/. The extent to which rural women village

leaders can actually access and use such a website is unclear – for instance, as of spring 2007, Li Huaqin did not have a computer in her home.

24. Xiaoling Zhang (2007: 77) finds that local media currently do not generally contribute to democratic discourses, but that they do 'open possibilities for fostering local people's notions of citizenship and for them to engage in and deliberate upon public affairs', including helping to raise 'people's awareness of such issues as accountability and transparency'.

25. Interview with Xu Fengqin, 16 April 2007.

26. Interview with Qinglong County Women's Federation officials, 16 April 2007. Judd (2002) examines the benefits but more the limitations of the 'Two Studies, Two Competitions' (*shuangxue, shuangbi*) programme at length; see also Jacka (2006a).

27 Interview with Xu Rong, *Nongjianü* programme officer, 14 May 2007. The relationship between the Women's Federation and *Nongjianü* is more complex that some of these assertions may make it seem; in fact, Xie Lihua, *Nongjianü*'s head, is also an associate editor at *Zhongguo Funü Bao*, the newspaper of the Women's Federation. However, *Nongjianü* does constitute a largely autonomous organization.

28. This sentiment is echoed in the words of Li Guimin, one of the leaders of the Women's Health Support Small Groups created by Xu's organization, who told Xie Lihua that changes in her village were the result of the activities of both *Nongjianü* and Xu's Health Promotion Association, and that the Women's Federation needs to reform or else it 'cannot do anything worthwhile' (Xie 2006b).

29. According to Article 22 of the Constitution of the All-China Women's Federation (2003), the village Women's Committee, which is the lowest representative body of the Women's Federation, should consist of a head, deputy head, and an unspecified number of committee members. In practice, most villages have a village Women's Committee head, but few have a functioning committee.

30. Interview with Li Huaqin, 8 May 2007.

31. Interview with Li Huaqin, 8 May 2007.

32. For instance, China's 'New Left' does discuss the increase in inequality in the reforms. Sometimes such critiques are suppressed, as in the case of Chen Guidi and Wu Chuntao's book *Will the Boat Sink the Water?* (2006).

33. Interview with Xie Lihua, 17 June 2009.

34. Interview with Xu Fengqin, 18 June 2009; personal correspondence October 2009.

9. Myths and realities: gender and participation in a donor-aided project in northern China

Yang Lichao

INTRODUCTION

Over the last two decades, both 'gender mainstreaming' and participatory approaches have shaped the goals and methods adopted in donor-aided development projects in China. This study explores one such project, conducted from 2002 to 2006 in north-western Inner Mongolia. Drawing on my own experience working on the project in the last two years of its implementation, I examine how far and in what ways gender and participation were incorporated into project policies, procedures and activities, and use the project as a case study to explore the political, institutional and cultural constraints affecting the gender outcomes of participatory approaches to development in the Chinese context.

The chapter contains five sections: It begins with a general review of the evolution of participatory approaches to gender issues in development, and explains how participation has become a discursive 'orthodoxy' in China. The second section outlines the background of the project and the gender aims, policies and implementation procedures set out in project documents. The third provides an ethnographic account of three episodes illustrating the extent to which participatory approaches were applied to achieve the project's gender equity aims in project interventions. The fourth section analyses the gender outcomes of the project, focusing specifically on why and how participatory project planning and activities were constrained by local political, institutional and cultural processes. The final section draws a brief conclusion.

This study does not mean to make an evaluation or a negative judgement on a specific project, nor does it aim to explain outcomes in terms of design or recommend solutions to problems. Rather, its interest is, first, to explore the political processes through which the project and, specifically, its interventions into gender relations came to be designed and implemented in the way they did, and second, to unravel the links between gendered institutions and practice in project villages.

GENDER AND PARTICIPATORY APPROACHES IN DEVELOPMENT DISCOURSE

During the past several decades, the terms 'women in development (WID)' and 'gender and development (GAD)' have been widely used in development thinking and practice. The term 'women in development' was coined by a Washington-based network of female development professionals who argued that women's rights and status had deteriorated in the modernization process (Tinker 1990: 30). WID goals and methods of achieving social justice and equity for women were incorporated as mainstream development concerns during the United Nations Decade for Women from 1976 to 1985. Focusing primarily on women as a separate category, WID development approaches aimed to improve women's status by remedying women's lack of access to resources and improving their income-earning capacities and opportunities. By the late 1970s, some women's activists and development scholars had begun to question the focus on women in isolation, and criticized approaches which merely emphasized integrating women into development processes via employment (Moore 1988). They further argued that WID was based on Western ideals that are not suited to the situation in underdeveloped countries (Beetham and Demetriades 2007). In development practice, it was argued that applying WID approaches tended to oppose individual women's needs to family welfare (Razavi and Miller 1995). Meanwhile, it became widely accepted that women's subordinate status and the unequal power relations between men and women cannot be explained by relations of production between men and women alone, and that women's inequality and development needs cannot be addressed without exploring the social construction of gender. A new term 'gender and development (GAD)' was introduced in development discourse. Rather than isolating women as a special category, GAD approaches explore the nature of women's subordinated status and focus on gendered power relations. However, a practical challenge for planners and policy makers has been how to operationalize gender in development plans, policies and practices. If development projects cannot meet this challenge, the discursive shift from WID to GAD might have little impact on women's experience of development.[1]

The evolution of GAD approaches inspired a growing emphasis on applying bottom-up or participatory methods in development projects. Participation has been a core value and goal in global development thinking and practice since the 1960s. A key method used in participatory approaches to development has been Participatory Rural Appraisal (PRA), through which 'poor and exploited people can and should be enabled to analyse their own reality' (Chambers 1997: 106). The emergence of PRA was followed by a rapid growth of development activities aimed at involving marginalized groups, including women, in an investigation of their own problems, determination of their own aims and reflection on their own achievements.

Commenting on the popularity of, and indeed almost the requirement for, 'participation' to be included in development work, or at least in development agencies' rhetoric, some scholars and activists have dubbed participation the 'new orthodoxy' (Green 2000: 68) or the 'new tyranny' (Cooke and Kothari 2001). Criticisms have taken two main forms: Some have addressed the technical and methodological limitations of participatory approaches, such as PRA; others have emphasized the 'theoretical, political and conceptual limitations' of participation (Cooke and Kothari 2001). Critiques inspire innovation. Since the late 1990s, the meaning of 'participation' has been enlarged to foster a sense of greater social inclusivity among development subjects (Hickey and Mohan 2004).

Plummer (2004: 19) notes that the first participatory project introduced into China was the Yunnan Upland Management Programme, funded by the Ford Foundation in the late 1980s and early 1990s. Since then, participation as both a method and an outcome of interventions has come to be accepted almost universally as 'a good thing' (Cooke and Kothari 2001: 36) by both international and Chinese development scholars and practitioners. Although participatory approaches to development periodically have been reviewed and updated at the international level, serious and objective reviews of participatory approaches have rarely been undertaken by development professionals in China, and there is a lack of discussion of the outcomes of 'participatory' projects that is based on empirical research rather than doctrinal conceit.

International links have, however, promoted debates about participatory approaches in gender development policies and procedures among women activists in China. Over the last decade, Chinese development agencies have shifted their attention from women-specific projects to mainstreaming gender in organizational and project policies. Large international non-governmental organizations (NGOs) and donor agencies have supported numerous initiatives to promote and localize the field. For example, the Ford Foundation supported a six-year Women and Gender Studies programme from 2001 to 2006; while Oxfam has claimed to institutionalize gender mainstreaming within its organization. As a consequence, greater emphasis has been placed on working with grassroots women's

NGOs and involving women in gender planning. Most donors and NGOs use the common language of 'bottom-up' and 'participation' to mark their commitment to promoting gender equity through participatory methods. In practice, however, relatively few donors have incorporated participatory methods effectively into the gender policies, project designs and procedures that shape their development interventions. Some critics have suggested that this occurs because international donor agencies and aid projects attempt to impose their own culturally and politically inappropriate assumptions and agendas in China (Plummer and Taylor 2004a: 87); others argue that it is due to a lack of convincing case studies and systematic research, and the resulting gap between theory and practice (Plummer and Taylor 2004a: 74). Moreover, neither participation nor gender have received public recognition and political support as development issues. In this study, I will take the critique one step further by making the following arguments: First, participatory goals have not been achieved because participatory methods are inconsistent with the political processes through which donor-aided projects are implemented in China; second, so-called 'participation' and 'participatory approaches' are in fact largely controlled by government elites and development practitioners; third, project gender policies and procedures are at odds with local institutions and cultural contexts that sustain gender power relations; and fourth, there is a need to address technical constraints, including the shortage of resources and skills, in participatory gender and development projects.

PROJECT BACKGROUND AND GENDER POLICY

The Grassland Management Project (GMP) was an international donor-funded project, located in Red League[2] in the north-western part of the Inner Mongolian Autonomous Region, aimed at addressing poor ecological management and gender inequalities.[3] The area is deficient in drinking water and vulnerable to drought. Grassland degradation had been exacerbated by over-grazing and the collection of medicinal plants during the rainy season. The Red League pattern of residence is based on sedentary and dispersed herders' households. The principal pastures surrounding villages previously were farmed collectively. Cattle and sheep also were herded collectively, with neighbourhoods taking turns in providing herders. Livestock were owned by individual households, but controlled by elders and men. After the introduction of economic reforms in 1978, however, the pattern of dispersed residence and collective herding was gradually no longer possible in most areas in Red League, as increasing individual claims on collective pasture holdings led to a decline in the reliability of the collective field as a basis for subsistence. As in Han areas, Mongolian women in Red League undertook most of the housework as well as working outside with their husbands. However, income earned was held and controlled by men.

The bulk of GMP activities were intended to trial methods of sustainably managing grassland through the participatory distribution of user rights, and technical improvements to livestock raising.[4] The Project designers viewed the adaptation and implementation of user rights as a 'last chance' to reverse the destruction of the grasslands and save the Mongolian tradition of herding. It was assumed that if participating herding households were allocated enforceable user rights, they would invest in grassland maintenance. In addition, the Project sought to include women's names on user rights certificates so as to ensure their access to land.

The overseas Managing Contractor was Bright Pty Ltd, working in association with the donor government, which had built up a bilateral aid relationship with China's government over a period of 20 years. The Chinese implementing agency was the Animal Husbandry Bureau (AHB) of the municipal government in Red Capital, the capital city of Red League. The Project involved cooperation between the overseas team and the Project Management Office (PMO), which was physically located in the AHB. The Chinese Project Director, the Vice-Director of the AHB, came under the authority of the city Vice-Mayor responsible for agriculture. The overseas team was appointed by the Managing Contractor and located in the PMO. The Board of Directors included the Chinese Project Director, the overseas Team Leader, the Community Development Expert and the Grassland Management Expert in the overseas team.

The donor agency had a long-standing practice of incorporating gender policy and addressing gender issues in all its development projects by 'improving the involvement of women in community participation' (GMP 2005: 27). According to design documents, the GMP aimed to conduct a series of activities to promote women's participation in public affairs in order to reduce gender inequality. The most important of these involved the provision of revolving microcredit to help women herders and farmers develop small businesses. Primary capital was issued to borrowers' groups in each village. Loans were granted on an eight-month cycle at a very low interest rate, and were to be used directly on income-generating activities. When repaid, the loans would be re-allocated to other women members of the groups.[5] The project also sought to create an enabling environment for women to participate in the user rights allocation process so they could play a larger role in land management. For example, the 2005 Annual Plan stated that 'women have equal rights with men to become involved in the grassland user rights allocation process . . . Women's names should be included in user rights certificates' (GMP 2005: 24). Other participatory activities included technical training and agricultural extension activities, women's participation in public affairs, village meetings and community governance. Through participation and demonstration, non-herding families as well as rich and poor herders, men and women, were to be introduced to alternative farming practices and income-generating activities. According to the design, about 350 women, especially poor women in project activity areas, were to be involved in a variety of training courses and revolving microcredit schemes.

A second gender objective of the project was to build the local partner's gender awareness and capacity. GAD training was provided for the Women's Federation of Red League. The project also cooperated with the Women's Federation of Red Capital. Women's Federation members took part in the main project activities, building connections between village leaders and project staff and carrying out day-to-day project work. During the course of the GMP, reporting was disaggregated by gender, and adjustments were made to the participatory procedures used to achieve gender objectives. The GMP Annual Plan in 2005, for example, recommended conducting separate meetings for smaller groups of women and men to ensure that education would be imparted first hand (GMP 2005: 36).

Project activities were conducted in villages in Left Banner. The election of Community Management Committees at the *aili* (natural village) level was intended to promote community participation in grassland monitoring and management. The responsibilities of the Community Management Committee, including organizing community meetings and facilitating project implementation, were clearly articulated and the committee regulations required women's participation. Participatory strategies were reviewed by the project's Board of Directors and villagers' representatives who were not members of the Community Management Committee. Women's participation was, at least formally, ensured through the organization of meetings. For example, in the needs assessment meeting held in the village of Baima in March 2006, participants were divided into four groups comprising men from poor, middle-income and better-off households, and women, and the priorities identified by the women differed from those articulated by the men's groups.

In summary, the GMP attempted to incorporate gender into participatory goals, policies, procedures and activities. As such, the project is illustrative of a wider trend in rural development interventions in China. But what happened in practice? Below, I describe instances of so-called 'participatory' interventions, discuss the political processes through which the project was organized and implemented, and explore the links between local gendered institutions and development practices in the GMP.

WOMEN'S PARTICIPATION IN PRACTICE

Ethnographic snapshots of three episodes involving encounters between project staff and women illustrate how women's participation in the project was mediated by staff's assumptions about the limited development potential of rural women and their lack of training in working from either a GAD or participatory perspective.

Episode 1: The Internal Project Meeting

It is a dry and hot Monday in July, 2005. A black marble stele has stood at the gate of the Animal Husbandry Bureau (AHB) for three years. It is carved with the words 'Grassland Management Project' in English, Chinese and Mongolian, and the national emblems of China and the donor country are sculpted on top. Behind the stele is the five-storied AHB building. The project offices are located on the fourth and fifth floors of this building, where the overseas team representing the donor agency and its domestic partner, the PMO, work together.

At 9:30am, the regular monthly meeting gets underway. Apart from me, the only other female present identifies herself as Liu, the Gender and Development Coordinator. The other six PMO staff are Community Development Officers, and Animal Husbandry and Grassland Technicians. The foreign team consists of a Team Leader, a Community Development Expert and a Policy Adviser. I am introduced as the new project officer of the foreign team.

Liu speaks first. She explains the microcredit activities conducted in Baima village. Small loans were given to women 10 months ago. Most borrowers wanted to raise pigs. Seven women from Baima had a field visit to a state farm in Left Banner where, for the past decade, the Women's Federation has been promoting women's pig raising activities. A village Women's Federation director, who is a successful pig breeder, offered training and advice to the women from Baima, and ten women subsequently bought landrace breed piglets from the state farm at a cost of about 370 yuan per pair. Three pairs of piglets cost about 1100 yuan, which was the maximum loan available to each borrower. Using feed concentrates, piglet fattening is expected to take 150 days, instead of the usual one and a half years. The potential profit per head is estimated to be at least 300 yuan, according to the trainer in Left Banner.

However, Liu complains that it has been extremely hard to get the last round of borrowers to repay their loans. A woman named Qiqige used the money to pay for her son's surgery instead of raising pigs as she had intended, and therefore has no money to return. The other women feel that, because Qiqige has defaulted, they should not be required to repay either, so none of the borrowers have returned the money. But according to Liu, this is just an excuse. In fact, most women did not manage to sell their pigs. Some of the pigs were kept for family consumption, and a few women bought more sows to generate more income. Liu says, 'The women refused to admit that they have made money from raising pigs. Most of the local women are illiterate. It is useless to explain the project to them. Their quality (*suzhi*) is so poor!'

Episode 2: The Participatory Village Consultative Meeting

It is a Monday morning in September, 2005. A village consultative meeting is being held in Baima Central Meeting Hall. After a long dry summer, the landscape is scrubbed clean by the return of rain. The wind and mild sunshine are withering the grassland. It is the start of autumn. At 10:00am, the project land cruiser arrives at Baima. People continue gathering in the yard. By 10:45am, about 45 villagers are in the meeting hall, including 15 women, some of whom have babies in their arms. This means attendance is better than usual. There are two project officials: Luo and myself.

Luo speaks first. He explains that the project goal is to reduce poverty and improve local people's livelihoods. Therefore, it is important to organize training to enhance their capability and technical skills. The goal of today's meeting is the participatory selection of training courses for all villagers in Baima. First, the villagers will identify their needs, and then they will select and prioritize a certain number of training courses together.

As the hamlet is relatively small, only men's and women's discussion groups are organized, instead of the usual 'better-off, middle income, poor and women's groups'. Men are divided into two groups. All of the women form one group. Each group is allocated a small white board, a pen and some brown paper. I remain with the women and spend several minutes learning their names.

'What are we doing today?' A young woman named Saiyin asks Rula, across me.

'I don't know. Maybe they will send us to Tongliao to learn how to raise pigs'. Rula giggles and rocks the baby in her arms. All the women look at me, expecting an answer.

'We want to know what problems there are in the village, what you want to learn to solve the problems,' I answer, 'For example, the grazing ban will be applied from next year, which means you cannot raise as many cattle and sheep by next spring as you do now. How will you maintain or improve your livelihood if you have to reduce animal numbers?'

'Oh yes, my husband will have to go out to find a job', says Rula.

'What can he do outside the village?' I ask.

'I think he will go to Changchun. His uncle is a builder there, he will get him a job on the construction site', she says with certainty.

'But what will you do while your husband is away?' I look at her, expecting an answer such as 'raise pigs', 'sew', or 'be a hairdresser'.

Rula sighs, lowers her head and grumbles: 'I will look after our 15 sheep, five goats, our daughters and one-year-old son, my mother-in-law who is blind and my 90-year-old grandmother-in-law alone, alone . . .'. She drags the last syllable out in a long, woeful tone.

The baby bursts out crying. Rula unbuttons her coat and suckles her son. There is a significant pause in the conversation. Two women leave to prepare the lunch to feed the project officials after the meeting.

'What do you wish to learn to improve your life?' I turn to the rest of the women and break the silence.

'My fiancé wants to be a driver; can you send him to learn driving?' Saiyin responds.

A woman next to her laughs, 'She is asking what you want to learn. Don't always think of the men. Women have the right to participate too. But I have to ask a question beforehand – does the project bear all the costs for the training?' I confirm that it does. Then she says that she wants to learn about bookkeeping. Two years previously, she borrowed from the microcredit project and says that if she knew how to keep accounts, she might run her small mill better. The speaker is Chunhua, a 40-year-old widow. Chunhua holds the distinction of being the most successful miller in the whole area.

I hand Chunhua the pen, asking her to write down her idea.

'But I can't write!' protests Chunhua. She passes the pen to Saiyin. Saiyin asks, 'What should I write?'

'Bookkeeping, and the things you want to learn. What you want to know,' replies Chunhua.

'Hairdressing!' says Saiyin. 'How to raise pigs!' says another woman, and the idea is echoed by several women. Rula says that she knows a woman who is an expert at pig raising and now successfully runs her own business in Tongliao. 'Maybe we can invite her to teach us', says Rula. Many women pick up on the idea. There is excitement in the air as the conversation turns to using microcredit loans to buy piglets and learning how to raise them. The enthusiasm spreads. Saiyin holds the pen and writes on the white board:

- bookkeeping (1)
- hairdressing (2)
- pig raising (5)

The number following each item indicates the number of women who want to learn it.

Luo comes from the other groups. He reads the list and frowns. 'Who wants to learn bookkeeping?' he asks, standing above the group of women, who remain seated on long benches.

Chunhua immediately responds.

'But can you read and write? If not, how will you get the information you need? I am afraid you have to think about that. It is impossible to learn bookkeeping if you do not know how to read.' Luo is not at all nervous when he talks to Chunhua, who gets frustrated by his words.

'Who wants to learn hairdressing?' Luo continues to ask.

No one answers.

Luo turns to me for an answer. I look away. He says, 'Don't be nervous to express yourself in public – actually I am going to say that hairdressing is a very good idea. But I am worried that there are only two people who want to learn it. It is generally very hard to organize a course for less than eight people. Let's see if the other two groups have similar intentions.'

'Do you mean we have to do the whole thing again then?' Chunhua stares at Luo, bravely I think.

'Yes, do it again.' Luo declares. 'Be practical. All training will be organized in the Left County Vocational Education School; but the school does not offer all courses. I have a list of recommended courses. Yang, please make sure that people select within that scope. You have five minutes to do it.' He gives me a note which lists five courses. Then he leaves to look in on the other discussion groups.

Chunhua walks off. Saiyin refuses to write anymore, and no one else wants to act as the group's scribe. Rula tells me to write down the first three courses listed in the note:

- driving
- motorcycle repair
- cooking

The other two groups come back and people all gather in the meeting hall. The three groups' lists are written in thick black markers on the brown paper. The men have lists almost identical to the women's:

- motorcycle repair
- driving
- veterinary
- cooking

The men's list becomes the joint men's and women's choices, and it is recorded as the participatory village training course selection priorities.

People disperse, and two women come in with the food they have been preparing for us.

Episode 3: The Meeting on the Second Round of Microcredit in Tala

I've come back to my hotel room late at night. Xiang, the Community Development Expert of the overseas team, and Liu, have just arrived back at the hotel after attending a microcredit meeting in Tala, another project village. I invite Liu to share a room with me in order to save her costs, as PMOs need to pay for food and accommodation from their per diem allowances.

Liu looks tired. After she moves to my room, I ask her how the meeting went. She says it was disappointing. The purpose of the meeting was to reorganize the microcredit groups using participatory approaches and help the borrowers to set up small businesses. The borrowers who did not return the loans from the first round, most of whom came from the poorest households in the village, were still invited to attend the meeting, although they were excluded from applying for loans in the second cycle. Two came, but they sat in the corner and listened without even raising their heads.

Liu complains that Xiang's speech was too long and boring. Xiang tried to explain theories of microfinance and the ideal of participatory approaches to the women, many of whom were illiterate. His speech lasted almost two hours and by the time he concluded, more than half of the women had left the meeting. Consequently, they failed to reorganize the groups of loan recipients because people had gone home.

Liu says: 'The time was also a problem. The meeting started at 7:30pm to allow most people to come after dinner. But I didn't expect Xiang to give such a long speech. By the time we got to the main points, it was too late to move on. At 8:30, several men came to collect their wives and mothers.'

'Actually, it was much better when I ran the first cycle of lending by myself', Liu claims: 'I didn't know much either about finance or about theories of participation. I just lived in the village for a week, chatting and working with the women. So eventually I formed a close personal relationship with them. Of course they are willing to pay attention to what I talk about and do', she explains proudly, her eyes blinking in the darkness.

'I guess people were bored with writing with coloured markers on the white board too', Liu says. 'Several women asked whether we could skip that section in today's meeting. They were more interested in how to apply for the loan and how much they could borrow in this second cycle.'

RETHINKING GENDER AND WOMEN'S PARTICIPATION IN THE PROJECT

These encounters are illustrative of how the day-to-day implementation of gender and participatory development projects in rural China is influenced by a complex constellation of political, institutional and cultural factors. Episode 1 exemplifies a project worker's elitist interpretation of how individual repayment defaults arising from women's lack of cultural capital result in collective default. However, the design of the microcredit scheme failed to establish a relationship between individual and collective borrowers within the community. As no sanctions were applied to defaulters or the community as a whole, there was no peer pressure to repay. Technical deficiencies, rather than women's shortcomings, were the real reason for the failure of the microcredit scheme. Episode 2 provides a powerful illustration of gender relations within the family and community. It demonstrates how women were socialized to identify as 'mothers' and 'wives' and accept their subordinate status in the village. As with the meeting on the second round of microcredit narrated in Episode 3, the 'participatory consultative meeting' reflected and reproduced local gendered power relations and hierarchies of knowledge. In both events, Chinese officials, including the GMP officials and experts, interacted as though they were following directives issued by upper level organizations or government rather than facilitating a 'bottom-up' process of needs assessment and resource allocation. Indeed, GMP officials negatively influenced gender roles and power relations in public decision-making processes: By ignoring women's choice of training courses, the elitist officials treated the community as a closed patriarchal system, and women as subordinate categories confined by strict notions of gendered divisions of labour and power. Women's knowledge and needs were not acknowledged, much less valued by men and the officials involved in the project. Moreover, as illustrated in Episode 3, the microcredit scheme not only excluded some relatively poor women who had defaulted on their loans, but also subjected them to the humiliation of having to participate in subsequent discussions about the scheme, further diminishing their standing in the community.

How can we explain these failures? In what follows, I argue that China's political processes, a disconnect between participatory theory and practice in GAD projects, and local cultural and institutional contexts impede the implementation of participatory methods.

The Effect of Political Processes

Since the 1980s, 'foreign-aid projects' have been viewed by China's leadership as a means of raising funds for social and economic development in areas where there is limited local revenue to invest in development. However, the Communist Party and government do not view 'foreign-aid programmes' as a preferable source of development funds. The state's main concern is that international aid projects import 'Western' values and concepts into China, thereby threatening social cohesion and social stability. Although a 'rights' discourse is now evident in China, the state still considers 'rights defence', including defence of villagers' 'land rights', 'women's rights' and 'human rights', as potentially destabilizing. Public participation in decision making similarly is viewed as potentially problematic. Therefore, on one hand, the central government has encouraged aid donors to 'contribute to social development and harmony'. On the other hand, donors' project designs and methods of implementation are subject to stringent regulation and oversight. Project design, organizational involvement, methodology and activities must all be approved by a Party or government agency. And all aid projects must 'cooperate' with a government or Party agency which supervises and works with the project team in the field. As officials in supervising agencies are held responsible for ensuring that the projects comply with regulatory requirements, and their performance evaluation and consequent promotion and salary prospects can be affected by project compliance and the extent to which projects promote local economic growth, their cooperation tends to be contingent on the project containing easily achievable, economically quantifiable targets and no political risk. Without official cooperation, the project cannot be implemented. Moreover, if the project is approved, it can only be implemented within the local cooperating agencies' administrative jurisdictions. As funding is tied to individual project activities as set out in the original design documents, project staff have little incentive or opportunity to make strategic changes to development plans, procedures or activities.

The GMP, like other donor-aided development projects, required the support of local state agencies. Support was conditional on three things. First, a relationship between the project and local government had to be established through introductions from higher level government. Second, the project had to operate under the guidance and supervision of the cooperating government. Third, the project had to conduct activities that were in the political and/or economic interests of local government. To gain cooperation from local government and the Women's Federation in Red League, the terms 'women's rights', 'right to participate' and, especially, 'human rights' were avoided in the GMP design, policies and training work. Having secured cooperation from the League government, the project worked with staff from the AHB at League level and the Women's Federation at county level to get permission to implement rural development activities in villages.

The objective of the League agencies in cooperating with the project was primarily to obtain donor funding. In addition to officials' instrumental approach to the project, to some extent the GMP also was constrained by staff capacity. PMO members were seconded from their respective state agencies to temporary positions as project staff. They generally lacked the education, skills, and, in particular, the attitudes necessary to carry out their roles in project implementation. They were trained to grasp community development theories within a very short time, and rarely understood and accepted participatory development concepts. For example, at the first stage of project implementation, PMO members were sent to a three-day workshop on 'Gender and Development'. Training in 'participation' and 'microcredit' was of similarly limited duration. Nor could the attitudes required to gain women's participation in project design and implementation be imposed. This was reflected, for example, in Luo's dismissal of the training needs identified by the women in the meeting at Baima. Project officials kept their bureaucratic work habits, and focused on the achievement of quantifiable targets, sidestepping thorny problems in project implementation, and writing reports highlighting the completion of designated tasks. Thus, they paid little attention to generating new ideas and ways of working. Moreover, when the GMP funding ended, the project was dissolved and there was no further direct engagement of the officials who had held responsibility for the areas of Project activity. Similar political constraints can be observed in other donor-funded development projects across China.

Theory and Participatory Practice in the GMP

According to Chambers, a key proponent of participatory approaches to development, there is a divide among rural development academics and practitioners. Whereas academics are trained to analyse and criticize rural development practices, practitioners rarely draw on those critiques to improve their practice (Chambers 1983: 30). In China, however, there has been little communication between practitioners and academics in the development field. There is a limited pool of domestic community development experts, and most of those experts work as full-time scholars and part-time development consultants. As scholars, they have no incentive to criticize their own work when putting participatory theories and methods into practice. Consequently, there has been little effort to improve 'participatory practice' since the concept was first introduced into China.

The disconnect between theory and practice was evident in the GMP. The project's Institutional Development Expert was absent throughout the final two years of project implementation because, as one of the most well-known academic experts on participatory approaches in China, he was engaged elsewhere. The 'foreign' Community Development Expert, Xiang, worked with great passion to share his theories with villagers. However, as an 'expert' he failed to listen to local voices and value local knowledge. Instead, as shown in his lecture on microcredit in Tala, by treating villagers like students, rather than equal participants, he failed to transmit information in a manner that would enable women to secure loans. PMO staff had little understanding of participatory practices and, following criteria given in the Chinese 'Community Participation Ladder', rated merely 'notifying' villagers of decisions reached by the PMO as a form of participation.[6]

Hence, women's involvement in project activities was particularly limited. At the Village Consultative Meeting in Baima, PMOs applied some participatory tools in conducting group discussions to identify villagers' needs and training preferences. However, the 'decisions' which were supposed to be reached through the 'participatory decision-making process' actually were pre-determined by the limited resources available, which already reflected a prioritization of skills typically sought and used by men, such as motorcycle repair and driving. By devaluing women's knowledge and skills and dismissing their training preferences as unrealistic, Luo reinforced gendered hierarchies of expertise. And, despite my own commitment to gender equality, I felt uneasy about imposing concepts of gender equality and participatory appraisal on local women.

The practical difficulties in applying participatory approaches to gender issues in international development are widely recognized (see for example, Mosse 2001). Operational limits certainly constrained the GMP. Nevertheless, the constraints on participatory practice in the project went far beyond the kinds of technical problems commonly found elsewhere, because of the attitudes and limited training, skills and resources of PMO staff. In 2004 the GMP appointed a gender officer, Liu, from among the staff of the AHB in order to promote gender equality and women's status more effectively. Liu was encouraged to work closely with local women in project villages to develop their understanding of, and participation in the microcredit scheme. However, Liu received only limited training in gender-awareness and microcredit management. Although committed to enhancing women's access to and use of credit, she was therefore poorly equipped to perform her role. Consequently, when women in Baima refused to repay their loans, she was unable to recognize the complex cultural, institutional and material factors contributing to their actions and attributed their loan default to the women's 'poor quality'. Nor, in the absence of support from Xiang, the Community Development Expert, was she able to propose alternative strategies to enable repayment and loan circulation. Moreover,

Liu complained that her work was 'the least important' component of the project. Her Director lacked interest in her work, her male colleagues were antagonistic to gender issues, and the budget and time allocated to work on gender issues were often cut. Because of the political, conceptual and operational limitations on the project, marginalized women received little practical assistance from microcredit or the allocation of user rights.

Gender and Participation in Cultural and Institutional Context

The gender participatory outcomes of the GMP were shaped not just by political processes and operational constraints, but also by local cultural and institutional limitations to participatory thinking and practice. The following discussion takes as examples the allocation of land user rights and the circulation of microcredit loans, to explore how local norms influenced gender practices during the GMP.

As in Han society, Mongolian marriage typically is exogamous and virilocal. Marrying and moving to their husbands' villages, women gradually lose close contact with their kin and social networks in their natal village. Household property usually is registered under the names of husbands, and few married women have registered rights to land or other assets. In cases of marital breakdown, land rights are not allocated to wives unless they are elderly. Divorced Mongolian women are among the most marginalized people in villages. Given the disadvantages confronting rural women divorcees, it is not surprising that divorce is still comparatively uncommon. Lin Zhibin (2007: 64) and others claim that the virilocal system is a fundamental cause of women's low social status and political participation, whilst scholars elsewhere have argued that the distribution of land-use rights to households is another important factor contributing to unequal gender relations (Gouthami and Rajgor 2008).

One of the main goals of the GMP was to enhance women's roles in agricultural production through the allocation of user rights. For example, Item 9 of the Constitution of the Herder's Shareholder Cooperative for Grassland Management and Development, developed by GMP project workers, states, 'the grassland will be allocated in priority to the women who married into this community and the newly born children' (GMP 2004: 2). However because the Constitution considered the shareholder unit to be an indivisible household, the project failed to require that women's names be included on certificates of land user rights.

In most project villages, women were included in discussions about allocation principles and the distribution of user rights certificates. Their participation in these activities was intended to foster their confidence and ability to speak in public, and acknowledge their role as members of, and producers in, the community.[7] Certainly, in the process of user rights allocation, some women did gain an understanding of women's land rights. As Chen, a woman in Tala Aili said:

> At the beginning [of the project], the women in our village identified grassland degradation as a major issue affecting our lives. Over time, we felt that there was a problem in that while you were doing the work on grassland restoration . . . men controlled the land, and I think this needed to be addressed . . . We feel that land should be women's land as well.

However, despite women's increasing awareness of their land rights, their ability to secure access to land was constrained by many factors. One of those factors was the political sensitivity associated with land rights' distribution in China. The Red Capital government closely scrutinized the user rights schemes, to ensure that laws relating to land ownership and use were not infringed during the allocation of use-rights to households. In the process, however, officials actually strengthened the patriarchal organization of unitary households by transferring land user rights to men, justifying women's subordination and restriction to the home. A deputy governor of Left Banner,[8] Liu, explained that 'It is usually this way in village governance – few women can communicate in Mandarin and most of them are illiterate, they should stay at home . . . Land issues have been men's topics'. Thus, the different ways that government officials treated men and women reflected local political processes and officials' stereotypical views of Mongolian village women. Given that both officials and village men considered the inclusion of women's names on user rights certificates to be culturally contentious, it is unlikely that this proposal would have been generated by participatory needs assessments in the communities, or by government fiat. Land rights are central to the realization of gender equality in rural China. But gender relations in land rights cannot be satisfactorily addressed within the time frame of a five-year donor-funded project or, in the absence of extended gender-awareness training for both men and women, by participatory approaches.

In the Red League, as in most areas of rural China, women rarely are entrusted to play important economic roles in public. By providing revolving loans to women to establish small businesses, the GMP aimed to assist women in improving their incomes, enhance their status in their households, participate in a broader range of social activities and, thus, empower them over the longer term. However, as Liu explained at the internal project meeting in 2005, in Baima a large portion of microcredit was used for consumption and emergency welfare rather than productive investment. In attributing loan defaults to rural women's 'poor quality',

Liu repeated an elitist discourse that has been propagated by governments and the Women's Federation, and which works against the promotion of rural women's self-confidence and entrepreneurship. The practical challenges posed by providing microcredit to the poorest members in Baima were overlooked, as were the obstacles preventing those women from repaying their loans. Further inquiries revealed two additional problems. First, although the loans were intended for women, like other household income they largely ended up in the hands of men. Among the 15 female loan borrowers interviewed, 13 said that the money eventually came under men's control. Rula confided that, of the 1000 yuan she received,

> I gave 800 yuan to my husband so that he could return to the construction site where he works in Tongliao . . . The money could be spent on any family members who are not eligible to access loans. Giving the money to my husband is normal because he can bring money back and make the repayment.

Saiyin, a widow supporting three children, gave the loan she received to her 18-year-old son to establish a small shop. When he could not manage the repayments, Saiyin drew on her profits from herding to return the loan. She explained: 'I want to create an opportunity for my son to learn to make a living. Also, I am too busy with domestic and herding responsibilities to run the shop, so I gave the money to my son'.

The second problem was that, as loans were issued at fixed intervals, they were not always available when women most needed them. Therefore, to invest in production or to meet urgent consumption needs at other times during the year, women borrowed from neighbours or relatives and repaid their debts when they subsequently received loans from the microcredit scheme. As one of the poorer women explained:

> We can get loans only in March because it is the season to buy lambs and calves. But I don't need the money in spring because I don't want to increase animal numbers. Rather, I may need it in January to buy fodder . . . I cannot get it from the project so I have to borrow from my brother.

These case studies demonstrate that microcredit schemes require critical attention to who actually controls the money and how loans function within households and production cycles. Women in the project areas were not able to control income, investment and expenditure within their households. Irrespective of their receipt of loans, they were still expected to conform to traditional gender roles and perform household tasks. Male power and resource control largely remained untouched. Consequently, in the short term the GMP income-generating activities only entailed women bearing extra responsibility for debt and workloads, while loan defaulters' attendance at microcredit meetings exposed them to disapproval from fellow villagers and PMO staff.

CONCLUSION

Rural women in Inner Mongolia depend on the grasslands for their livelihoods. In the initial stages of the GMP, women were very concerned about environmental degradation, but through the process of project implementation, local women came to realize that grassland degradation was not the only issue affecting their lives. Although there was little evidence that the project had achieved its aims with regard to assisting women to meet their practical needs, there was some sign that the project improved women's gender consciousness, their understanding of their land rights and selfesteem. In Baima and Tala, for example, women realized that they were more capable than they had thought, and should enjoy land rights and more respect from their husbands and families. After project completion, a few young women from Baima and Tala went to work in neighbouring towns and cities. Women were very keen to acquire knowledge and experiences that would generate income and a broader perspective on gender relationships.

However, as discussed above, achievement of the GMP goals, of using participatory approaches to improve the livelihoods of the rural poor and improve women's participation in public affairs, was hampered by a range of factors. At the most superficial level of analysis, it is clear that the attitudes and capacities of local officials, project workers and local people impeded women's participation. To improve the outcomes of projects such as these, much greater investment needs to be made in staff training, and in gender and public awareness campaigns. Few single resource management projects have sufficiently large budgets to cover these costs. Therefore, support from government is essential to bring about the fundamental attitudinal changes necessary for the success of participatory GAD projects.

At a broader level, women's participation in foreign-funded rural development projects remains constrained by China's political processes, the gap between theory and participatory practice, and local cultural and institutional contexts. Without fundamental changes in each of these areas, women's participation in rural development cannot be ensured. Recent research points out that state institutions play an important role in advancing women's position and in enabling women's economic and political participation. Over the past few decades, the Chinese government has drawn on ideological, legislative and institutional measures to shape gender norms and values, and women's economic, social and political status has greatly improved (Howell 2008). However, dominant top-down approaches and patterns of male dominance in state institutions continue to set key limitations to women's empowerment. At all government levels, women are placed in less important positions. In the Red League government, for example, in 2005 only 5 per cent of leadership positions were occupied by women.[9] This phenomenon of women's under-participation widely exists at the national, provincial, county and township levels as well as in Village Committees and village Party Branches (Howell 2008).

Efforts to overcome gender inequality also need to take account of local political processes and values. As this study has demonstrated, the GMP attempted to promote women's participation in decision making in households and communities. However, during the five years of its implementation, the project made few gains in assisting women to participate, be heard, and shape their roles in families and village communities. One key reason for this failure was that there was a lack of attention paid to the policy and political barriers to women's participation, and the elitism and discriminatory gender attitudes of the officials cooperating in the project. Examples have been provided of men being given more respect, decision-making clout, resources and training opportunities than women, and of women's knowledge being discredited, and their needs and priorities ignored.

Promoting more equal gender relations requires sustained efforts by governments and society, as well as fundamental shifts in political institutions and social norms. Without a clear framework establishing what gender equality and participation are and could be in the political, institutional and cultural contexts in which development projects are formulated and implemented in China, projects cannot achieve gender equality and participation. These goals can only be achieved by understanding and adapting to the specific cultural, political and institutional contexts in the country and locality, and working, at least to some extent, to reduce the constraints imposed by those contexts.

NOTES

1. For references and a discussion of the shift from WID to GAD see Razavi and Miller (1995).
2. A league (*meng* in Pinyin) is an administrative unit in Inner Mongolia. It belongs to the prefecture level of the Chinese administrative hierarchy. Inner Mongolia is made up of leagues, which are divided into county-level divisions (banners), and then divided into township-level divisions (sumu).
3. The project discussed in this chapter was undertaken in north-western Inner Mongolia.

However, the name, Grasslands Management Project, the name of the project's managing contractor, and all local place names referred to in the chapter, are pseudonyms.

4. Grassland User Rights Allocation is a land contracting scheme under which herders acquire land contracting rights for grazing on collective land. Under the scheme, land users acquire land-use rights without being required to pay any fees to the government. The community sets a fixed term for land-use rights, issuing licenses to herders' households to graze on collective pasture on a rotational grazing basis.

5. It is worth mentioning here that the microcredit scheme conducted by the GMP was distinct from credit-based group-lending schemes. The latter make use of borrowers' community standing as collateral for loans. For example, if one borrower defaults, the loans will be cut off to the whole community and the individual defaulter will become very unpopular. See Duffy-Tumasz (2009: 248) for further discussion.

6. The ladder of community participation in China includes notification, attendance, expression, discussion, decision making and initiative/self-management. See Plummer and Taylor (2004b: 42).

7. See Arun (1999) for further discussion.

8. Left Banner is one of the banners of the Red League.

9. Interview, League Women's Federation, 2005.

References

Adam, Barbara (1995), *Timewatch: The Social Analysis of Time*, Cambridge: Polity Press.

Agarwal, Bina (1997), '"Bargaining" and gender relations: within and beyond the household', *Feminist Economics*, **3** (1), 1–51.

Ahlers, Anna and Gunter Schubert (2009), '"Building a new socialist countryside" – only a political slogan?' *Journal of Current Chinese Affairs*, **38** (4), 35–62.

Aikman, Sheila and Elaine Unterhalter (2005), *Beyond Access: Transforming Policy and Practice for Gender Equality in Education*, London: Oxfam.

All China Women's Federation (2003), *The Constitution of the All China Women's Federation*, available at: http://www.women.org.cn/zhuanti/9da/dhwj/zhangchengzongze.htm (accessed 28 January 2011).

Anderson-Levitt, Kathryn (2004), 'Reading lessons in Guinea, France and the US', *Comparative Education Review*, **48** (2), 229–253.

Anhui People's Congress (APC) (2004), 'Anhui sheng jinzhi fei yixue xuyao jianding tai'er xingbie he xuanze xingbie zhongzhi renshen de guiding' [Anhui province regulation on the prohibition of foetal sex identification and sex-selective termination of pregnancy for non-medical purposes], Public announcement number 12 of the APC, available at: http://www.chinacourt.org/flwk/show1.php?file_id=93465 (accessed 1 January 2010).

Anhui Population and Family Planning Commission (APFPC) (2002), 'Anhui sheng renkou yu jihua shengyu tiaoli' [Population and family planning regulations of Anhui province].

Arnove, Robert F. and Carlos Alberto Torres (eds) (2003), *Comparative Education: The Dialectic of the Global and the Local* (2nd edition), Lanham, MD: Rowman & Littlefield.

Arun, Shoba (1999), 'Does land ownership make a difference? Women's roles in agriculture in Kerala, India', *Gender and Development*, **7** (3), 19–27.

Attané, Isabelle and Christophe Guilmoto (2007), 'Introduction', in Isabelle Attané and Christophe Guilmoto (eds), *Watering the Neighbour's Garden: The Growing Demographic Female Deficit in Asia*,

Paris: Committee for International Cooperation in National Research and Demography, pp. 1–24.

Augustine-Adams, Kit (2002), '"With notice of the consequences": liberal political theory, marriage and women's citizenship', *Citizenship Studies*, **6** (1), 5–20.

Bai Lu and Du Fangqin (2009), 'Yige guangcha shijie de xin shijiao: nüxing zhuyi nanquanzhi lilun zai Zhongguo de chuanbo yu yunyong' [A new perspective on the world: the dissemination and application of feminist theories of patriarchy in China], *Jiangxi shehui kexue*, **4**, 179–185.

Banister, Judith (2004), 'Shortage of girls in China today', *Journal of Population Research*, **21** (1), 20–25.

Beaver, Patricia D., Hou Lihui and Wang Xue (1995), 'Rural Chinese women: two faces of economic reform', *Modern China*, **21** (2), 205–232.

Beetham, Gwendolyn and Justina Demetriades (2007), 'Feminist research methodologies and development: overview and practical application', *Gender and Development*, **15** (2), 199–216.

Bian, Yanjie, John R. Logan and Xiaoling Shu (2000), 'Wage and job inequalities in the working lives of men and women in Tianjin', in Barbara Entwisle and Gail Henderson (eds), *Re-drawing Boundaries, Work, Households, and Gender in China*, Berkeley: University of California Press, pp. 111–133.

Bittman, Michael and Judy Wajcman (2000), 'The rush hour: the character of leisure time and gender equity', *Social Forces*, **79** (1), 165–189.

Bossen, Laurel (1994), 'Zhongguo nongcun funü: shenme yuanyin shi tamen liu zai nong tian li?' [Chinese rural women: what keeps them down on the farm?], in Li Xiaojiang, Hong Zhu and Xiuyu Dong (eds), *Xingbie yu Zhongguo*, Beijing: SDX Joint Publishing Company, pp. 128–154.

Bossen, Laurel (2002), *Chinese Women and Rural Development: Sixty Years of Change in Lu Village*, Yunnan, Lanham, MD: Rowman & Littlefield.

Bossen, Laurel (2007a), 'Missing girls, land and population controls in rural China', in Isabelle Attané and Christophe Z. Guilmoto (eds), *Watering the Neighbour's Garden: The Growing Demographic Female Deficit in Asia*, Paris: Committee for International Cooperation in National Research in Demography, pp. 207–228.

Bossen, Laurel (2007b), 'Village to distant village: the opportunities and risks of long-distance marriage migration in rural China', *Journal of Contemporary China*, **16** (50), 97–116.

Bourdieu, Pierre (1977), *Outline of a Theory of Practice*, Cambridge: Cambridge University Press.

Bourdieu, Pierre (1986), 'The forms of capital', in John G. Richardson (ed.), *Handbook of Theory and Research for the Sociology of Education*, New York, Westport and London: Greenwood Press, pp. 241–258.

Bray, Mark (2003), 'Control of education: issues and tensions in centralization and decentralization', in Robert F. Arnove and Carlos Alberto Torres (eds), *Comparative Education: the Dialectic of the Global and the Local* (2nd edition), Lanham, MD: Rowman & Littlefield, pp. 204–228.

Bu, Wei (2004), 'An issue of bachelors' or girls' human rights?', paper presented at Workshop on Sex Ratio Imbalance (0–4 years), Beijing.

Cai, Yong and William Lavely (2007), 'Child sex ratios and their regional variation', in Zhao Zhongwei and Fei Guo (eds), *Transition and Challenge: China's Population at the Beginning of the 21st Century*, Oxford: Oxford University Press, pp. 103–123.

Care for Girls Campaign (CGC) (2006a), 'Guan'ai nühai xingdong – zhishi jingsai tiku' [The Care for Girls Campaign – a resource of knowledge], The Office of the National Expert Group of the Care for Girls Campaign, Beijing: China Population House.

Care for Girls Campaign (CGC) (2006b), 'Guan'ai nühai xingdong – gongzuo zhinan' [Operational guidelines for the Care for Girls Campaign], Beijing: China Population House.

Carnoy, Martin (1999), *Globalization and Educational Reform*, Paris: UNESCO.

Chambers, Robert (1983), *Rural Development – Putting the Last First*, Essex, UK: Longmans Scientific and Technical Publishers; New York: John Wiley & Sons.

Chambers, Robert (1997), *Whose Reality Counts? Putting the First Last*, London: Intermediate Technology Publications.

Chang, Leslie T. (2008), *Factory Girls: From Village to City in a Changing China*, New York: Speigel and Grau.

Chen Fang (2008), *Zhongguo nüxingxue lingyu yu xuewei jiaoyu* [Women's studies program and higher degree education], Zhonghua nüzi xueyuan xuebao, **20** (6), 40–45.

Chen Guidi and Tao Chun (2004), 'Zhongguo nongmin diaocha' [An investigative report on the Chinese peasantry], Beijing: Renmin Wenxue Chubanshe.

Chen, Guidi and Chuntao Wu (2006), *Will the Boat Sink the Water? The Life of China's Peasants*, New York: Public Affairs.

Chen, Hsiao-hung Nancy and Tsung-hsi Fu (2009), 'Older people's income security in China', in Tsung-hsi Fu and Rhidion Hughes (eds), *Ageing in East Asia: Challenges and Policies for the Twenty-First Century*, London: Routledge, pp. 37–53.

Chen, Lanyan (2008), *Gender and Chinese Development: Towards and Equitable Society*, London: Routledge.

Chen Shengli (2006), 'Nühai shenghuo huanjing yanjiu – guan'ai nühai xingdong jixian diaocha yanjiu baogao' [Research on living conditions of girl children – report of the baseline survey of the Care for Girls Campaign], Beijing: China Population House.

Chen, Xiwen (2009), 'Review of China's agricultural and rural development policy changes and current issues', *China Agricultural Economic Review*, **1** (2), 121–135.

Chen, Yiyun (1994), 'Out of the traditional halls of academe: exploring new avenues for research on women', in Christina Gilmarten, Gail Hershatter, Lisa Rofel and Tyrene White (eds), *Engendering China: Women, Culture, and the State*, Cambridge: Harvard University Press, pp. 69–79.

Cheng, Kai-ming (1998), 'Reforms in the administration and financing of higher education', in Michael Agelasto and Robert Adamson (eds), *Higher Education in Post-Mao China*, Hong Kong: Hong Kong University Press, pp. 11–28.

Cheng, Kai-ming (2010), 'The challenges of running the world's largest classroom', Global Asia, Summer, available at: http://globalasia.org/V5N2_Summer_2010/Cheng_Kai_ming.html

China Development Brief (2002–2003), China Contemporary Girls Research Network, www.cgedu.net 5: p. 3, available at http://www.chinadevelopmentbrief.com/.

China, Ministry of Education (2010) 'A blueprint for educational modernization – the birth of the outline of China's national plan for medium and long-term education reform and development', available at: http://202.205.177.9/edoas/en/level3.jsp?tablename=1245221141523299&infoid=1286874547640206&title=A%20Blueprint%20for%20Educational%20Modernization (accessed 22 January 2011).

China Women's News (2006), 'Restrictions and solutions: new socialist countryside construction and women's development', available at: http://www.womenofchina.cn/Issues/Politics/12413.jsp (accessed 14 May 2010).

Choe, Hyun (2003), 'National identity and citizenship in China and Korea', PhD thesis, University of California, Irvine.

Christiansen, F. and Heather X. Zhang (2009), 'The political economy of rural development in China: reflections on current rural policy', *Duisburg Working Papers on East Asian Studies*, No. 81, Duisburg, Germany: Institute of East Asian Studies, Universität Duisburg-Essen.

Chu, Junhong (2001), 'Prenatal sex determination and sex-selective abortion in rural central China', *Population and Development Review*, **27** (2), 259–281.

Chuxiong zhou Fulian (2009), 'Chuxiong zhou Fulian guanyu fuke bing chazhi gongzuo de qingkuang baogao' [Report from the Chuxiong Prefecture Women's Federation on the examination and treatment of gynecological diseases in Chuxiong Prefecture], in Yunnan sheng Fulian huibao cailiao ji (Unpublished collection), pp. 30–34.

Colclough, Christoper (1996), 'Education and the market: which parts of the neo-liberal solution are correct', *World Development*, **24** (4), 589–610.

Communist Party of China (CCP) (2007), 'Guanyu quanmian jiaqiang renkou yu jihua shengyu gongzuo tongchou jiejue renkou wenti de jueding' [Decision on fully enhancing population and family planning programmes and comprehensively addressing population issues], Central Committee of the CCP and the State Council.

Communist Party of China (CCP) (2008), 'Zhonggong Zhongyang guanyu tuijin nongcun gaige fazhan ruogan zhongda wenti de jueding' [Resolution of the Communist Party of China Central Committee on some major issues in rural reform and development], available at: http://www.gov.cn/jrzg/2008-10/19/content_1125094.htm (accessed 1 November 2008).

Cooke, Bill and Uma Kothari (eds) (2001), *Participation: The New Tyranny?* London and New York: Zed Books Ltd.

Cortina, Regina and Nelly P. Stromquist (eds) (2000), *Distant Alliances: Promoting Education for Girls and Women in Latin America*, New York: Falmer.

Costello, Marilou, Marlina Lacuesta, Saumya RamaRao and Anrudh Jain (2001), 'A client-centered approach to family planning: the Davao project', *Studies in Family Planning*, **32** (4), 302–314.

Croll, Elisabeth (2000), *Endangered Daughters: Discrimination and Development in Asia*, London: Routledge.

Datta, Rekha and Judith Kornberg (2002), 'Introduction: empowerment and disempowerment', in Rekha Datta and Judith Kornberg (eds), *Women in Developing Countries: Assessing Strategies for Empowerment*, Boulder: Lynne Rienner Publishers, pp. 1–9.

Davin, Delia (1975), 'Women in the countryside of China', in Margery Wolf and Roxane Witke (eds), *Women in Chinese Society*, Stanford: Stanford University Press.

Davis, Angela (2006), 'Mama's got the blues: Rivals, girlfriends and advisors', in Elizabeth Hackett and Sally Haslanger (eds), *Theorizing Feminisms: A Reader*, New York and Oxford: Oxford University Press, pp. 431–444.

Davis, Deborah and Stevan Harrell (eds) (1993), *Chinese Families in the Post-Mao Era*, Berkeley: University of California Press.

Davis, Sara (2005), *Song and Silence: Ethnic Revival on China's Southwest Borders*, New York: Columbia University Press.

Deem, Rosemary (1988), *Work, Unemployment and Leisure*, London: Routledge.

Diamant, Neil (2000), *Revolutionizing the Family*, Berkeley: University of California Press.

Ding Juan (2006), 'Zhongguo funü de zhengzhi canyu zhuangkuang' [The condition of Chinese women's political participation], in Tan Lin (ed.), *1995–2005 nian: Zhongguo xingbie pingdeng yu funü fazhan baogao*, Beijing: Shehui Kexue Wenxian Chubanshe, pp. 52–64.

Dongzu Jianshi Bianxiezu and Dongzu Jianshi Xiudingben Bianxiezu (eds) (2008), *Dongzu jianshi* [A brief history of the Kam], Beijing: Minzu Chubanshe.

Dongzu lüyou (2009), chat site at Dongzu lüyou sheying wang [Kam tourism photography net], available at: http://www.dongzulvyou.com/bbs (accessed 29 April 2009).

Du, Jie (2004), 'Gender and governance: the rise of new women's organizations', in Jude Howell (ed.), *Governance in China*, Lanham: Rowman & Littlefield, pp. 172–192.

Du Juan (2005), 'Mingsheng yu shengji: Lijiang Dongbazi Naxiren de shehui xingbie guannian yu xingwei fangshi' [Reputation and livelihood: gender concepts and behavioural norms among the Dongbazi Naxi people of Lijiang], in Yunnan shehui xingbie yu fazhan xiao zu (ed.), *Canyu xing fazhan zhong de shehui xingbie zhuji*, Beijing: Zhongguo Shehui Kexue Chubanshe, pp. 83–113.

Duffy-Tumasz, Amelia (2009), 'Paying back comes first: why repayment means more than business in rural Senegal', *Gender and Development*, **17** (2), 243–254.

Edwards, Louise (2007), 'Strategizing for politics: Chinese women's participation in the one-party state', *Women's Studies International Forum*, **30** (5), 380–390.

Edwards, Louise (2008), *Gender, Politics and Democracy: Women's Suffrage in China*, Stanford: Stanford University Press.

Eklund, Lisa (2009), 'Demasculinization of agriculture – exploring the impact of rural–urban migration on son preference in rural Anhui', paper presented at ECARDC IX conference, Leeds.

Enloe, C. (1990), 'Womenandchildren: making feminist sense of the Persian Gulf War', *The Village Voice*, 25 September, 29–32.

Entwisle, Barbara and Gail Henderson (2000), 'Introduction', in Barbara Entwisle and Gail Henderson (eds), *Re-drawing Boundaries, Work, Households, and Gender in China*, Berkeley: University of California Press, pp. 1–15.

Escobar, Arturo (1995), *Encountering Development: The Making and Unmaking of the Third World*, Princeton, NJ: Princeton University Press.

Evans, Harriet (2005), *Women and Sexuality in China: Dominant Discourses of Female Sexuality and Gender since 1949*, Cambridge: Polity Press.

Fan, Maureen (2007), 'In rural China, a bitter way out', *Washington Post*, 15 May, A10.

Fan Zuyin (2003), '"Zhongguo shaoshu minzu yinyue xuehui dijiu jie nianhui ji Dongzu dage yantaohui" kaimuci' [Opening remarks for 'The Ninth Annual Conference on Chinese Minority Music and the Symposium on Kam big song'], in Yang Xiuzhao and Wu Dingguo (eds), *Dongzu dage yu shaoshu minzu yinyue yanjiu – Dongzu dage yantaohui ji Zhongguo shaoshu minzu yinyue xuehui di jiujie nianhui lunwenji*, Beijing: Zhongguo Wenlian Chubanshe, pp. 4–5.

Fei Xiaotong and Zhiyi Zhang (1990), *Yunnan sancun* [Earthbound China: a study of rural economy in Yunnan], Tianjin Renmin Chubanshe.

Ferguson, James (1994), *The Anti-Politics Machine: Development, Depoliticization and Bureaucratic Power in Lesotho*, Minneapolis: University of Minnesota Press.

Fong, Vanessa L. (2004), 'China's one-child policy and the empowerment of urban daughters', *American Anthropologist*, **104** (4), 1098–1109.

Friedman, Sara L. (2006), *Intimate Politics: Marriage, the Market, and State Power in Southeastern China*, Cambridge MA and London: Harvard University Press.

Fu, Jing (2010), 'Urban-rural income gap widest since reform', *China Daily*, available at http://www.chinadaily.com.cn/china/2010-03/02/content_9521611.htm (accessed 4 February 2011).

Fujian sheng Minzhengting (2006), 'Yidian daimian zhenghe ziyuan jiji tuijin chengxiang shehui qiuzhu tixi jianshe' [Promote work in all areas and appropriate resources to actively advance construction of a system of urban and rural social relief], 6 June, available at: http://www.gov.cn/ztzl/2006-01/06/content_149681.htm (accessed 11 June 2008).

Fuzhou shi (n.d.), 'Fuzhou shi bei zhengdi nongmin xiangshou dibao' [Fuzhou city expropriated villagers receive dibao], *Zhongguo guotu ziyuan wang*, available at: http://www.clr.an/front/read/read.asp?ID =15829 (accessed 6 November 2008).

Gaetano, Arianne and Tamara Jacka (eds) (2004), *On the Move: Women in Rural to Urban Migration in Contemporary China*, New York: Columbia University.

Gaige, Mark (2008), 'Citizenship: past practices, prospective patterns', in Jose V. Ciprut (ed.), *The Future of Citizenship*, Cambridge: MIT Press, pp. 121–144.

Gao Lina (2007), 'Zhaoxing Dongzhai de baohu yu lüyou kaifa' [Protection and tourist development of Zhaoxing Kam Village], *Xiao chengzhen jianshe* **3**, 77–80.

Gao Xiaoxian (2005), 'Tuidong shehuixingbie yu fazhan bentuhua de nuli – shehui xingbie yu fazhan zai zhongguo: huigu yu fazhan wang yantaohui zongshu' [Promoting the indigenization of gender and development: a report on the Forum on Gender and Development in China: Reflections and Hopes for Development], in Gao Xiaoxian, *Zhongguo shehui zhuanxing: Nongcun funü yanjiu*, Xi'an: Shaanxi Chubanshe, pp. 240–254.

Goldstein, Harvey (2004), 'Education for all: the globalization of learning targets', *Comparative Education*, **40** (1), 7–14.

Goodman, David S.G. (2004), 'The campaign to "Open Up the West": national, provincial-level and local perspectives', *The China Quarterly*, Special Issue 5 (July), 317–334.

Gouthami and Meena Rajgor (2008), 'Women's perceptions of land ownership: a case study from Kutch District, Gujarat, India', *Gender and Development*, **16** (1), 41–54.

Grassland Management Project (GMP) (2004), 'The constitution of the herder's shareholder cooperative for grassland management and development' (unpublished).

Grassland Management Project (GMP) (2005), 'Annual plan 2005' (unpublished).

Green, Maia (2000), 'Participatory development and the appropriation of agency in southern Tanzania', *Critique of Anthropology*, **20** (1), 67–89.

Greenhalgh, Susan and Edwin Winckler (2005), *Governing China's Population: From Leninist to Neoliberal Biopolitics*, Stanford: Stanford University Press.

Greenhalgh, Susan and Jiali Li (1995), 'Engendering reproductive policy and practice in peasant China: for a feminist demography of reproduction', *Signs: Journal of Women in Culture and Society*, **20** (3), 601–641.

Gu Wenfeng (2008), 'Yi xuehui wei pingtai, tuidong miao zu shehui xingbie pingdeng' [Pushing gender equality among the Miao, using the minorities association as a platform], Yunnan Province Minorities Association Newsletter, annual (2008), p. 50.

Guilmoto, Christophe and Isabelle Attané (2007), 'The geography of deteriorating child sex ratio in China and India', in Isabelle Attané and Christophe Guilmoto (eds), *Watering the Neighbour's Garden: The Growing Demographic Female Deficit in Asia*, Paris: Committee for International Cooperation in National Research and Demography, pp. 113–134.

Guldin, Gregory E. (2001), *What's a Peasant To Do? Village Becoming Town in Southern China*, Boulder: Westview Press.

Guo, Xiajuan, Yongnian Zheng and Li Yang (2009), 'Women's participation in village autonomy in China: evidence from Zhejiang', *China Quarterly*, **197**: 145–164.

Guo, Xiangyu, Zhi-Gang Yu, Todd Schmit, Brian Henehan and Dan Li (2009), 'Evaluation of new socialist countryside development in China', *China Agricultural Economic Review*, **1** (3), 314–326.

Guo Yuhua (2001), 'Daiji guanxi zhong de gongping luoji jiqi bianqian – dui Hebei nongcun yanglao moshi de fenxi' [The logic of fairness and transition in intergenerational relations – an analysis of elderly care patterns in rural Hebei Province], *Zhongguo xueshu*, **4**, 221–254.

Guojia Tongji Ju Yunnan Diaocha Zong Dui (2007), 'Yunnan nongcun funü canyuxing nongcun jianshe de diwei he zuoyong de zai renshi' [Recognition of Yunnan rural women's role and status in participating in the construction of the new countryside], available at: http://www. caein.com/index.asp?xAction=xReadNews&NewsID=23127 (accessed 29 March 2010).

Guonei tuanti: Guizhou Liping Dongzu dage yishutuan [Chinese groups: Liping Kam big song arts troupe from Guizhou] (2008), available at: http://ent.sina.com.cn/y/2008-09-18/16142174315.shtml (accessed 22 December 2008).

Han Xuedan and Ronggua Su (2006), 'Zhongguo renkou zhengce de zhuangbian ji qi dui xingbie pingdeng yu funü fazhan de yingxiang' [Changes in China's population policies and their effects on gender equality and women's development], in Lin Tan (ed.), *1995–2005 nian: Zhongguo xingbie pingdeng yu funu fazhan baogao*, Beijing: Shehui Kexue Wenxian Chubanshe, pp. 160–167.

Hannum, Emily (2003), 'Poverty and basic education in rural China: an analysis of community and household influences on girls and boys enrollment', *Comparative Education Review*, **47** (2), 141–159.

Hannum, Emily, Meiyan Wang and Jennifer Adams (2010), 'Rural–urban disparities in access to primary and secondary education under market reforms', in Martin Whyte (ed.), *One Country, Two Societies*, Cambridge: Harvard University Press, pp. 125–146.

Hansen, Mette Halskov (1999), *Lessons in Being Chinese*, Seattle: University of Washington Press.

Harrington, K., V. Armstrong, J. Freeman, J. Aquilina and S. Campbell (1996), 'Fetal sexing by ultrasound in the second trimester: maternal preference and professional ability', *Ultrasound in Obstetrics and Gynecology*, **8** (5), 318–321.

Harris, Rachel (2004), *Singing the Village: Music, Memory and Ritual among the Sibe of Xinjiang*, Oxford and New York: Oxford University Press (for The British Academy).

Hawkesworth, Mary (2004), 'Global containment: the production of feminist invisibility and the vanishing horizon of justice', in Manfred Steger (ed.), *Rethinking Globalism*, Lanham: Rowman & Littlefield, pp. 51–65.

Hawkesworth, Mary (2006), *Globalization and Feminist Activism*, Lanham: Rowman & Littlefield.

He, Baogang (2005), 'Village citizenship in China: a case study of Zhejiang', *Citizenship Studies*, **9** (2), 205–219.

He Fuping (2004), 'Fujian sheng shixing "tudi chengbao fa" zhong nongcun funü tudi chengbao quanyi baozhang yanjiu' [Study of the protection of rural women's land contract rights during Fujian Province's implementation of the 'Land Contract Law'], *Zhonggong Fujian shengwei dangxiao xuebao*, **12**, 61–66.

He Lirong (2008), '"Chujia nü" tudi quanyi baohu de yinjing yu chulu' [Difficulties and solutions in protecting 'out–married women's' land rights], *Hebei faxue*, **9**, 128.

Henderson, Karla A. (1990), 'The meaning of leisure for women: an integrative review of the research', *Journal of Leisure Research*, **22** (3), 228–243.

Hershatter, Gail (2004), 'State of the field: women in China's long twentieth century', *The Journal of Asian Studies*, **63** (4), 991–1065.

Hickey, Samuel and Giles Mohan (eds) (2004), *Participation: From Tyranny to Transformation? Exploring New Approaches to Participation in Development*, London and New York: Zed Books Ltd.

Hindess, Barry (2001), 'The liberal government of unfreedom', *Alternatives*, **26**, 93–111.

Ho, Peter, Jacob Eyferth and Eduard B. Vermeer (eds) (2004), *Rural Development in Transitional China*, London: Frank Cass.

Howell, Jude (2002), 'Women's political participation in China: struggling to hold up half the sky', *Parliamentary Affairs*, **55** (1), 43–56.

Howell, Jude (2003), 'Women's organizations and civil society in China: making a difference', *International Feminist Journal of Politics*, **5** (2), 191–215.

Howell, Jude (2006), 'Women's political participation in China: in whose interests elections?' *Journal of Contemporary China*, **15** (49), 603–619.

Howell, Jude (2008), 'Gender, institutions, and empowerment: lessons from China', in Kartik Roy, Hans Blomqvist and Cal Clark (eds), *Institutions and Gender Empowerment in the Global Economy, Part 1*, Singapore: World Scientific, pp. 103–130.

Hsiung, Ping-chun, Maria Jaschok and Cecilia Milwertz (eds) (2001), *Chinese Women Organizing: Cadres, Feminists, Muslims, Queers*, Oxford: Berg.

Huang Hui (2006), 'Shi yi wu' fazhan wu zhong zou' [Five gains from the development of the 11th five year plan], *Liaowang*, 3 June, 29–30.

Huang, Yuqin (2009), 'Transforming the gendered organisation of labour and leisure: women, labour, leisure and family in an inland Chinese village, 1926–2006', PhD thesis, University of Essex, UK.

Hudson, Valerie M. and Andrea M. den Boer (2004), *Bare Branches: The Security Implications of Asia's Surplus Male Population*, Cambridge: MIT Press.

Hultqvist, Kenneth and Gunilla Dahlberg (eds) (2001), *Governing the Child in the New Millennium*, New York: Routledge Falmer.

Ingram, Catherine (2007), '"If you don't sing, friends will say you are proud": how and why Kam people learn to sing big song', *Context: A Journal of Music Research*, **32**, 85–104.

Ingram, Catherine (2010), 'Hwun hwun jon ka [Listen] . . . Kam villagers singing big song in early twenty-first-century china', PhD thesis, University of Melbourne.

International Fund for Agricultural Development (IFAD) (1995), *The Status of Rural Women in China*, Rome: IFAD.

Jacka, Tamara (1997), *Women's Work in Rural China: Change and Continuity in an Era of Reform*, Cambridge: Cambridge University Press.

Jacka, Tamara (2006a), 'Approaches to women and development in rural China', *Journal of Contemporary China*, **15** (49), 585–602.

Jacka, Tamara (2006b), *Rural Women in Urban China: Gender, Migration, and Social Change*, Armonk, NY: M.E. Sharpe.

Jacka, Tamara (2008), 'Increasing women's participation in village government in China: is it worth it?' *Critical Asian Studies*, **40** (4), 499–529.

Jacka, Tamara (2010), 'Women's activism, overseas funded participatory development, and governance: a case study from China', *Women's Studies International Forum*, **33** (2), 99–112.

Jakobson, Linda (2004), 'Local governance: village and township direct elections', in Jude Howell (ed.), *Governance in China*, Lanham: Rowman & Littlefield, pp. 97–120.

Janke, Terri (1999), 'Our culture our future: a report on australian indigenous cultural and intellectual property rights', *Australian Indigenous Law Reporter*, **4** (4), available at: http://www.austlii.edu.au/journals/AILR/1999/51.html#fnB1 (accessed 6 August 2009).

Jeffery, Lyn (2001), 'Placing practices: transnational network marketing in mainland China', in Nancy N. Chen, Constance D. Clark, Suzanne Z. Gottschang and Lyn Jeffery (eds), *China Urban: Ethnographies of Contemporary Culture*, Durham: Duke University Press, pp. 23–42.

Jin, Xiaoyi, Shuzhuo Li and Marcus Feldman (2007), 'Marriage form and son preference in rural China: an investigation in three counties', *Rural Sociology*, **27** (4), 511–536.

Jing Niyan (2007), 'Shehui wenhua yu funü de shengyu jiankang – yi ge Jingpo cunzhuang de shengyu wenhua xisu yu funü jiankang de ge'an' [Collective culture and women's reproductive health – a case study of women's health and reproductive culture and customs in a Jingpo village], in Yunnan Shehui Xingbie yu Fazhan Xiaozu (ed.), Bianyuan de tupo, Kunming: Yunnan Shehui Kexue Chubanshe, pp. 121–136.

Jing, Zhao and Wenbin Hu (2007), 'China country case study: Country profile commissioned for the EFA Global Monitoring Report 2008, Education for All by 2015: will we make it?' Available at: http://unesdoc. unesco.org/images/0015/001555/155595e.pdf (accessed 2 June 2009).

Johnson, Kay Ann (2004), *Wanting a Daughter, Needing a Son: Abandonment, Adoption, and Orphanage Care in China*, St Paul, MN: Yeong & Yeong.

Judd, Ellen R. (1990), '"Men are more able": rural Chinese women's conceptions of gender and agency', *Pacific Affairs*, **63** (1), 40–61.

Judd, Ellen R. (1994), *Gender and Power in Rural North China*, Stanford, CA: Stanford University Press.

Judd, Ellen R. (2002), *The Chinese Women's Movement: Between State and Market*, Stanford, CA: Stanford University Press.

Judd, Ellen R. (2007), 'No change for thirty years: the renewed question of women's land rights in rural China', *Development and Change*, **38** (4), 689–710.

Judge, Joan (2002), 'Citizens or mothers of citizens? Gender and the meaning of modern Chinese citizenship', in Merle Goldman and Elizabeth J. Perry (eds), *Changing Meanings of Citizenship in Modern China*, Cambridge: Harvard University Press, pp. 23–43.

Kabeer, Naila (2002), 'Citizenship and the boundaries of the acknowledged community: Identity, affiliation and exclusion', Brighton: Institute of Development Studies IDS Working Paper No. 171.

Kabeer, Naila (2005), 'Introduction: the search for inclusive citizenship', in Naila Kabeer (ed.), *Inclusive Citizenship: Meanings and Expressions*, London: Zed Books, pp. 1–30.

Kaufman, Joyce and Kristen Williams (2004), 'Who belongs? Women, marriage and citizenship', *International Feminist Journal of Politics*, **6** (3), 416–435.

Klenk, Rebecca M. (2004), '"Who is the developed woman?": women as a category of development discourse, Kumaon, India', *Development and Change*, **35** (1), 57–78.

Kristof, Nicholas D. and Sheryl WuDunn (2010), *Half the Sky: Turning Oppression into Opportunity for Women Worldwide*, New York: Random House, Inc.

Kung, James K. (2000), 'Common property rights and land reallocations in rural China: evidence from a village survey', *World Development*, **28** (4), 701–719.

Lee, Felicia A. (2004), 'Engineering more sons than daughters', *New York Times*, July 3, A17.

Lee, Mary Jo Benton (2001), *Ethnicity, Education and Empowerment: How Minority Students in Southwest China Construct Identities*, Aldershot: Ashgate Publishing.

Lee, Sing and Arthur Kleinman (2003), 'Suicide as resistance in Chinese society', in Elizabeth J. Perry and Mark Selden (eds), *Chinese Society: Change, Conflict, and Resistance* (2nd edition), New York: Routledge, pp. 289–311.

Lei, Guang (2010), 'Bringing the city back in: the Chinese debate on rural reforms', in Marton King White (ed.), *One Country, Two Societies: Rural–Urban Inequality in Contemporary China*, Cambridge: Harvard University Press, pp. 311–334.

Levinson, Bradley, Douglas E. Foley and Dorothy C. Holland (eds) (1996), *The Cultural Production of the Educated Person*, Albany: State University of New York Press.

Lewis, Maureen and Marlaine Lockheed (2006), *Inexcusable Absence: Why 60 Million Girls Still Aren't in School and What To Do About It*, Washington, DC: Center for Global Development.

Li Changping (2002), *Wo xiang zongli shuo shihua* [I spoke the truth to the premier], Beijing: Guangming Ribao Chubanshe.

Li Chunri (2005), 'Fazhan zhong de funü: di ba ci Yunnan funü lilun yanjiu hui zongshu' [Women in development: overview of the 8th Yunnan women's theory study conference], paper presented at the 8th Yunnan Women's Theory Study Conference, Kunming, 10 November.

Li, Danke and Mun C. Tsang (2003), 'Household decisions and gender inequality in education in rural China', *China: An International Journal*, **1** (2), 224–248.

Li, Lianjiang (2003), 'The empowering effect of village elections in rural China', *Asian Survey*, **43** (4), 648–662.

Li, Lianjiang and Kevin O'Brien (2008), 'Protest leadership in rural China', *China Quarterly*, **193**, 1–23.

Li, Shuzhuo (2007), 'Imbalanced sex ratio at birth and comprehensive intervention in China', report presented at the 4th Asia Pacific Conference on Reproductive and Sexual Health and Rights, Hyderabad, India, available at: www.unfpa.org/gender/docs/studies/china.pdf (accessed 25 June 2009).

Li Shuzhuo, Xiaoyi Jin, Marcus Feldman, Nan Li and Chuzhu Zhu (eds) (2006), *Dangdai Zhongguo nongcun de zhaozhui hunyin* [Uxorilocal marriage in contemporary rural China] [bilingual], Beijing: Social Sciences Academic Press.

Li, Shuzhuo, Wei Jan, Jiang Quanbao and Marcus W. Feldman (2007), 'Imbalanced sex ratio at birth and female child survival in China: issues and prospects', in Isabelle Attané and Christophe Guilmoto (eds), *Watering the Neighbour's Garden: The Growing Demographic Female Deficit in Asia*, Paris: Committee for International Cooperation in National Research and Demography, pp. 25–47.

Li, Xiaojiang and Liang Jun (1998), 'Women in China', in Nelly P. Stromquist (ed.), *Women in the Third World, an Encyclopedia of Contemporary Issues*, New York: Garland Publishing, pp. 593–600.

Li, Xiaorong (1995), 'Gender inequality in China and cultural relativism', in Martha C. Nussbaum and Jonathan Glover (eds), *Women, Culture and Development: A Study of Human Capabilities*, Oxford: Clarendon Press, pp. 407–425.

Li, Xiaoyun, Liu Xiaoqian, Zhang Keyun, Dong Qiang, Wang Dongmei, Li Linyi, Guo Zhanfeng, Luo Rumin, Yang Hongping and Wu Jie (2006), 'Gender and poverty in China: qualitative analysis', in *China: Research Report on Gender Gaps and Poverty Reduction*, Beijing: World Bank, pp. 147–266.

Li, Xing (2010), 'Urban–rural divide put under spotlight at conference', *China Daily* 9 August, available at: http://www.chinadaily.com.cn/bizchina/2010-08/09/content_11118659.htm (accessed 8 August 2010).

Liaw, H. Ray (2008), 'Women's land rights in rural China: transforming existing laws into a source of property rights', *Pacific Rim Law and Policy Journal*, 17 (1), 237–264.

Lin Chun (2001), 'Whither feminism: a note on China', *Signs*, 26 (4), 1281–1286.

Lin, George (2009), *Developing China: Land, Politics and Social Conditions*, London: Routledge.

Lin, Jing and Heidi Ross (1998), 'The potentials and problems of diversity in Chinese education', *McGill Journal of Education*, 33 (1), 31–49.

Lin Mei (2006), 'Cong xingbie pingdeng shijiao kan "guan'ai nühai" xingdong' [The Care for Girls Campaign from a gender equality perspective], *Zhonghua nüzi xueyuan bao*, 18 (6), 28–33.

Lin, Zhibin (2007), 'Gender and rural reforms in China: a case study of population control and land rights policies in northern Liaoning', *Feminist Economics*, 13 (3–4), 63–92.

Link, Perry, Richard P. Madsen and Paul G. Pickowicz (eds) (2001), *Popular China, Unofficial Culture in a Globalizing Society*, Lanham: Rowman and Littlefield.

Liping, Xianwei Xuanchuanbu (2008), *Dongzu dage yishutuan dazao baozhuang zhaoshang xiangmu* [Invitation of outside investment for the Kam big song arts troupe marketing project], available at: http://www.liping.gov.cn/Article/ShowArticle.asp?ArticleID=1015 (accessed 22 December 2008).

Lister, Ruth (1997), *Citizenship and Feminist Perspectives*, London: Macmillan.

Liu, Chengfang, Linxiu Zhang, Renfu Luo and Scott Rozelle (2009), 'Infrastructure investment in rural China: is quality being compromised during quantity expansion?' *The China Journal*, **61**, 105–129.

Liu Feng and Long Yaohong (eds) (2004), *Dongzu: Guizhou Liping xian Jiulong cun diaocha* [The Kam: an investigation in Jiulong Village, Liping County, Guizhou], Kunming: Yunnan Daxue Chubanshe.

Liu, Serena (2007), 'Social citizenship in China: continuity and change', *Citizenship Studies*, **11** (5), 465–479.

Liu, Sisi (2004), 'Where have all the young girls gone?', *China Rights Forum*, **4**, 50–55.

Liu Xiaochun (2007), 'Minsu lüyou de wenhua zhengzhi' [The cultural politics of folklore tourism], available at: http://www.21ctcm.com.cn/Article/ShowArticle.asp?ArticleID=158&Page=5 (accessed 29 March 2010).

Liu, Xin (2000), *In One's Own Shadow: An Ethnographic Account of the Condition of Post-reform Rural China*, Berkeley: University of California Press.

Liu Yong (2005), 'Wenhua lüyou yu chuantong yinyue de chuancheng' [Cultural tourism and the transmission of traditional music], *Zhongguo yinyue*, **97**, 109–110.

Lou, Jingjing and Heidi Ross (2008), 'From fee to free: achieving the right to education in China' (guest editor's introduction), *Chinese Education and Society*, **41** (1), 4–8.

Lu, Yiyi (2008), 'NGOs in China: development dynamics and challenges', in Zheng Yongnian and Joseph Fewsmith (eds), *China's Opening Society: The Non-state Sector and Governance*, New York: Routledge, pp. 83–105.

Ma, Quisha (2002), 'The governance of NGOs in China since 1978: how much autonomy?', *Nonprofit and Voluntary Sector Quarterly*, **31** (3), 305–328.

Mak, Grace C.L. (ed.) (1996), *Women, Education and Development in Asia*, New York: Garland Publishing.

Mancheng Women's Federation (n.d.), 'Chushi Li Huaqin' [Getting to Know Li Huaqin], unpublished report.

Marshall, Thomas H. (1963), *Sociology at the Crossroads and Other Essays*, London: Heineman.

McLaren, Anne E. (2008), *Performing Grief: Bridal Laments in Rural China*, Honolulu: University of Hawai'i Press.

Mei Lin (2006), 'Cong xingbie pingdeng shijiao kan "guan'ai nühai" xing-dong' [The Care for Girls Campaign from a gender equality perspective], *Zhonghua nüzi xueyuan bao*, **18** (6), 28–33.

Meyer, John W. and Ronald L. Jepperson (2000), 'The "actors" of modern society: the cultural construction of social agency', *Sociological Theory*, **18** (1), 100–120.

Miao, Jing (1991), 'Tradition and its future in Chinese folksongs', in Tokumaru Yosihiko et al. (eds), *Tradition and its Future in Music: Report of SIMS 1990 Osaka*, Tokyo and Osaka: Mita Press, pp. 489–494.

Michelson, Ethan and William L. Parish (2000), 'Gender differentials in economic success: rural China in 1991', in Barbara Entwisle and Gail Henderson (eds), *Re-drawing Boundaries, Work, Households, and Gender in China*, Berkeley: University of California Press, pp. 134–156.

Min, Dongchao (1999), 'The development of women's studies: from the 1980s to the present', in Jackie West, Zhao Minghua, Chang Xiangqun and Cheng Yuan (eds), *Women of China: Economic and Social Transformation*, New York: St Martin's Press, Inc, pp. 211–225.

Ministry of Education (2003), *2002 nian jiaoyu tongji baogao* [2002 statistical report on education Beijing], available at: http://www.moe.edu.cn/stat/tjgongbao/ (accessed 2 February 2004).

Mittelman, James H. (2006), 'Globalization and development: learning from debates in China', *Globalizations*, **3** (3), 377–391.

Moghadam, Valentine M. (2005), *Globalizing Women: Transnational Feminist Networks*, Baltimore: Johns Hopkins University Press.

Mok, Ka-Ho (ed.) (2003), *Centralization and Decentralization: Educational Reforms and Changing Governance in Chinese Societies*, Hong Kong: Comparative Education Research Centre, The University of Hong Kong, and Kluwer Academic Publishers.

Moore, Henrietta L. (1988), *Feminism and Anthropology*, Cambridge, UK: Polity Press.

Mosse, David (2001), '"People's knowledge", participation and patronage: operations and representations in rural development', in Bill Cooke and Uma Kothari (eds), *Participation: The New Tyranny?* London and New York: Zed Books Ltd, pp. 16–35.

Movius, Lisa (2004), 'Cultural devolution', *The New Republic*, 1 March, 116–121.

Mueggler, Erik (2001), *The Age of Wild Ghosts, Memory, Violence, and Place in Southwest China*, Berkeley: The University of California Press.

Mungello, David (2008), *Drowning Girls in China: Female Infanticide since 1650*, Lanham, MD: Rowman & Littlefield.

Murphy, Rachel (2003), 'Fertility and distorted sex ratios in a rural Chinese county: culture, state, and policy', *Population and Development Review*, **29** (4), 595–626.

Murphy, Rachel (2004), 'Turning peasants into modern Chinese citizens: "population quality" discourse, demographic transition and primary education', *The China Quarterly*, **177**, 1–20.

Naroditskaya, Inna (2000), 'Azerbaijanian female musicians: women's voices defying and defining the culture', *Ethnomusicology*, **44** (2), 234–256.

National Population and Family Planning Commission (NPFPC), Ministry of Health (MOH) and State Food and Drug Administration (SFDA) (2003), 'Guanyu jinzhi fei yixue xuyao de tai'er xingbie jianding he xuanze xingbie de rengong zhongzhi renshen de guiding' [Regulation on the prohibition of foetal sex identification and sex-selective abortion for non-medical purposes], available at: http://www.chinapop.gov.cn/zcfg/bmgz/200806/t20080627_155804.html (accessed 6 January 2010).

Nilsson, Erik (2010), 'Rural political reform for the benefit of all', *China Daily*, 27 January, available at: http://www.chinadaily.com.cn/english/Opinion/2010-01/27/content_9381090.htm (accessed 14 July 2010).

Nongjianü Wenhua Fazhan Zhongxin (2003), *2003 nianbao* [2003 annual review], Beijing: Cultural Development Centre for Rural Women.

Nongjianü Wenhua Fazhan Zhongxin (2004), *2004 nianbao* [2004 annual review], Beijing: Cultural Development Centre for Rural Women.

Nongjianü Wenhua Fazhan Zhongxin (2005a), *2005 nianbao* [2005 annual review], Beijing: Cultural Development Centre for Rural Women.

Nongjianü Wenhua Fazhan Zhongxin (2005b), *Shengming weiji ganyu shequ xingdong* [Community action for life crisis intervention], Beijing: Cultural Development Centre for Rural Women.

Nongjianü Wenhua Fazhan Zhongxin (2006), *2006 nianbao* [2006 annual review], Beijing: Cultural Development Centre for Rural Women.

Nongjianü Wenhua Fazhan Zhongxin (2008), *Nannü gongtong canyu shengming weiji ganyu xiangmu yingji* [Photo album of the project for joint male–female participation in life crisis intervention], Beijing: Cultural Development Centre for Rural Women.

O'Brien, Kevin (1996), 'Rightful resistance', *World Politics*, **49** (1), 31–55.

O'Brien, Kevin (2002), 'Villagers, elections and citizenship', in Merle Goldman and Elizabeth J. Perry (eds), *Changing Meanings of Citizenship in Modern China*, Cambridge: Harvard University Press, pp. 212–231.

O'Brien, Kevin and Lianjiang Li (2006), *Rightful Resistance in Rural China*, New York: Cambridge University Press.

O'Byrne, Darren J. (2005), 'Toward a critical theory of globalization: a Habermasian approach', in Richard P. Appelbaum and William I. Robinson (eds), *Critical Globalization Studies*, New York: Routledge, pp. 75–87.

Ogletree, Charles J. and Rangita de Silva-de Alwis (2004), 'The recently revised marriage law of China: the promise and the reality', *Texas Journal of Women and the Law*, **13** (2), 251–312.

Ong, Aihwa (2006), *Neoliberalism as Exception: Mutations in Citizenship and Sovereignty*, Durham, NC: Duke University Press.

Ong, Aihwa and Donald M. Nonini (eds) (1997), *Ungrounded Empires: The Cultural Politics of Modern Chinese Transnationalism*, New York: Routledge.

Ortner, Sherry B. (2006), *Anthropology and Social Theory: Culture, Power and the Acting Subject*, Durham: Duke University Press.

Pan Yongrong (2005), 'Liping xian Yongcong xiang Jiulong cun Dongyu diaocha baogao' [A report on the investigation of the Kam language of Jiulong Village, Yongcong Township, Liping County], in *Guizhou minzu diaocha juan ershiyi 2003*, Guiyang: Guizhou Sheng Minzu Yanjiusuo and Guizhou Sheng Minzu Yanjiuhui, pp. 486–503.

Parpart, Jane L. (1993), 'Who is the "other"? A postmodern feminist critique of women and development theory and practice', *Development and Change*, **24** (3), 439–464.

Parpart, Jane L. (1995), 'Deconstructing the development "expert": gender, development and the "vulnerable groups"', in Marianne H. Marchand and Jane L. Parpart (eds), *Feminism/Postmodernism/Development*, London: Routledge, pp. 221–243.

People's Daily, 22 December 2010, http://english.peopledaily.com.cn/90001/90778/90862/6848826.html (accessed 9 February 2011).

People's Republic of China (2005), *Government White Paper: Gender Equality and Women's Development in China*, available at: http://china.org.cn/e-white/20050824/index.htm (accessed 3 July 2010).

Perry, Elizabeth and Merle Goldman (2007), *Grassroots Political Reform in Contemporary China*, Cambridge, MA: Harvard University Press.

Phillips, Michael R., Xianyun Li and Yanping Zhong (2002), 'Suicide rates in China, 1995–99', *The Lancet*, 9 March, **359**, 835–840.

Plummer, Janelle (2004), 'Introduction', in Janelle Plummer and John G. Taylor (eds), *Community Participation in China: Issues and Process for Capacity Building*, London and Sterling, VA: Earthscan, pp. 1–20.

Plummer, Janelle and John G. Taylor (2004a), 'Key factors and processes affecting participation', in Janelle Plummer and John G. Taylor (eds), *Community Participation in China: Issues and Process for Capacity Building*, London and Sterling, VA: Earthscan, pp. 55–90.

Plummer, Janelle and John G. Taylor (2004b), 'The characteristics of community participation in China', in Janelle Plummer and John G. Taylor (eds), *Community Participation in China: Issues and Process for Capacity Building*, London and Sterling, VA: Earthscan, pp. 36–54.

Po, Lanchih (2008), 'Redefining rural collectives in China: land conversion and the emergence of rural shareholding cooperatives', *Urban Studies*, **45** (8), 1603–1623.

Population Census Office and National Bureau of Statistics of China (1985), *Tabulations of the 1982 Census of the PRC*, Beijing: China Statistics Press.

Population Census Office and National Bureau of Statistics of China (2002), *Tabulations of the 2000 Census of the PRC*, Beijing: China Statistics Press.

Postman, Neil (1996), *The End of Education*, New York: Vintage Press.

Pu Hong (1991), 'Dongzu dage de guoqu xianzai he jianglai' [The past, present and future of Kam big song], Zhongguo shaoshu minzu yinyue xuehui di san jie nianhui, pp. 44–50.

Pu Hong and Zhang Tiehong (2003), 'Dongxiang yiyuan qipa – galao (dai xu)' [The exquisite work of art of the Kam region – big song (additional introduction)], in Guizhou sheng shaoshu minzu guji zhengli bangongshi, *Al Laox – Dongzu dage*, Guiyang: Guizhou Minzu Chubanshe, pp. 4–18.

Qian, Tina and Nick Young (2006), 'Profile: veteran fighter for "ugly duckling" that serves rural women', *China Development Brief*, 3 April, available at: www.chinadevelopmentbrief.com/node/526 (accessed 20 October 2009).

Qin, Hui (2003), 'Dividing the big family assets', in Wang Chaohua (ed.), *One China, Many Paths*, London: Verso, pp. 128–159.

Quanguo Fulian and Guojia Tongjiju (2001), 'Di'erqi Zhongguo funü shehui diwei chouyang diaocha zhuyao shuju baogao' [Report on the main statistical data from the second Chinese sample survey on women's status], available at: www.stats.gov.cn/tjgb/qttjgb/qgqttjgb/t20020331_15816.htm (accessed 30 August 2009).

Rahini, May (2006), *Keeping the Promise: Five Benefits of Girls' Secondary Education*, Washington, DC: Academy for Educational Development.

Razavi, Shahrashoub and Carol Miller (1995), *From WID to GAD: Conceptual Shifts in the Women and Development Discourse*, United Nations Research Institute for Social Development, United Nations Development Programme, available at: http://kms1.isn.ethz.ch/serviceengine/Files/ISN/38688/ipublicationdocument_singledocument/219634F2-9FFE-4205-8B02-26E41F4FC81F/en/OP+001c.pdf (accessed 22 December 2009).

Redlich, Fritz (1976), 'Generations: a critique and reconstruction', *Belgisch*

Tijdschrift voor Nieuwste Geschiedenis **7**, 243–271, also available at: http://www.flwi.ugent.be/btng-rbhc/pdf/BTNG-RBHC,%2007,%20 1976,%201-2,%20pp%20243-271.pdf (accessed 15 December 2006).

Rees, Helen (2000), *Echoes of History: Naxi Music in Modern China*, Oxford: Oxford University Press.

Rees, Helen (2002), 'Cultural policy, music scholarship and recent developments', in Robert C. Provine, Tokumaru Yosihiko and J.L. Witzleben (eds), *The Garland Encyclopedia of World Music, Volume 7: East Asia – China, Japan and Korea*, New York & London: Routledge, pp. 441–493.

Rofel, Lisa (1998), *Other Modernities: Gendered Yearnings in China after Socialism*, Berkeley: University of California Press.

Rofel, Lisa (1999), 'Museums as women's space: displays of gender in post-Mao China', in Mayfair Mei-hui Yang (ed.), *Spaces of Their Own: Women's Public Sphere in Transnational China*, Minneapolis and London: University of Minnesota Press, pp. 116–131.

Ross, Heidi and Jing Lin (2006), 'Social capital formation through Chinese school communities', in Emily Hannum and Bruce Fuller (eds), *Children's Lives and Schooling Across Societies: Research in the Sociology of Education, Vol. 15*, Oxford: Elsevier, pp. 43–69.

Ross, Heidi and Jing Lin (guest editors) (2001), Special issue on 'Educating girls in a different way: teaching and learning in Chinese girls' schools', *Chinese Education and Society*, **34** (1).

Ross, Heidi and L. Wang (2008), 'Educating girls as community leaders: contradictions in one Spring Bud Project in rural Shaanxi, China', *Girlhood Studies: An Interdisciplinary Journal*, **1** (1), 81–113.

Sahlfeld, Miriam (2008), 'Commercializing cultural heritage? Criteria for a balanced instrumentalization of traditional cultural expressions for development in a globalised digital environment', in Christoph B. Graber and Mira Burri-Nenova (eds), *Intellectual Property and Traditional Cultural Expressions in a Digital Environment*, Cheltenham, UK and Northampton, MA, USA: Edward Elgar, pp. 256–286.

Sai, Fred T. (1997), 'The ICPD Programme of Action: pious hope or a workable guide?' *Health Transition Review*, **7** (Supplement 4), 1–5.

Sargeson, Sally (2004), 'Full circle? Rural land reforms in globalizing China', *Critical Asian Studies*, **36** (4), 637–656.

Sargeson, Sally (2006), 'Introduction: women and policy and institutional change in rural China', *Journal of Contemporary China*, **15** (49), 575–583.

Sargeson, Sally and Yu Song (2010), 'Land expropriation and the gender politics of citizenship in the urban frontier', *The China Journal*, **64**, 19–45.

Sassen, Saskia (2005), 'The many scales of the global: implications for theory and for politics', in Richard P. Appelbaum and William I. Robinson (eds), *Critical Globalization Studies*, New York: Routledge, pp. 155–166.

Sassen, Saskia (2007), 'Response', *European Journal of Political Theory*, **6** (4), 431–444.

Scharping, Thomas (2007), 'The politics of numbers: fertility statistics in recent decades', in Zhao Zhongwei and Fei Guo (eds), *Transition and Challenge: China's Population at the Beginning of the 21st Century*, Oxford: Oxford University Press, pp. 34–53.

Schein, Louisa (1996), 'Multiple alterities: the contouring of gender in Miao and Chinese nationalisms', in Brackette F. Williams (ed.), *Women out of Place: The Gender of Agency and the Race of Nationality*, New York and London: Routledge, pp. 79–102.

Schein, Louisa (1997), 'Gender and internal orientalism in China', *Modern China*, **23** (1), 69–98.

Schein, Louisa (1999), 'Performing modernity', *Cultural Anthropology*, **14** (3), 361–395.

Schein, Louisa (2000), *Minority Rules: The Miao and the Feminine in China's Cultural Politics*, Durham and London: Duke University Press.

Seeberg, Vilma and Heidi Ross (2007), 'The case for prioritizing education for girls left behind in remote rural China', in David Baker and Alexander Wiseman (eds), *International Perspectives on Education and Society, Volume 8, Education for All: Global Promises, National Challenges*, Oxford: Elsevier Science Ltd, pp. 111–158.

Sen, Amartya (1993), 'Capability and well-being', in Martha Nussbaum and Amartya Sen (eds), *The Quality of Life*, Oxford: Clarendon Press, pp. 30–53.

Sen, Amartya (1999), *Development as Freedom*, Oxford and New York: Oxford University Press and Alfred A. Knopf.

Sen, Amartya (2000), *Development as Freedom*, New York: Alfred Knopf.

Shelton, Beth Anne (1992), *Women, Men, and Time: Gender Differences in Paid Work, Housework, and Leisure*, New York: Greenwood Press.

Shiva, Vandana (2000), *Stolen Harvest: The Hijacking of the Global Food Supply*, Cambridge, MA: South End Press.

Sifabu Faxue Jiaocai Bianjibu (ed.) (1996) *Zhongguo minzu faxue* [Studies of Chinese nationalities' law], Beijing: Falu Chubanshe.

Siim, Birte (2000), *Gender and Citizenship: Politics and Agency in France, Britain and Denmark*, Cambridge: Cambridge University Press.

Smith, Graeme (2009), 'Political machinations in a rural county', *The China Journal*, **62**, 29–59.

So, Alvin Y. (ed.) (2003), *China's Developmental Miracle: Origins, Transformations and Challenges*, Armonk: M.E. Sharpe.

Solinger, Dorothy (1999), *Contesting Citizenship in Urban China: Peasant Migrants, the State and the Logic of the Market*, Berkeley: University of California Press.

Somers, Margaret R. (1994), 'Rights, relationality and membership: rethinking the making and meaning of citizenship', *Law and Social Inquiry*, **19** (1), 63–112.

Song, Yiching, Linxiu Zhang and Ronnie Vernooy (2006), 'Empowering women farmers and strengthening the local seed system: action research in Guangxi, China', in Ronnie Vernooy (ed.), *Social and Gender Analysis in Natural Resource Management*, New Delhi: Sage, pp. 129–154.

Srivastava, I. (1991), 'Women as portrayed in women's folk songs of North India', *Asian Folklore Studies*, **50** (2), 269–310.

Stacey, Judith (1983), *Patriarchy and Socialist Revolution in China*, Berkeley: University of California Press.

Standard Service Delivery Protocol (SSDP) (n.d.), 'Standard Service Delivery Protocol on family planning'.

State Council of the People's Republic of China (2005), 'Guowuyuan guanyu dali fazhan zhiye jiaoyu de jueding' [A decision to promote the development of vocational education in China], available at: http://www.gov.cn/zwgk/2005-11/09/content_94296.htm (accessed 4 February 2011).

State Family Planning Commission (SFPC) (2002), 'Guanyu zonghe zhili chusheng renkou xingbiebi shenggao wenti de yijian' [Suggestions about comprehensively managing increased sex ratio at birth imbalance].

Stromquist, Nelly P. (2003), 'Women's education in the twenty-first century: balance and prospects', in Robert F. Arnove and Carlos Alberto Torres (eds), *Comparative Education* (2nd edition), Lanham: Rowman and Littlefield, pp. 176–203.

Stromquist, Nelly P. (2004), 'The intersection of public policies and gender: understanding state action in education', paper presented at the Comparative and International Education Society annual conference, Salt Lake City, Utah, March.

Su Cuiwei (2005), 'Nüren de fangzi, nanren de jia: lahuzu "lunxie di" bianqian zhong de shehui xingbie fenxi' [Women's house and men's family: gender analysis of Lahu swidden land transition], in Yunnan shehui xingbie yu fazhan xiao zu (ed.), *Canyu xing fazhan zhong de shehui xingbie zhuji*, Beijing: Zhongguo Shehui Kexue Chubanshe, pp. 159–204.

Su Cuiwei (2008), 'Lahu chuanton yu xiandai de xingbie hexie' [The traditional culture of Lahu ethnic group and gender equality currently], Yunnan Province Minorities Association Newsletter, annual (2008), p. 55.

Su, Minzi (2009), *China's Rural Development Strategy: Exploring the 'New Socialist Countryside'*, Boulder: First Forum Press.

Sutton, Margaret (1998), 'Girls' educational access and attainment', in Nelly P. Stromquist (ed.), *Women in the Third World: An Encyclopedia of Contemporary Issues*, New York: Garland Publishing, pp. 381–396.

Tan, Liangying (2008), 'Changing mindsets: how China's abnormal sex ratio is turning its government into a champion of gender equality', *Asian Journal of Comparative Law*, **3** (1), Article 2.

Tan Lin (ed.) (2006), *1995–2005 nian: Zhongguo xingbie pingdeng yu funü fazhan baogao* [1995–2005: report on gender equality and the development of women in China], Beijing: Shehui Kexue Wenxian Chubanshe.

Tan Lin and Bohong Liu (eds) (2005), *Zhongguo funü yanjiu shi nian 1995–2005* [Ten years of research on women in China, 1995–2005], Beijing: Shehui Kexue Wenxian Chubanshe.

Tian Cuiqin (2004), *Nongmin xianxia* [The leisure of Chinese peasants], Beijing: Social Science Document Press.

Tinker, Irene (ed.) (1990), *Persistent Inequalities: Women and World Development*, New York and Oxford: Oxford University Press, cited in Shahrashoub Razavi and Carol Miller, *From WID to GAD: Conceptual Shifts in the Women and Development Discourse*, United Nations Research Institute for Social Development, United Nations Development Programme, available at: http://kms1.isn.ethz.ch/serviceengine/Files/ISN/38688/ipublicationdocument_singledocument/219634F2-9FFE-42 05-8B02-26E41F4FC81F/en/OP+001c.pdf (accessed 22 December 2009).

Tinsman, Heidi (2000), 'Reviving feminist materialism: gender and neoliberalism in Pinochet's Chile', *Signs*, **26** (1), 145–188.

Tomasevski, Katarina (2003), 'United Nations Report on Economic, Social, and Cultural Rights: The Right to Education', New York: United Nations, 6, available at: http://www.unhchr.ch/Huridocda/Huridoca.nsf/e06a5300f90fa0238025668700518ca4/d2a0154274b5f3f3c 1256dff002ff8f4/$FILE/G0317038.pdf (accessed 4 December 2010).

Tomba, Luigi (2009), 'Of quality, harmony and community: civilization and the middle class in urban China', *positions*, **17** (3), 591–616.

Tong Jiqing (2006), 'Nücunguan, tianye de xiwang [Women village heads, the hopes of the fields]', *Zhongguo funü bao*, 20 June, available at: http://www.nongjianv.org/web/Html/mtbd/2006-11/24/14_39_37_06101313295326898_06112414393745291.html (accessed 11 August 2008).

Tuohy, Sue (2001), 'The sonic dimensions of nationalism in modern China: musical representation and transformation', *Ethnomusicology*, **45** (1), 107–131.

UN Millennium Project (2005), *Taking Action: Achieving Gender Equality and Empowering Women*, New York: Task Force on Education and Gender Equality.

United Nations (1995), 'The United Nations fourth world conference on women: platform for action', available at: www.un.org/womenwatch/daw/beijing/platform/plat1.htm (accessed 25 October 2009).

United Nations Children's Fund (UNICEF) (2003), 'The state of the world's children report: girls' education and development', available at: http://www.unicef.org/sowc03/ (accessed 7 April 2011).

United Nations Development Programme (UNDP) (2008), *China Human Development Report. 2007–2008: Basic Public Services Benefiting 1.3 Billion Chinese People*, Beijing: China Translation and Publishing Corporation.

United Nations Development Programme (UNDP) (2009), 'Women's empowerment', available at: www.undp.org/women/ (accessed 26 October 2009).

United Nations Development Programme (UNDP) (2010), *Assessment of Development Results: China*, available at: http://www.undp.org/evaluation/documents/ADR/ADR_Reports/China/ADR-China-2010.pdf (accessed 14 January 2011).

United Nations Educational, Scientific and Cultural Organization (UNESCO) (2000), *Education For All: The Year 2000 Assessment Final Country Report of China*. (Chapter Five), available at: http://www.unesco.org/education/wef/countryreports/china/contents.html (accessed 7 April 2011).

United Nations Educational, Scientific and Cultural Organization (UNESCO) (2004), 'Gender and education for all – the leap to equality. EFA global monitoring report 2003–2004', available at: http://www.unesco.org/new/en/education/themes/leading-the-international-agenda/efareport/reports/20034-gender/.

United Nations Educational, Scientific and Cultural Organization (UNESCO) (2009), *Grand Song of the Dong Ethnic Group*, Representative List of the Intangible Cultural Heritage of Humanity, available at: http://www.unesco.org/culture/ich/index.php?RL=00202 (accessed 30 October 2009).

United Nations Population Fund (UNFPA) (2005), 'Easing family planning rules leads to fewer abortions and more baby girls, Chinese province finds', available at: www.unfpa.org/news/news.cfm?ID=734 (accessed 25 June 2009).

United Nations Population Fund (UNFPA) (2007), 'Sex ratio – facts and figures', UNFPA China, October 2007, available at: http://www.un.org.cn/cms/p/resources/30/1359/content.html (accessed 7 April 2011).

Unterhalter, Elaine, Emily Kioko-Echessa, Rob Pattman, Fatmatta

N'Jai, Rajee Rajagopalan and Junu Shrestha et al. (2004), 'Scaling up girls' education: towards a scorecard for Commonwealth countries in Africa', paper prepared for conference on scaling up girls' education in Africa, Nairobi, June, available at: www.ioe.ac.uk/research/27053.html (accessed 2 February 2011).

Voet, Rian (1998), *Feminism and Citizenship*, London: Sage.

Wang, Fei-Ling (2005), *Organizing Through Division and Exclusion: China's Hukou System*, Stanford, CA: Stanford University Press.

Wang, Shanshan (2007), '30m men face bleak future as singles' *China Daily*, available at: http://www.chinadaily.com.cn/china/2007-01/12/content_781804.htm (accessed 10 February 2011).

Wang Zhuqing (2007),'Shehui xingbie shijiao xia de nongcun funü tudi quanyi baohu' [The protection of rural women's land rights from a gender perspective], *Nongcun jingji* 3, 36–38.

Wei Xinghe (2006), '"Guan'ai nühai xingdong" gonggong zhengce de jiedu' [Understanding the public policies of the Care for Girls Campaign], *Jiangxi xingzheng xueyuan xuebao*, 8 (3), 61–64.

Wei Xinghe and Lijuan Gao (2007), 'Guan'ai nühai xingdong de zhengce fenxi ji jianyi – jian shehui xingbie shijiao' [Analysis and recommendations on the policies of the Care for Girls' Campaign – a gender perspective], *Sixiang zhanxian*, 33 (3), 80–85.

Wen Jiabao (2004), 'Jianchi yi ren wei ben shi kexue fazhan guan de benzhi he hexin' [Establishing people centredness is the essence and core of a scientific development view], available at: http://www.china.com.cn/chinese/2004/Feb/507198.htm (accessed 8 August 2010).

Wen Jiabao (2006), 'Report on the work of the government, delivered at the third session of the 10th National People's Congress', 5 March, available at: http://www.chinability.com/2005%20government%20work%report.htm (accessed 4 June 2010).

Wen, Tiejun (2001), 'Centenary reflections on the "three dimensional problem" of rural China', *Inter-Asia Cultural Studies*, 2 (2), 287–295.

Werbner, Pina and Nira Yuval-Davis (1999), 'Introduction: women and the new discourse of citizenship', in Nira Yuval-Davis and Pina Werbner (eds), *Women, Citizenship and Difference*, London: Zed Books, pp. 1–38.

Wesoky, Sharon (2002), *Chinese Feminism Faces Globalization*, New York: Routledge.

Wesoky, Sharon (2007), 'Rural women knowing all: globalization and rural women's organizing in China', *International Feminist Journal of Politics*, 9 (3), 339–358.

White, Tyrene (2006), *China's Longest Campaign: Birth Planning in the People's Republic, 1949–2005*, Ithaca: Cornell University Press.

Whyte, Martin (ed.) (2010), *One Country, Two Societies, Rural-Urban Inequality in Contemporary China*, Cambridge: Harvard University Press.

Wolf, Margery (1985), *Revolution Postponed: Women in Contemporary China*, Stanford, CA: Stanford University Press.

Wong, Linda (2004), 'Market reforms, globalization and social justice in China', *Journal of Contemporary China*, **13** (38), 151–171.

Woo, Margaret Y.K. (2002), 'Law and the gendered citizen', in Merle Goldman and Elizabeth J. Perry (ed.), *Changing Meanings of Citizenship in Modern China*, Cambridge: Harvard University Press, pp. 308–329.

World Bank (2005), 'Gender issues and best practices in land administration projects: synthesis report', available at: http://siteresources.worldbank.org/INTARD/Resources/Gender_land_fulltxt.pdf (accessed 9 November 2009).

World Bank (ed.) (2006), 'China: research report on gender gaps and poverty reduction', Beijing: World Bank, available at: http://siteresources.worldbank.org/INTEAPREGTOPGENDER/Resources/China-Gender-Gaps&Poverty-Reduction.pdf (accessed 6 April 2011).

World Bank (2007), 'China and the World Bank: a partnership for innovation', Washington, DC: World Bank, available at: http://siteresources.worldbank.org/INTCHINA/Resources/318862-1121421293578/cn_bank_part nershp_innovation.pdf (accessed 14 July 2010).

World Bank Gender and Development Group (2003), *Gender Equality and the Millennium Development Goals*, Washington, DC: World Bank, available at: http://siteresources.worldbank.org/INTGENDER/Publications/20706126/gendermdg.pdf (accessed 7 April 2011).

Wu Dingguo (ed.) (2005), *Dongxiang Liping guojia zhongdian fengjing mingshengqu jianming shouce* [A concise handbook to the Kam home of Liping, a national level scenic area], Liping County: Liping Xian Lüyou Fazhan Weiyuanhui Bangongshi.

Wu Fei (2005), 'Gaizao renxin de zhengzhi – "Nongjianü" nongcun funü jiankang zhichi xiaozu pinggu' [Politics concerning the soul: an evaluation of the rural women's health support group], in Nongjianü Wenhua Fazhan Zhongxin (ed.), Shengming weiji ganyu shequ xingdong, Beijing: Cultural Development Centre for Rural Women, pp. 14–22.

Wu Pei'an (2003), 'Dongzu yinyue minjian chuancheng yu xuexiao jiaoyu tan' [A discussion of Kam music in folk transmission and school education], *Guizhou daxue xuebao – yishuban*, **17** (2), 28–32.

Wu Xingwen (2008), *Liping yi Dongzu dage wei pinpai tuijie guoji luyou shichang chengji xiren* [The Liping Kam big song cultural symbol is promoted on the international tourist market with successful

results], available at: http://www.zgmdlyw.cn/Article/ShowArticle.
asp?ArticleID=803 (accessed 28 December 2008).

Wu Yunhe (2008),'Rural buzzwords in 30 years', *China Daily*, 10
November, available at: http://www.chinadaily.com.cn/bizchina/2008-
11/10/content_7190344.htm (accessed 19 August 2010).

Xie Lihua (2006a), 'Pilu zisha shuzi yu difang zhengji youhe xiangguan?'
[What is the relationship between revealing suicide figures and local
official achievements?], weblog entry of Xie Lihua, 17 December, http://
blog.sina.com.cn/xielihua (accessed 5 June 2008).

Xie Lihua (2006b), 'Wo ye xiang chang shouge – zhongzi kaihua le' [I
am also thinking of singing a song – the seed is producing flowers],
weblog entry of Xie Lihua, 20 December, http://blog.sina.com.cn/xieli
hua (accessed 5 June 2008).

Xie Lihua (2008), '2008, Women yingjie tiaozhan' [2008, we greet the chal-
lenge], *Nongjianü*, 1 January.

Xie Lihua (2009), 'Wo lijie de funü fuquan' [My understanding of women's
empowerment], weblog entry of Xie Lihua, 26 October, http://blog.sina.
com.cn/xielihua (accessed 28 October 2009).

Xu Chuanxin (2009), 'Nongcun liushou funü yanjiu: huigu yu qianzhan'
[Studies on left-behind women in rural areas: review and prospects],
Renkou yu fazhan, **15** (6), 54–73.

Xu Fengqin (2007), 'Hebei Qinglong xian: 36 Gunzi cun funümen de xin
shenghuo' [Hebei's Qinglong County: the new lives of the women of 36
Rollers Village], *Nongjianü*, 10–11 February.

Xu Fengqin and Xu Rong (2004), 'Qinglong xian funü jiankang xiangmu
honghong huohuo' [The Qinglong county women's health project is
flourishing], *Zhongzi*, December, Beijing: Cultural Development Centre
for Rural Women.

Xu Xiang and Li Xinde (2006), 'Hongta jituan bamai nongtian da gai
haohua bieshu neimu' [The inside story on Hongta Group's forcible
acquisition of farmland to build luxury villas], *Shijie shangye baodao*, 10
October, available at: http://www.biz.icxo.com (accessed 17 December
2008).

Xu Xu (2007), 'Nü nengren "cong zheng" zhihou – nücunguan Li Huaqin
de gushi' [After a capable woman 'engages in politics' – the story of the
female village head Li Huaqin], *Nücunguan*, 10–15 March.

Ya Wen (2003), 'Dongzu dage fazhan shi shangde yici huihuang – Liping
Dongzu minjian hechangyuan dui Dongzu dage fazhan de lishixing
gongxian' [The unique brilliance of the historical development of Kam
big song – the historical contribution to the development of big song
made by the members of the Liping folk chorus], *Zhongguo yinyue*, **4**,
71–72.

Yan, Yunxiang (2003), *Private Life under Socialism: Love, Intimacy, and Family Change in a Chinese Village 1949–1999*, Stanford, CA: Stanford University Press.

Yang Dianhu (2003), 'Jichu jiaoyu kecheng gaige yu Dongzu dage yinyue chuancheng' [Basic educational teaching reforms and the ongoing musical transmission of Kam big song], in Yang Xiuzhao and Wu Dingguo (eds), *Dongzu dage yu shaoshu minzu yinyue yanjiu – Dongzu dage yantaohui ji Zhongguo shaoshu minzu yinyue xuehui di jiujie nianhui lunwenji*, Beijing: Zhongguo Wenlian Chubanshe, pp. 128–139.

Yang Guoren (2003), 'Dongzu dage fazhan shishang de yizuo fengbei – Liping xian Dongzu minjian hechangtuan chengli qianhou de nanwang suiyue' [A monument in the historical development of Kam big song – Unforgettable years preceding and following the establishment of the Liping county Kam folk chorus], in Zhang Zhongxiao and Yang Fanggang (eds), *Dongzu dage yanjiu wushi nian*, Guiyang: Guizhou Minzu Chubanshe, pp. 486–500.

Yang Jing (2007), 'Yunnan shehui xingbie pingdeng yu cunmin zizhi luntan' [Forum on gender equality and democratic management of village autonomy in Kunming, Yunnan, available at: http://www.china-gad. org/Article/ShowArticle..asp?ArticleId=2668 (accessed 10 June 2010).

Yang, Li and Yinsheng Xi (2006), 'Married women's rights to land in China's traditional farming areas', *Journal of Contemporary China*, **15** (49), 621–636.

Yang Xiao (2000), 'Xiangjian yu xiaoyuan: Dongge chuancheng de liangzhong xingtai' [Countryside and schools: the two forms of Kam song transmission], *Yinyue tansuo*, **4**, 9 pages (page numbers not supplied).

Yang Xiuzhao (2003), 'Dongzu dage shi renlei wenhua de zhengui yichan' [Kam big song is the precious legacy of human culture], in Yang Xiuzhao and Wu Dingguo (eds), *Dongzu dage yu shaoshu minzu yinyue yanjiu – Dongzu dage yantaohui ji Zhongguo shaoshu minzu yinyue xuehui di jiujie nianhui lunwenji*, Beijing: Zhongguo Wenlian Chubanshe, pp. 14–28.

Yang Yujing (2009), 'Gaige kaifang 30 nian zhongguo funü/xingbie yanjiu' [A summary of the women's/gender studies in the 30 years of reform and opening-up era], *Zhongguo funü luncong*, **90** (1), 71–78.

Yang Zhengquan (2003a), 'Dazao Dongzu wenhua lüyou pinpai de goux- iang' [Ideas for creating the Kam cultural tourism symbol], in Yang Xiuzhao and Wu Dingguo (eds), *Dongzu dage yu shaoshu minzu yinyue yanjiu – Dongzu dage yantaohui ji Zhongguo shaoshu minzu yinyue xuehui di jiujie nianhui lunwenji*, Beijing: Zhongguo Wenlian Chubanshe, pp. 148–153.

Yang Zhengquan (2003b), 'Xu – Dongzu dage zhi yuan' [Preface – the destiny of Kam big song], in Yang Xiuzhao and Wu Dingguo (eds), *Dongzu dage yu shaoshu minzu yinyue yanjiu – Dongzu dage yantaohui ji Zhongguo shaoshu minzu yinyue xuehui di jiujie nianhui lunwenji*, Beijing: Zhongguo Wenlian Chubanshe, pp. 1–3.

Yang Zongfu (2000), 'Dongge jinru yishu yuanxiao jishi' [A record of actual events concerning Kam song entering arts colleges], in 'Dongzu bainian shilu' bianweihui (ed.), *Dongzu bainian shilu*, Beijing: Zhongguo Wenshi Chubanshe, pp. 391–394.

Yao Lijuan and Shi Kaizhong (2005), *Dongzu diqu de shehui bianqian* [Societal changes in Kam areas], Beijing: Zhongyang Minzu Daxue Chubanshe.

Yardley, James (2004), 'The new uprooted', *New York Times*, 12 September, Section 4, p. 6.

Ye, Jingzhong (2008), 'The disempowered participation of the Women's Federation in international development projects', *Chinese Sociology and Anthropology: A Journal of Translations*, **40** (4), 38–48.

Ye, Xingqing (2009), 'China's urban-rural integration policies', *Journal of Current Chinese Affairs*, **38** (4), 117–143.

Yen, Fang-Tzu (2007), 'The impact of gender and hierarchy on women's reproductive health in a Kam village, Guizhou province, China', *Culture, Health and Sexuality*, **9** (1), 55–68.

Young, Marilyn (1989), 'Chicken Little in China: women after the cultural revolution', in Sonia Kruks, Rayna Rapp and Marilyn B. Young (eds), *Promissory Notes: Women in the Transition to Socialism*, New York: Monthly Review Press, pp. 233–247.

Young, Nick (2003), 'Does this cat catch mice?' *China Development Brief* (July), available at: http://www.chinadevelopmentbrief.com/node/143 (accessed 23 February 2011).

Yunnan Funü Ertong Gongzuo Weiyuanhui (2003), '2003 nian Yunnan funü fazhan gangyao zhixing qingkuang de pinggu baogao' [Evaluation report on the implementation of Yunnan women's development plan in 2003], Kunming.

Yunnan sheng Fulian (2008), 'Chuangye chuangxin fazhan xiandai xin nongye – ji Yunnan jingguo keji zhifu daitou ren Ting Meitao' [Ting Meitao, the woman leader of science and technology enriching modern agriculture in rural development in Yunnan] , available at: http://www.ynwoman.cn/chpages/html/info1.asp?id=434&catid=115&cattype =2 (accessed 10 June 2010).

Yuxi Fenghuang Jiedao Banshichu (2006), 'Guanyu shidi nongmin jiuye fuwu wu xiang tixi ji shengcun fazhan de sikao' [Reflections on a system of five principles for the sustainable development of employment services for landless villagers], 13 November.

Yuxi nianjian 2007 [Yuxi yearbook 2007], Kunming: Yunnan Renmin Chubanshe.

Yuxi shi (2008), Yuxi shi beizhengdi nongmin yanglao baoxian shishi xize [Implementation regulations on Yuxi City old age insurance for expropriated villagers], 1 November.

Zeng Jianguo, Zhang Duolai, Zhou Xiaoyang and Xiao Feili (2006), 'Guan'ai nühai xingdong shidian gongzuo zhong cunzai de zhuyao wenti yiji qi duice yanjiu – yi Hunan wei lie' [Research on the main problems in the Care for Girls Campaign and countermeasures to them – a case study of Hunan], *Nanhua daxue xuebao (shehui kexue ban)*, **7** (4), 12–14.

Zeng, Yi (2007), 'Options for fertility policy transition in China', *Population and Development Review*, **33** (2), 215–246.

Zhang, Jeanne H. (2003), 'Gender in post-Mao China', *European Review*, **11** (2), 209–224.

Zhang, Linxiu, Chengfeng Liu, Haomiao Liu and Lerong Yu (2008), 'Women's land rights in rural China: current situation and likely trends', in Bernadette P. Resurreccion and Rebecca Elmhirst (eds), *Gender and Natural Resource Management: Livelihood, Mobility and Interventions*, Ottowa, ON: IDRC, available at: http://www.idrc.ca/en/ev-126261-201-1-DO_TOPIC.html (accessed 28 October 2009).

Zhang Qiang (2004), 'Erzhi guai mai: cong da dao fang lu you duo yuan' [People trafficking: how great is the gap between combating and preventing?], available at: http://bjyouth.ynet.com/article.jsp?oid=2985805 (accessed 10 June 2010).

Zhang, Weiguo (2002), *Economic Reforms and Fertility Behaviour: A Study of a North China Village*, London: China Library.

Zhang, Weiguo (2006), 'Marketization, democratization, and women's participation in village elections in contemporary rural China: a study of a north China village', *Journal of Women, Politics and Policy*, **28** (2), 1–28.

Zhang, Weiguo (2008), 'State, gender, and uxorilocal marriage in contemporary rural north China', *The China Journal*, **60**, 111–132.

Zhang, Xiaoling (2007), 'Seeking effective public space: Chinese media at the local level', *China: An International Journal*, **5** (1), 55–77.

Zhang, Zhihong (1999),'Rural industrialization in China: from backyard furnaces to township and village enterprises', *East Asia*, **17** (3), 61–87.

Zhao Guanjun (2006), 'Shishi zhengming, zisha shi keyi yufang de' [The facts will bear out, suicide can be prevented], *Gongyi shibao*, 12 December, weblog entry of Xie Lihua, 13 December 2006, http://blog.sina.com.cn/xielihua (accessed 5 June 2008).

Zhao Jie (2009), 'Aizi fangzhi lingyu zhong de xing he "shehui xingbie huayu'" [Sexuality and 'gender discourse' in HIV/AIDS prevention], speech given at the International Conference of Women Studies, Fudan University, Shanghai 26–29th June 2009.

Zhao Jie and Li Yi (2007), 'Fuquan yu hudong – yi ci chenggong de hangdao huodong: Zhong Ying xiangmu Yunnan da ling nütong luntan yu nühai yiqi gongzuo de anli yanjiu' [Empowerment and interaction – a successful advocacy activity: the forum on adolescent girls and work with girls in Yunnan in the Sino-British Project], *Funü luncong*, **2** (79), 33.

Zhao, Jing and Wenbin Hu (2007), 'China country case study: country profile commissioned for the EFA global monitoring report 2008. Education for all by 2015: will we make it?', available at: http://unesdoc. unesco.org/images/0015/001555/155595e.pdf (accessed 2 June 2009).

Zhao Qun (2004), 'Yunnan nongcun funü zai fazhan zhong mianlin de zhuyao wenti' [The main issues Yunnan rural women face in development], *Gender and Development in China*, available at: http://www. china-gad.org/Treasure/ShowArticle.asp?ArticleID=4049 (accessed 10 June 2010).

Zhao Yan (2004), 'Qingkou zhen xiandaihua de daijia' [The costs associated with Qinkou Township's modernization], available at: http:// www.Chinaelections.org/PrintNews.asp?NewsID=67166 (accessed 5 November 2008).

Zhen Yan (ed.) (2008), 'Zhongguo nongcun funü zhuangkuang diaocha' [Report on the situation of rural women in China], Beijing: Shehui Kexue Wenxian Chubanshe.

Zheng, Yongnian (2008), *Technological Empowerment: The Internet, State, and Society in China*, Stanford: Stanford University Press.

Zheng, Zhenzhen (2007), 'Interventions to balance sex ratio at birth in rural China', in Isabelle Attané and Christophe Z. Guilmoto (eds), *Watering the Neighbour's Garden: The Growing Demographic Female Deficit in Asia*, Paris: Committee for International Cooperation in National Research in Demography, pp. 327–346.

Zhong, Zangbao and Jinhua Di (2005), 'Tudi liuzhuan zhong funü de diwei yu quanyi [Women's status and rights in land transfers]', in Tan Lin and Liu Bohong (eds), *Zhongguo funü yanjiu shi nian*, Beijing: Shehui kexue wenxian chubanshe, pp. 424–432.

Zhongguo Kexueyuan Minzu Yanjiusuo Guizhou Shaoshu Minzu Shehui Lishi Diaochazu and Zhongguo Kexueyuan Guizhou Fenyuan Minzu Yanjiusuo (eds) (1963), *Guizhou sheng Liping xian Sanlong xiang Dongzu shehui jingji diaocha ziliao* [Research materials on the society and economy of Sanlong Township, Liping County, Guizhou Province] in Guizhou shaoshu minzu shehui lishi diaocha ziliao zhi shi'er [Vol. 12,

Research Materials on the Society and History of Guizhou's Minority Groups], no publication details.

Zhongguo xibu kaifa wang [China Great Western Development Net] (2009), available at: www.chinawest.gov.cn/web/index.asp (accessed 11 June 2009).

Zhonghua Renmin Gonghe Guo (1999), Tudi guanli fa [Land administration law], Beijing: Zhongguo Fazhi Chubanshe.

Zhonghua Renmin Gonghe Guo (2005), Funü quanyi baozhang fa [Law on the protection of women's rights and interests], available at: http://www.law-lib.com/law/law_view.asp?id=97595 (accessed 25 May 2010).

Zhou Feizhou (2007), 'Shengcai you dao: tudi kaifa he zhuanrang zhong de zhengfu he nongmin' [Creating wealth: governments and villagers in the development and transfer of land], Shehuixue yanjiu, 1, 49–82.

Zhou Heping (ed.) (2006), Diyipi guojiaji feiwuzhi wenhua yichan minglu tudian (shang, xia) [An illustrated register of the first series of national-level intangible cultural heritage], Beijing: Wenhua Yishu Chubanshe.

Zhou, Kate Xiao (1996), How the Farmers Changed China: Power of the People, Boulder, CO: Westview Press/Harper Collins.

Zhu Heshuang (2005), 'Zhongguo xinan shaoshu minzu funü xingxiang xiandai jiangou' [Modern construction of minority women's profiles in southwest China], Guizhou minzu yanjiu, 25 (3), 72–80.

Zui gaodang de Dongzu yinshi wenhua fangshi jiedai nin! [The highest style of Kam culinary culture to receive you!] (2008), Guangxi Sanjiang Luyou Wenhua Wang [Cultural Tourism in Sanjiang Guangxi Net], available at: www.dongzuwang.com/dxly/show.php?itemid-327.html (accessed 29 April 2009).

Zweig, David (2002), Internationalizing China: Domestic Interests and Global Linkages, Ithaca: Cornell University Press.

Index